The Liberty Way

The Liberty Way

Falwell's Path to Christian Zionism

Dr. Kobby Barda

ANTHEM PRESS

Anthem Press
An imprint of Wimbledon Publishing Company
www.anthempress.com

This edition first published in UK and USA 2026
by ANTHEM PRESS
75–76 Blackfriars Road, London SE1 8HA, UK
or PO Box 9779, London SW19 7ZG, UK
and
244 Madison Ave #116, New York, NY 10016, USA

© 2026 Kobby Barda

The author asserts the moral right to be identified as the author of this work.

All rights reserved. Without limiting the rights under copyright reserved above,
no part of this publication may be reproduced, stored or introduced into
a retrieval system, or transmitted, in any form or by any means
(electronic, mechanical, photocopying, recording or otherwise),
without the prior written permission of both the copyright
owner and the above publisher of this book.

British Library Cataloguing-in-Publication Data
A catalogue record for this book is available from the British Library.

Library of Congress Cataloging-in-Publication Data: 2025941517
A catalog record for this book has been requested.

ISBN-13: 978-1-83999-609-2 (Hbk)/978-1-83999-610-8 (Pbk)
ISBN-10: 1-83999-609-9 (Hbk)/1-83999-610-2 (Pbk)

Cover Credit: Bernard Gotfryd photograph collection (Library of Congress)

This title is also available as an eBook.

CONTENTS

Foreword by Dr. Rev. Johnnie Moore   ix

Acknowledgments   xi

Introduction   1
    The Visionary Leader: Dr. Jerry Falwell   2
    The Church Planting Movement   2
    The Unique Relationship with Menachem Begin   3
    The Moral Majority and Its Lasting Impact   4
    Catalyzing the Embassy Move Under Trump   4
    Contextual Background   4

1. Introduction to the Modern Evangelical Political Power   7
    Background on Christian Theology and Its Affinity to Israel   7

2. The Beginning of Dr. Jerry Falwell's Journey and the Establishment of Liberty University   17
    The Beginning of Jerry Falwell's Journey   17
    The Formative 1960s   22
    The Decision to Establish an Academic Institution   26
    About the Growth of Liberty University   29

3. The Grassroots Planting Method on Campuses   33
    What Is the Church Planting Movement?   33
    On the Importance of Church Planting in Falwell's Vision   35
    Church Planting: Supportive and Motivational Activities   37
    Competition "The Fastest-Growing Church"   39
    Did Falwell Succeed in His Vision to Plant 5,000 Churches?   41
    Status Report on Falwell's Economic Empire in the Mid-1980s and How the Grassroots Movement Operation Was Supported from Lynchburg   42

4. The Centrality and Importance of Israel in the Vision of Falwell in Promoting Political Action from Liberty University   45
    The Religious Context of Falwell's Connection with the State of Israel   45

How Does Falwell Convey the Importance of Israel to Students
and Future Pastors? 47
The Importance of Jerry Falwell's Organized Excursions to the
Holy Land, with Students and Graduates 48
Converting Support into Politics Influencing U.S.-Israel Relations 51
The Vision to Move the American Embassy to Jerusalem 53

5. The Relationship with Menachem Begin and the Political
Alliance with Israel 59
Introduction to Falwell's Relationship with Menachem Begin 59
Carter, the Palestinian Issue, and the Beginning of the Alliance
Between the American Right-Wing and Menachem Begin 65
Falwell as Mediator Between Menachem Begin and Anwar Sadat 68
Menachem Begin's Decision to Award Falwell with the
Jabotinsky Medal and the Rift vis-a-vis the Jewish World 75
Bombing Iraq's Nuclear Reactor and the Phone Call from
Begin to Falwell 84
Begin's Decision to Annex the Golan Heights and Falwell's
Support of That Move 88
Falwell Endorses Menachem Begin and the Israeli Government
with Regard to the Lebanon War 91
The Sale of AWACS Planes to Saudi Arabia 94
Summary of the Special Relationship Between Begin and Falwell 97

6. Establishing the Moral Majority and Breaking Away from It:
Case Studies from the 1980s of the Moral Majority's Lobby
Congressional Activities 101
About the Decision to Enter Politics 101
Establishment of the Moral Majority Movement in Response to
Supreme Court Rulings 102
How Was the Mailing List Created, or—a Story About Sugar
and a Horse on a Farm 105
The Rise to Power of Jerry Falwell and His Role in the Struggle
Against President Carter 106
The Principles of the Moral Majority and Its Activity in
Support of Israel 109
About Falwell's Political Power Before the 1980 Election 112
The Moral Majority Blitz in the 1980 Elections 113
Dividing the Spoils Following Reagan's Election in 1980 115
Jerry Falwell's Political Ascent 119
Toward the 1984 Elections 121

CONTENTS

	The Decision to Retire from Political Life and Dissolve the Moral Majority	124
	Falwell's Retirement to Liberty University and Adapting It to the Twenty-First Century	127
	Falwell's Relationship with the Likud Prime Ministers After His Retirement from Politics	129
	Falwell's Death	131
7.	A Follow-Up Study on Liberty University Graduates Who Have Planted Churches	137
	Methodology and Approach	137
	The Graduates' Expansion Trend	138
	Liberty University Graduates and Church Planting	141
	Closeness Forms a Family That Leads to a Mission	142
	All Beginnings Are Difficult	143
	On the Importance of Marketing in the Life of a Pastor	146
	The Importance of Israel in the Daily Lives of Liberty University Graduates Who Lead Churches	151
8.	Findings and Discussion	157
	Summary and Recommendations for Future Research	161

Bibliography — 165

Appendices — 173
Appendix A—Data of Liberty Graduates Who Planted Churches — 173
Appendix B—Stenogram of a Conversation Between Falwell and a Team of Pastors with Menachem Begin — 177

Index — 191

FOREWORD
BY DR. REV. JOHNNIE MOORE

In an age of unprecedented information access, the discovery of overlooked historical narratives becomes all the more remarkable. Dr. Kobby Barda's scholarship stands as just such an achievement—unearthing crucial yet forgotten connections that illuminate our present moment.

Where others have relied on assumptions about Evangelical-Jewish relations, Dr. Barda approached his research with extraordinary objectivity and scholarly persistence. What emerged from his meticulous investigation was not merely isolated historical fragments, but a rich tapestry revealing the depth and complexity of a once-unimaginable alliance: the profound friendship between hundreds of millions of Christians and the Jewish people worldwide.

By opening this new scholarly domain, Dr. Barda has revealed compelling narratives that demonstrate how Jewish-Christian relations have fundamentally shaped both modern Israel and America during its period of global preeminence. His initial discoveries provided the catalyst for my own doctoral research, allowing me to further develop crucial aspects of this historical relationship.

My life's work centers on transforming Jewish-Christian relations—particularly regarding the hundreds of millions of Christian Zionists—from sentimental goodwill into substantive partnership. In this mission, Dr. Barda's research proves invaluable. We must acknowledge uncomfortable truths: Jewish communities often question Christian motivations, while Christians frequently fail to recognize how history justifies such wariness. Yet Dr. Barda reveals that we stand at the threshold of a new era in this relationship.

Fascinatingly, Theodor Herzl, modern Zionism's visionary founder, anticipated this alliance. At the first Zionist World Congress, Herzl personally invited Christian supporters as observers. Among them was Henry Dunant, the Red Cross founder who, though illness prevented his attendance, received Herzl's public gratitude in his closing address. Equally significant was Reverend William Hechler, referenced over one hundred times in

Herzl's diaries. Despite Herzl's commitment to secular Zionism, he noted that Hechler reminded him of his movement's inescapable theological dimensions.

My profound hope is that Dr. Barda's groundbreaking work inspires a renaissance of historical scholarship when our academic institutions desperately need such intellectual renewal. For in these recovered historical narratives lie essential lessons that illuminate not just our past, but our path forward. This is always important but especially now amidst a haunting rise in anti-Semitism from our universities. However, I am optimistic that history's most ancient hate will finally meet its match when confronted by hundreds of millions of Christians who cherish the Jewish people everywhere. Dr. Barda's crucial research helps reveal why the Jewish community and the State of Israel have more allies now than at any point in their ancient history. I, for one, am intent on keeping it this way.

Blessings,
Rev. Johnnie Moore, PhD
President, The Congress of Christian Leaders
Washington, DC

ACKNOWLEDGMENTS

I extend my heartfelt gratitude to **Dr. Eli Cook**, Head of the American Studies Program and the Department of General History at the University of Haifa, for his patient and dedicated guidance in shaping and writing the doctoral dissertation that eventually evolved into the book you are now reading. Dr. Cook also made it possible for me to complete the research through a generous fellowship from his research funds, which enabled me to conduct archival work in the United States. He previously supervised my MA thesis, and for more than six years has provided ongoing academic support with unwavering commitment and intellectual generosity.

My sincere thanks go to **Prof. Zach Levey**, Head of the School of International Relations, for his trust, patience, and guidance. He graciously agreed to supervise this interdisciplinary project and provided invaluable advice throughout the journey.

Special thanks to the Rector of the University of Haifa, Prof. Gur Alroey, whom I first met when he headed the Ruderman Program. Since that time, he has always been there to offer academic support with great patience and a genuine sense of mission.

In acknowledging those who supported my research, I must begin by thanking the Chaikin Chair in Geostrategy for their generous fellowship support during my studies and for their future assistance in the process of transforming this dissertation into an English-language book.

I am especially grateful to **Prof. Uriel Simonsohn** of the University of Haifa's Religious Laboratory, who supported me not only through fellowships but, more importantly, through intellectual engagement with the religious and political dimensions at the heart of my research.

I extend my deep appreciation to the team at **Anthem Press**—especially **Golda, Jebaslin, and Tej**—for their trust, dedication, and patience in shepherding this book from dissertation to publication, always with a generous spirit and a true desire to help.

I wish to thank the many pastors who agreed to be interviewed for this study, with special appreciation to **Dr. Rev. Johnnie Moore**, Senior Vice

President of Liberty University, for his valuable insights as a former student of the university, as someone who served under Dr. Jerry Falwell, and as a participant in President Trump's Evangelical Advisory Board. I am also deeply grateful to **Dr. Elmer L. Towns**, co-founder of Liberty University and father of the church planting methodology, who generously dedicated over two hours of his time to help me piece together key elements of the project.

Thanks, are also due to the staff at the Falwell Library, particularly **Ms. Abigail Ruth Sattler**, who assisted me greatly in locating and identifying many of the sources that make up the mosaic of this work. Deep thanks as well to **Ms. Jennifer Newby** at the Ronald Reagan Presidential Library Archive, for her endless patience and assistance in finding the files that significantly supported my research.

Above all, I extend my deepest and most heartfelt thanks to my wife, **Michal Franco-Barda**. It is no easy task to support someone who works, studies, and researches almost around the clock—while holding down a full-time job and being a devoted mother to our three children: **Ronny, Yehonatan, and Gili**. If I was able to meet the ambitious timelines I set for myself, it is entirely thanks to her, the guiding light of my life, for which I offer my eternal gratitude.

To my parents, **Aryeh and Mazal Barda**, I owe everything. Your belief in me and your lifelong investment brought me to this point. From my father, Aryeh Barda Rip., I inherited a passion and love for history. I regret that you did not live to read this dissertation, Dad, but I know you would have absorbed every word and asked follow-up questions with the curiosity of a child.

To my dear mother, Mazal Barda—may you be blessed with many long and good years. Thank you for moving mountains for me at every stage of my life, offering strength, support, and wise counsel that paved my way forward.

Finally, I cannot conclude without a brief word about the subject of this work, Dr. Jerry Falwell. I believe that this is the first doctoral dissertation to examine how Falwell established and realized his visionary model for the world—a model grounded, in his view, in the Hebrew Bible that he revered so deeply:

> *Where there is no revelation, people cast off restraint; but blessed is the one who heeds wisdom's instruction. 19 Servants cannot be.* (Proverbs 29:18)

This book aims to offer readers a perspective on how Falwell sought to disseminate the Word of God through a strategic prism that translated his theology into both domestic and international political activism—with a special emphasis on U.S.-Israel relations.

INTRODUCTION

The intersection of religion and politics in the United States has often been a potent force, shaping not only domestic policies but also international relations. Among the many religious movements that have influenced American politics, the rise of Christian Zionism stands out as a particularly powerful and complex phenomenon. This book, *Jerry Falwell, Liberty University, Church Planting, and the Rise of Christian Zionism in the United States*, delves into the life and legacy of Dr. Jerry Falwell, a man whose vision and actions have left an indelible mark on both American politics and the relationship between the United States and Israel.

This book is an extension of my doctoral dissertation, which was awarded by the University of Haifa in November 2023. The aim of this book is to provide a comprehensive examination of Dr. Falwell's impact on American politics, particularly through the lens of the church planting movement initiated by Liberty University graduates and the unique relationship Falwell cultivated with Israeli prime minister Menachem Begin.

From its inception, Liberty University was envisioned by Dr. Falwell as more than just an educational institution; it was to be a hub for training and mobilizing a new generation of Evangelical leaders who would carry forward the conservative Christian agenda. This agenda was not limited to domestic issues; it had a significant international dimension, particularly in its support for Israel. The book traces the roots of this movement, exploring how the Evangelical community in the United States, under Falwell's leadership, became one of the staunchest supporters of Israel, influencing U.S. foreign policy in profound ways.

The terms "evangelical" and "fundamentalist" refer to two historically interrelated yet distinct movements within American Protestantism. Evangelicalism developed as a broad, trans-denominational movement centered on the authority of the Bible, the necessity of personal conversion, the atoning work of Christ, and a mandate to evangelize. It gained institutional and cultural strength through the Great Awakenings and reached national prominence in the mid-twentieth century through figures like Billy Graham.

Fundamentalism, by contrast, emerged in the early twentieth century as a response to the rise of theological liberalism and higher criticism. It emphasized the inerrancy of scripture, the virgin birth, the substitutionary atonement, the bodily resurrection of Christ, and his imminent return—doctrines collectively known as "the fundamentals." Fundamentalists often separated from mainline denominations, forming independent churches and institutions while adopting a posture of resistance to secular culture and modernity. While both traditions affirm biblical authority and orthodox Christian doctrine, Evangelicals have typically been more open to cultural and political engagement, whereas fundamentalists have historically preferred withdrawal. By the late twentieth century, however, distinctions blurred as elements of the fundamentalist camp joined Evangelical efforts in the political arena, particularly around social issues such as abortion, school prayer, and religious freedom.[1]

The Visionary Leader: Dr. Jerry Falwell

Dr. Jerry Falwell was a man of immense vision and determination. His influence on American society and politics cannot be overstated. Born in Lynchburg, Virginia, Falwell's early life and education laid the groundwork for his later achievements. After studying at Bible College in Springfield, Missouri, he returned to Lynchburg with a mission: to build a community rooted in conservative Christian values. This mission began with the establishment of a small church and a Bible study group, but it quickly expanded into a much larger project.

In 1971, Falwell founded Liberty University, an institution that would grow to become one of the largest Christian universities in the world. But Falwell's ambitions did not stop there. He saw Liberty University as a launching pad for a broader movement, one that would spread conservative Christian values across the United States through the planting of new churches. This movement, known as the Church Planting Movement, became a cornerstone of Falwell's strategy for expanding Evangelical influence.

The Church Planting Movement

The Church Planting Movement, as envisioned by Falwell, was not just about establishing new places of worship. It was about creating a network of

---

1 George M. Marsden, *Understanding Fundamentalism and Evangelicalism* (Grand Rapids, MI: William B. Eerdmans, 1991), 1–15.

churches that would serve as centers of political and social influence. Liberty University graduates, trained in theology and leadership, were sent out across the country to plant these churches. Their mission was not only to spread the gospel but also to promote the conservative Christian agenda that Falwell championed.

This book tracks the journeys of nearly 200 Liberty University graduates who planted churches across the United States. Through these case studies, we can see how the church planting movement became a powerful force in American politics, particularly in the promotion of Christian Zionism. Falwell's graduates were not just pastors; they were also political activists, mobilizing their congregations to support causes that aligned with Falwell's vision.

One of the key aspects of this movement was its use of mass media. Falwell understood the power of television, radio, and print media in spreading his message. He used these tools to great effect, not only to grow his own ministry but also to promote the church planting movement. The book explores how Falwell's media empire supported the growth of the movement and helped to shape public opinion on key issues, including U.S. support for Israel.

The Unique Relationship with Menachem Begin

A central theme in the narrative of Jerry Falwell's life is his unique and profound relationship with Israeli prime minister Menachem Begin. This relationship was more than just a political alliance; it was a bond forged through shared values and mutual respect. Begin, who saw in Falwell a steadfast ally, was instrumental in deepening the ties between the American Evangelical community and the state of Israel.

Falwell's unwavering support for Israel was not just ideological but also deeply personal. He saw himself as a defender of the Jewish state and worked tirelessly to promote Israel's interests within the United States. His relationship with Begin allowed him unprecedented access to Israeli leadership, enabling him to act as a bridge between Israel and the American Evangelical community. This partnership played a crucial role in mobilizing American Evangelical support for Israel, which in turn had significant implications for U.S. foreign policy.

One of the most notable outcomes of this alliance was the effort to move the U.S. embassy from Tel Aviv to Jerusalem. Falwell's advocacy for this cause began in the 1980s, long before it became a reality. He leveraged his influence within the Reagan administration, Congress, and among the American public to push for this move, seeing it as both a political and a spiritual imperative.

The Moral Majority and Its Lasting Impact

The establishment of the Moral Majority in 1979 marked a turning point in American politics. This movement, founded by Falwell, sought to mobilize conservative Christians to become politically active, particularly on issues such as abortion, school prayer, and the defense of Israel. The Moral Majority quickly grew into a powerful political force, playing a pivotal role in the election of Ronald Reagan in 1980.

Under Falwell's leadership, the Moral Majority became a key player in the Republican Party, influencing policy decisions and shaping the party's platform on a range of issues. The movement's impact extended beyond the 1980s, laying the groundwork for the continued involvement of Evangelical Christians in American politics.

One of the most significant legacies of the Moral Majority is its role in fostering the close relationship between the United States and Israel. Falwell's advocacy for Israel within the Moral Majority helped to solidify Evangelical support for the Jewish state, creating a powerful political bloc that would continue to influence U.S. policy toward Israel for decades to come.

Catalyzing the Embassy Move Under Trump

The foundation laid by Falwell and the Moral Majority had far-reaching consequences, one of the most significant being the decision by President Donald Trump to move the U.S. embassy to Jerusalem in 2017. This move, which fulfilled a long-standing Evangelical goal, was a direct result of the groundwork laid by Falwell and the Evangelical movement he helped to build.

Falwell's vision of a strong U.S.-Israel relationship was realized in this historic moment, underscoring the lasting impact of his efforts. The embassy move was not just a political victory but also a symbolic affirmation of the deep ties between the American Evangelical community and the state of Israel. It demonstrated the power of grassroots political activism and the ability of religious movements to shape national and international policy.

Contextual Background

The Liberty Way: Falwell's Path to Christian Zionism offers a detailed and nuanced exploration of one of the most influential figures in modern American politics. By examining Falwell's life and legacy, the book sheds light on the complex interplay between religion and politics in the United States, and how this interplay has shaped not only domestic policies but also international relations.

This book is not just a biography of Jerry Falwell; it is also a study of the broader movement he helped to create. It provides insights into the ways in which Evangelicalism has shaped American political discourse and policy, particularly in relation to Israel. Through its detailed analysis of the church planting movement, the Moral Majority, and Falwell's relationship with Menachem Begin, the book offers a new perspective on the rise of Christian Zionism and its impact on U.S. foreign policy.

This book is structured chronologically and thematically to trace the theological and political evolution of Christian Zionism through the life and work of Jerry Falwell. The opening chapters establish the theological roots of Christian Zionism in nineteenth-century dispensationalism and trace its journey through early advocates like William Blackstone and evolving through the interwar and postwar periods. From there, the book explores the post–World War II revival of Evangelicalism and its growing engagement with Zionism, including the influence of prominent figures such as Billy Graham and Reinhold Niebuhr. Subsequent chapters examine the founding of Liberty University and Falwell's strategic use of education as a means to foster a new generation of Christian leaders committed to conservative values and pro-Israel politics. Special attention is given to the Moral Majority and its alignment with the Republican Party, offering insights into how theological convictions translated into political mobilization. The final sections of the book delve into Falwell's direct engagement with Israeli leaders, his theological framing of U.S.-Israel relations, and the institutional legacy he left behind. In this way, the book not only provides a comprehensive biography of Falwell but also offers a broader exploration of how American Evangelicalism has intersected with the Zionist cause, reshaping political landscapes in both the United States and the Middle East.

As you embark on this journey through the life and legacy of Jerry Falwell, I invite you to consider the profound influence that one man, driven by faith and conviction, can have on the course of history. This book is a testament to that influence, and I hope it will provide readers with a deeper understanding of the forces that have shaped the modern Evangelical movement and its role in American politics.

Chapter 1

INTRODUCTION TO THE MODERN EVANGELICAL POLITICAL POWER

Background on Christian Theology and Its Affinity to Israel

The period after the Six-Day War (The 1967 War), which was also Israel's 25th Jubilee year, was a period of "rebirth" for Evangelical theology in general and the Christian Lobby that supported Israel in particular. David Katz claims that one of the influential connections to Evangelical theology in the modern era is the book *The Late Great Planet Earth* by Hal Lindsey, first published in 1970 with the help of Carol Carlson. According to the author and editor, 25 million copies of the book were sold, making it the best-selling book in Christian tradition, other than the Bible itself. According to Katz, this book has had such a significant impact, partly due to its dynamic description of the vision of John of Patmos, which unrolls before our eyes, starting with the establishment of the State of Israel in 1948.[1] According to the belief of observant Christians, this period, which comes every 50 years and is called in Hebrew "The Jubilee year," is a substantial milestone in the development of the relationship between the Evangelical Church and the people and State of Israel. Jason Olson also refers to 1967 as a turning point, claiming in his book that: "1967 was a vindication for fundamentalists. GOD proved that he stood by Israel. History has proven this."[2] Later in the book, he added that: "Post '67, the new Evangelicals, saw in the Israeli occupation of Jerusalem and the West Bank future proof of the religious prophecy; One that would serve as a full justification for biblical literature and the Eschaton."[3] However, before

---

1 David Katz, "Gog, Magog and Demagog" (Hebrew Text) in *Panim – Culture, Society and Education*, Issue 12, February 2012, https://www.itu.org.il/?CategoryID=549 &ArticleID=1748, accessed January 26, 2020.
2 Jason Olson, *America's Road to Jerusalem: The Impact of the Six-Day War on Protestant Politics* (Lanham, MD: Lexington Books, 2018), 116.
3 Ibid., 205.

discussing the 1970s, it is advisable and appropriate to take a brief look at the earlier development of the Evangelical Church in the nineteenth century.

The relationship of the Evangelical movement toward Israel and Judaism has undergone several changes over the years. To understand the theological roots of the movement's relationship to Israel, examining its connection to the land of Israel in the mid-nineteenth century is necessary. According to Donald Akenson, it was the Reverend John Nelson Darby who developed the theory.[4] The Anglo-Irish origin pastor, John Nelson Darby, was the one who promoted "The Theology of Dispensationalism," which sets Christianity as the "true Israel" and replaces Judaism in its exclusive proximity to the Creator. According to Donald Wagner, the British Protestants were those who developed the Theology of Parallel Covenants for Christians and Jews, and not necessarily the replacement of Judaism with Christianity.[5] The "new" Christian Zionism has vigorously emerged in the early decades of the twentieth century with the rise of the Evangelical movement in Britain and a new translation of the prophecy. Jarmila Drozdikova described in her article the significant theological influence of Darby on modern Evangelicalism.[6] According to Drozdikova, pastor John Nelson Darby (1800–1882) relinquished his position in the Church of England as a minister and became a member of a separatist Christian group in Plymouth, which called itself "The Plymouth Brethren."

Darby developed and honed the unique theology of this sect, with a particular emphasis on the Eschaton. Darby divided history into several periods (Dispensations), which, although not a new concept in and of itself, was Darby's idea to divide the approximate time of human existence into seven segments, beginning with the creation and ending in the thousand-year kingdom of Jesus after the battle of Armageddon. During each of these periods, GOD tests humanity through a different salvation scheme. Humanity fails all tests, and each historical period ends in a disaster of divine judgment. The first pericope ended with the fall of Adam and Eve and their eviction from the Garden of Eden; the second ended with the Flood, and the third with the Tower of Babylon, for example. In the Book of Daniel, 9:24–25, which served as Darby's inspiration, it is written:

---

4 Donald Harman Akenson, *Exporting the Rapture: John Nelson Darby and the Victorian Conquest of North American Evangelicalism* (New York: Oxford University Press, 2018).

5 Donald Wagner, "Christian Zionists, Israel and the 'Second Coming'," miftah.org, October 14, 2003, available at: http://www.miftah.org/Display.cfm?DocId=2545&CategoryId=5, accessed September 9, 2023.

6 J. Drozdíková, "History of the Future," *Asian and African Studies* 16, no. 1 (2007): 86–87.

> *Seventy "sevens" are decreed for your people and your holy city to finish transgression, to put an end to sin, to atone for wickedness, to bring in everlasting righteousness, to seal up vision and prophecy and to anoint the Most Holy Place. Know and understand this: From the time the word goes out to restore and rebuild Jerusalem until the Anointed One, the ruler, comes, there will be seven "sevens," and sixty-two "sevens." It will be rebuilt with streets and a trench, but in times of trouble. After the sixty-two "sevens," the Anointed One will be put to death and will have nothing. The people of the ruler who will come will destroy the city and the sanctuary. The end will come like a flood: War will continue until the end, and desolations have been decreed.*

Darby explained the hint as an explanation for further developments. It is written that 70 weeks of years shall pass between the return of the Jews from the Babylonian captivity to the reign of the Messiah. After the end of the sixth era, Jesus appeared, but the Jews refused to accept him. Then began the new division, that of the Church. We live in the sixth era, the Christian era, and refer to the seventh era, which is the era of the final cataclysm. At the end of this era, after seven years of war and mayhem, Jesus will establish his kingdom in Jerusalem and reign for a millennium. The innovation in this interpretation is depicted in the fact that only through the dramatic return of Jesus to establish his kingdom in Jerusalem will salvation come to the world. Believers must give up the illusion of "Christian civilization" until the return of Christ. Reverend Darby argued that Israel would replace the role of the Church.[7]

The theory of those called "Dispensationalists" defines the church as a body of true believers who have undergone inner experiences of conversion, received Jesus as their personal Savior, and committed themselves to living holy lives. From this comes the theological term that has become a definition in political discussions—"Born Again Christians"—referring to people who were not physically reborn but experienced the same revelation that brought them to the recognition and understanding of their new lives that were created after that rebirth. Only those who have undergone this revelation and been reborn will be spared the terrors that will precede the coming of the Messiah. The Messianic times will begin when the true believers are taken from Earth in a process called the "Rapture," when their souls will be detached from their bodies and ascend to heaven, where they will meet Jesus in the air. The believers will stay with Jesus for seven years, and thereby, they will be spared the terrible torment that will befall those who remain on

---

[7] It is important to emphasize that Darby's vision pre-dates the modern Zionist movement, founded only at the First Zionist Congress in Basel in 1897. In the Sixth Congress held in 1903, Uganda was even proposed as an alternative to the Jewish homeland.

Earth. During these seven years, two-thirds of humanity will perish from plagues, wars, and various forms of death. Based on their literal, interpretive principle, Dispensationalists argue that the promises given to Abraham by GOD and through him to the Jews, are eternal and unconditional, and they are waiting for their fulfillment. This means that the borders of the land GOD had promised to Abraham and his descendants, from the Nile to the Euphrates, are the will of GOD, and hence the importance given to Jewish settlement in the places GOD promised to Abraham, which has become an essential part of conservative politics. According to their prophecy, the final battle (Armageddon) will take place in the city of Megiddo, at the end which, Jesus the Messiah will return to a Jewish theocratic kingdom centered around the rebuilt Temple in Jerusalem. This theology seeks to promote the importance of multiphase, thus, first and foremost, to gather all the People of Israel in their land, to prepare for the coming of the false prophet, after whom Jesus will emerge.

This eschatological framework deeply influenced late nineteenth-century American Evangelicalism. American revivalist leaders such as William E. Blackstone brought these ideas into the public square. His best-selling book *Jesus Is Coming* (1878) popularized literalist prophecy interpretation and declared that the Jewish people had a biblically mandated right to the Land of Israel.[8]

Yaakov Ariel notes that Blackstone's legacy extended well beyond his immediate context. His theological framework, particularly the assertion that Jewish restoration to the Land of Israel was a biblical imperative—became foundational to a broader Protestant missionary discourse that gained momentum in the late nineteenth and early twentieth centuries. Ariel explains that dispensationalist theology, with its premise of separate divine plans for Jews and Christians, provided an ideological structure that legitimized missionary work among Jews without demanding complete assimilation. This allowed Christian evangelists to present conversion not as a betrayal of Jewish identity, but as its prophetic fulfillment—a notion that aligned well with pre-millennialist expectations and growing sympathy for Zionism.[9] Ariel further emphasizes that this theological-philosophical synthesis gave missionaries both motivation and method for engaging Jewish immigrants, especially amid the mass arrivals from Eastern Europe. Missions like the "Hope of Israel" in New

---

8 William E. Blackstone, *Jesus Is Coming* (Chicago: Fleming H. Revell Company, 1898), 186.

9 Yaakov Ariel, *Evangelizing the Chosen People: Missions to the Jews in America, 1880–2000* (Chapel Hill: University of North Carolina Press, 2000), 21–25.

York adopted rituals and cultural markers that affirmed Jewish distinctiveness, while simultaneously incorporating Christian eschatological meaning. This dual strategy—preserving Jewish identity while redirecting its purpose toward a Christological telos—helped establish an ideological bridge to what would later become Christian Zionism. Ariel argues that this theological platform gained heightened relevance in the years leading up to the famous 1925 Scopes Trial, when American Protestant fundamentalism entered a phase of cultural backlash and theological retrenchment. In this way, Ariel provides a critical link between the nineteenth-century dispensationalist foundations and the religious climate of early twentieth-century America—a period increasingly defined by resistance to secularism and renewed urgency to evangelize both Jews and Christians in light of perceived apocalyptic signs.

Historian George Marsden noted that by the early twentieth century, premillennial dispensationalism had become a cornerstone of American fundamentalist theology, fostering a perpetual expectation that biblical prophecy was being fulfilled in contemporary events.[10]

Darby's prophecy, which began in the mid-nineteenth century, received significant backing from events that seemingly supported his prophecies in the chronicle of the generations and even increased expectations for the fulfillment of other parts of the prophecy. The first event in the prophetic sequence began in February 1867 when British archaeologist Sir Charles Warren, who arrived in the holy land as part of the second expedition of the British Palestine Exploration Fund (PEF), discovered "Underground Jerusalem." The fund, which had only recently been established, lacked resources and was manned by a young engineer and three corporals. Warren enthusiastically assumed leadership of the expedition. As a devout Protestant, he saw great value in uncovering the mysteries of the biblical land hidden beneath the layers of rubbish and debris. As a military man, he sought to assist his country, which, unlike other powers, paid little attention to the territories of the decaying Ottoman Empire. The combination of religious, archaeological, and political missions was represented in the mapping and land exploration work that could also serve as a basis for military intelligence activities.[11] After 100 years of British struggle against Ottoman forces, on the night of December 8, 1917, the British Army, led by General Allenby succeeded in

---

10 George M. Marsden, *Fundamentalism and American Culture* (Oxford: Oxford University Press, 2006), 56–60.
11 Pierre Warren, "The Subterranean Water System within the Ancient City of David Site in Jerusalem," available at: https://www.cityofdavid.org.il/virtual_tour/water-system-warrens-shaft-city-david, retrieved on August 8th, 2021. (Hebrew Source)

capturing Jerusalem. Nirit Shalev-Khalifa, Director of the Department for Visual History, Archives and Documentation at the Yad Ben-Zvi Institute, explains the religious significance of the conquest for Christians: "He was received as a hero, awarded the rank of Field Marshal, and considered a crusader of his time. When he had to choose his title, it was expected he would choose Jerusalem, but he chose Megiddo instead," said Shalev-Khalifa. The title of "Megiddo" was considered his noblest title, and according to her, "there is a kind of connection to the story of Armageddon, even though Allenby was quite cold in terms of religion. His choice was mainly because the battle of Megiddo actually concluded the conquest of Greater Syria. This choice also symbolized Allenby's perception of himself as a soldier and that this was his role. He fulfilled his duties to the best of his abilities in the service of the King's Empire."[12]

Simultaneously, in the 1920s, the "Monkey Trial" issue became part of the Evangelical identity in the United States. Rami Shalheveth, in his article about the "Monkey Trial," describes the background: "Immediately after the publication of Darwin's book 'On the Origin of Species,' who for the first time provided a scientific explanation for the evolution of life on earth without the involvement of a higher power, thus denied the idea that man is the 'crown of creation.' In the popular discourse, the debate focused on Darwin's claim that man evolved from an ancient primate and is related to chimpanzees and gorillas. The common claim against him was, "You mean my father was a monkey?" Hence, the name "Monkey Trial" was born. He then adds: "In the 1920s, the debate heated up when opponents of evolution-initiated attempts to give scientific validity to the story of creation and produced the pseudo-science called 'Creationism.' Almost by chance, a member of the Tennessee State Legislature, the southern farmer and devout Christian John Washington Butler, entered this debate. Butler's motivations for the bill were a combination of deep religious faith and ignorance, as he himself admitted. During the trial, he said, "I knew nothing about evolution when I raised the bill. I read in the newspapers that boys and girls come home from school and tell their fathers and mothers that the Bible is nonsense." Yet, even after reading Darwin's books, he remained firm in his opinion that teaching the theory of evolution was dangerous. The bill passed the legislature in late January 1925, passed the Tennessee Senate on March 13, and went into effect eight

---

12 Eli Ashkenazi, "The Gentleman Who Conquered the Land: 100 Years since the Arrival of General Allenby to Jerusalem," *Walla News*, December 11, 2017, available at: https://news.walla.co.il/item/3118375, retrieved on August 8th, 2021. (Hebrew Source).

days later. Its supporters argued that since Creationism is prohibited from being taught in public schools, being a religious doctrine, the teaching of evolution should also be prohibited to prevent giving its supporters an advantage in public discourse. The bill provoked much opposition, and the American Civil Liberties Union (ACLU) sought a teacher who would agree to put it to the test. Eventually, it found Scopes, a novice math and science teacher who agreed to teach evolution when entering a biology class as a substitute teacher. The monkey trial created a buzz and ended with Scopes' conviction and a $100 fine, which was later overturned on appeal on technical grounds.

Butler's bill itself remained in effect for 42 years, until teacher Gary L. Scott was fired from his job for teaching evolution and started a fight to repeal the law. In May 1967, three days after the lawsuit he filed in federal court, the Tennessee House of Representatives and the Senate repealed Butler's law, and on May 18, the governor added his signature and brought an end to that infamous law.[13]

The period from the 1920s to the beginning of the 1970s was marked by the construction of community infrastructure and distancing from activity in the public arena.

Following the Scopes Trial, the theological and political landscape of American Protestantism diversified significantly. One influential figure who stood out during the mid-twentieth century was Reinhold Niebuhr, a leading Protestant theologian and public intellectual associated with the neo-orthodox movement. Unlike the fundamentalist strain of dispensationalism, Niebuhr's Christian realism emphasized the moral ambiguities of politics and the need for justice through democratic means. In the wake of World War II and the Holocaust, Niebuhr became an outspoken advocate for the establishment of a Jewish state. In 1942, he co-founded the Christian Council on Palestine and consistently argued that the moral obligation of Christians demanded support for Jewish self-determination in the land of Israel. He saw this not merely as a biblical prophecy fulfilled, but as a response to historical injustice and an imperative of Christian ethics. His writings and activism helped shift segments of mainline Protestantism toward a more favorable stance on Zionism, paving the way for broader Christian support of Israel in the decades to follow.[14]

---

13 Rami Shalheveth, "Today Before: The Background for the 'Monkey Trial'," Davidson Institute, March 21, extracted from the website: https://davidson.weizmann.ac.il/online/sciencehistory/%D7%94%D7%99%D7%95%D7%9D-.

14 Richard W. Fox, *Reinhold Niebuhr: A Biography* (New York: Pantheon Books, 1985), 250–255.

After a long period when Zionism was pushed to the sidelines of Evangelical Christianity, a revival of interest in Zionism began among Evangelical Christians after World War II. This revival coincided with a broader transformation within American fundamentalism. Historian Joel A. Carpenter explains that "the quiet years provided a haven for thoughtful reflection," enabling fundamentalist leaders to regroup and develop new strategies for mass evangelism through media and institutional outreach.[15] It was due, in part, to the efforts of the evangelist, Billy Graham, who began incorporating Zionist themes into his "crusades" across the United States and his visit to Israel in 1960 for a high-profile meeting with then-foreign minister Golda Meir and President Yitzhak Ben-Zvi.[16] Billy Graham was an American evangelist and pastor whose great missions and friendships with many U.S. presidents made him an international figure. Graham was one of the first "Televangelists" and successfully utilized the opportunities offered by new media technologies in his time, especially radio and television, to spread his Christian message. He made his breakthrough in 1949, when he moved to Los Angeles and befriended Hollywood stars during the religious crusades he held in a circus tent. In the 1950s, he moved to New York, where he began his relationships with presidents starting from the Eisenhower era, which earned him international recognition. In the 1970s, during Yitzhak Rabin's tenure as Israeli ambassador to Washington, their years-long friendship was established. Rabin wrote in his book: "I have close ties with the religious leader, Billy Graham. His unconditional support for Israel always excites me. He never misses an opportunity to speak about Nixon, whom he greatly loves and respects, and the need to strengthen Israel."[17] On the importance and contribution of Billy Graham to the spread of the Evangelical movement, Sarah Yeshayahu Leibman, together with Eddie Zeltzer, write in their book: "More than anything else, the activity of evangelist Billy Graham symbolized the beginning of the return of American fundamentalists to the public stage in their country. Graham's crusades, which were held in the large cities of America, drew Millions of listeners."[18]

---

15 Joel A. Carpenter, *Revive Us Again: The Reawakening of American Fundamentalism* (New York: Oxford University Press, 1997), 78.
16 Bader Mansour, "When Billy Graham Visited Israel," Baptist.org, February 21, 2018, http://www.baptist.org.il/news/post/173/When-Billy-Graham-Visited-Israel-%E2%80%93-Bader-Mansour, retrieved on August 8th, 2021.
17 Yitzhak Rabin, *Service Notebook* (Tel Aviv: Ma'ariv Publications, 1979), 280. (Hebrew Source).
18 Sarah Yeshayahu Leibman and Eddie Zeltzer, *Religion and Politics – Selected Aspects* (Open University Press, 2011), 128. (Hebrew Source).

The Six-Day War in 1967, which seemed to be the war in which Arab armies would annihilate Israel, ended with a great victory and the occupation of the biblical lands, including Jerusalem, Judea, Samaria, and the Golan Heights. This victory occurred precisely in the Jubilee year of the Crusader Allenby's entry on horseback into Jerusalem and was perceived by many as a prophetic preparation for the fulfillment of prophecy. Israel's ability to defeat all its enemies in such a short period of time was described by Christian author Nelson Bell, editor of the prominent *Christianity Today* newspaper, who wrote in July 1967 about the Israeli army's entry into Jerusalem from a place seeking to strengthen the prophecy, that "it gives Bible students joy and assurance of the accuracy and validity of the Bible [...] If we say, as the Arabs say, that Israel has no right to exist, we may be proven wrong in our blindness by GOD, under His providence."[19]

A political scientist, Sotiris Roussos, argues that the 1967 War was a significant turning point for American political involvement. "Evangelical Americans interpreted [the war] as a sign that the end of days is approaching and humanity is getting closer to it. Therefore, the Evangelical Americans experienced a religious revelation that manifested in increased political involvement in the Republican Party, which, inter alia, required creating a 'lobby' for Israel within the Republican Party. However, the idea of the Christian Party was to work and fortify unconditional US support for Israel, which began in the 1980s and continues until today."[20] It is also necessary to add, against the backdrop of that era, that the Evangelical movement grew as a counter-phenomenon vis-à-vis the sexual liberation of the 1960s in America, and promoted Christian family values, as described by Kristin Du Mez in her book: "Since the 1960s, Evangelicals have been committed to the term 'law and order'. What started as a reaction against hippies, anti-war activists, beauty-seeking freedom-lovers, and urban minorities grew into a movement [...]"[21] The connection between the biblical story and family values was one of the core topics in Christian Sunday schools in America, as described by Michael Ryan and Caroline Kinane, who gained momentum in these years: "In the United States, Sunday schools took a religious direction intertwined with Christian values. Schools that promoted the Dispensationalist view provided students with the message about the future and the importance of Israel

---

19 Melani McAlister, *Epic Encounters: Culture, Media, and U.S. Interests in the Middle East since 1945* (Oakland, CA: University of California Press, 2005), 170.
20 Sotiris Roussos, *Religion and International Relations in the Middle East* (Basel: MDPI, 2020), 81.
21 Kristin Kobes Du Mez, *Jesus and John Wayne: How White Evangelicals Corrupted a Faith and Fractured a Nation* (New York: Liveright Publishing, 2020), 298.

toward the end of days."²² Hence, we can see the combination of a rising need to return to family values and educational frameworks that foster Christian values on the one hand, who meet the "manifested miracle" of GOD's assistance to the People of Israel in obtaining parts of the Land of Israel, led by the ancient city of Jerusalem, on the other hand. At the end of the 1960s, this encounter was perceived as a significant catalyst, leading into the decade of "rebirth" of the Evangelical movement in general and within the context of Christian Zionism in particular.

However, above all, during that same period of the late 1960s and early 1970s, the movie *The Pastor of America* that had the most significant impact. It was the film of the late Reverend Billy Graham, called *His Land*, which became a significant catalyst for the growth of the Christian Zionist movement in the 1970s. According to Daniel Hummel's affirmation, the importance of the film, which was shot against the backdrop of Israeli landscapes and released to theaters in 1970, was that it broke through Christian consciousness to the importance of Israel for Evangelical faith: "The film captivated the Evangelical world, watched by hundreds of thousands and perhaps millions of people, in a blend of Messianic beliefs and cultural arguments, which later turned into the Christian-Zionist movement, that in turn will become a major part of the religious Right."[23]

---

22 Michael A. Ryan and Karolyn Kinane, *End of Days: Essays on the Apocalypse from Antiquity to Modernity* (Jefferson, NC: McFarland & Co., 2009), 204.

23 Daniel G. Hummel, "His Land and the Origins of the Jewish-Evangelical Israel lobby," *Church History* 87, no. 4 (American Society of Church History, December 2018): 1119–1151.

Chapter 2

THE BEGINNING OF DR. JERRY FALWELL'S JOURNEY AND THE ESTABLISHMENT OF LIBERTY UNIVERSITY

The Beginning of Jerry Falwell's Journey

Jerry Falwell (1933–2007) was a Fundamentalist Evangelical Baptist denomination pastor from Lynchburg, Virginia. He was born on August 11, 1933, into a family that suffered trauma. His father, Carey Falwell, killed his uncle, who was considered Lynchburg's "troublemaker." This event shaped the future of his father and the rest of his family. Although the court acquitted his father, it did not change the course of his life. Instead, he became an alcoholic and suffered from it until his death. Jerry was only 15 years old at the time; however, his father's memory continued to shape his life over time.[1] His father's fondness for alcohol was a significant trigger in his life to engage in the rescue and healing of alcoholism: "I believe that observing my father drinking heavily throughout my childhood has affected me, and that's why I have a hatred for that bitter drop, and why it has never been a problem in my personal life."[2] The Mother, Helen Falwell was an Evangelical Born-Again Christian who grew up in a family of 16 siblings, all working in their father's tobacco field, harvesting tobacco leaves.[3] Jerry's mother raised her children according to Evangelical Christian values, and he absorbed his love for Christianity from her. "I owe my personality to my mother; there's no question about it. Everything I know about the difference between good and

---

1 *"Why does Jerry Falwell Support Israel?"* comeandsee.com, November 4, 2003, available at: http://www.comeandsee.com/view.php?sid=504, accessed May 9, 2021.
2 Liberty University Archive, Fal 1: Falwell Family Materials. FAL 1:1-2 Box 1. Patricia Pingry, *Jerry Falwell: Man of Vision* (Milwaukee: Ideals Publishing Corporation, 1980), 19.
3 Ibid., 20.

evil comes from her [...] My mother was the one who shaped my morality and the significance of honesty, personality, humility, and respect for others."[4]

Falwell testifies that his love for Israel began with the reading of the Old Testament and how the commitment of GOD to the children of Israel is presented. In his autobiography, he repeatedly emphasizes the divine commitment to the children of Israel. Still, he also describes his understanding of the importance of Israel at the beginning of his journey:

> *The Bible tells us that for those many generations after Adam and Eve sinned, GOD did everything to save the children of Israel from their own sins. The righteous side of GOD longed to erase creation and start over, but His mercy prevailed and GOD called upon Noah to build an ark and save creation. After the flood, GOD made a covenant with Noah and his family to give the world another chance. Chapter after chapter, book after book, the records of the Bible describe GOD's efforts to save His creation from His own sin. He made a covenant with the fathers: Abraham, Isaac, and Jacob. He promised them a great nation that would live in the Promised Land. "And from the People of Israel," GOD promised, "will come a Messiah who will save all people from their sins."*[5]

Further down the road, Falwell will revisit the commitment of GOD to the children of Israel thousands of times. By so doing, he will fulfill the commitment of every Christian believer to assist the People of Israel in the Land of Israel to the best of his ability. As mentioned, Falwell grew up in the town of Lynchburg, Virginia, founded in the eighteenth century by John Lynch, an Irish American tobacco farmer. Some claim that the town was named after his brother's practice, Colonel Charles Lynch, who established an informal court during the Civil War that judged and hanged the rebellious rebels by their thumbs, and from there, the town's name was derived. In 1950, Falwell entered Lynchburg College and began studying courses that would lead him to specialize in mechanical engineering. He planned to transfer to Virginia Polytechnic Institute in his freshman year, and by the end of his sophomore year, there was no reason he wouldn't do so: he scored the highest math average in the college that year. However, come fall, Falwell had already registered for the Bible Baptist College in Springfield, Missouri, and was on his way to becoming a pastor.[6] During his senior year, Falwell served as an assis-

---

4 Ibid., 22.
5 Jerry Falwell, *Strength for the Journey: An Autobiography* (New York: Simon & Schuster, 1987), 163.
6 Frances FitzGerald, "A Disciplined, Charging Army," *The New Yorker*, May 18, 1981, available at: https://www.newyorker.com/magazine/1981/05/18/a-disciplined-charging-army, accessed May 9, 2021.

tant pastor at the Kansas City Baptist Temple, over 200 kilometers away from the college where he studied. He would travel on weekends to help prepare for Sunday service, after which he would return to start his college week.[7] Later in life, Falwell was awarded three honorary doctorate degrees: Doctor of Divinity from the Theological Seminary of Tennessee, Doctor of Letters (D. Litt) from the School of Advanced Theology in California, and Doctor of Law from the Central University in Seoul, South Korea.

On January 20, 1952, Falwell joined the Baptist Church of Park Avenue. The church's youth coordinator, Pastor Jack Dinsbeer, trained and encouraged him to become a full-time pastor. As a result, he studied at the Baptist College in Springfield, Missouri, and shortly after completing his studies gained his BA. In 1956 he became the pastor of a 35-members community that he founded on June 21, as part of an induction service that took place in the hall of "Mountain View" elementary school, where he had studied as a child. The service was conducted further to a dispute that led him and his followers to leave the Park Avenue Baptist Church and pursue their love for GOD in the way that Falwell interpreted the Holy Scriptures. This aspect is vital for understanding the place of Israel and the Jewish People, who have received the divine promise to be the chosen people. Falwell recalled in his memoires that "the Bible, being the word of GOD, contains everything that is needed for the doctrine of the worship of GOD."[8] Equipped only with the word of GOD, at 22, Jerry Falwell decided to hoist the flag of faith above a new church. This church, founded in an abandoned bottling plant and acquired through the contributions of its members for $5,000, was called the Thomas Road Baptist Church and would become one of the largest Baptist churches worldwide, with more than 24,200 members to date.[9] From the beginning of the church's journey, Falwell laid the foundation for its development with a quote from the Book of Apostles: "But you will receive power when the Holy Spirit comes on you; and you will be my witnesses in Jerusalem and in all Judea and Samaria, and to the end of the earth" (Acts 1:6–8). Falwell hung a map of Lynchburg on the wall and marked circles of influence on it, with the first circle, which was in the center and was named "Judea," being the church he founded, and his goal was to spread the gospel in circles around the church. For each circle around the church, he recorded the head of the household's name and address. Every morning at 9:00, he began knocking

---

[7] Ibid., *Jerry Falwell: Man of Vision*, 27.
[8] Ibid., *Jerry Falwell: Man of Vision*, 31.
[9] Park Avenue Baptist Church History official website, available at: https://trbc.org/history/, accessed May 9, 2021.

on doors in the circles he marked and started his speech: "Hello, I'm Jerry Falwell, the pastor of the new church here. I stopped by to say hello and invite you to our prayers." Thus, he managed to create the first contact and develop a conversation in which he asked about the children's details and ages in a friendly conversation. Before moving on to the next house, he updated his notebook with the family's details so that he could create a more intimate acquaintance with the community. When he finished the first circle—"Judea"—he moved on to his second circle called "Samaria," and after a few years, he completed knocking on most of the doors of Lynchburg residents. He kept lists of all the relevant details he collected.[10] These lists, with all the relevant details, were handed to the female volunteers who distributed his manifest to families in the circles he visited. On Saturdays, Falwell would phone to remind these families about the Sunday service, and invite them to attend. Newcomers received a worshipper card, and their contact information was cataloged in the church's system. Thus, in the first year, Falwell managed to increase his congregation from a parish of 35 at the beginning of the journey to 864.[11]

Simultaneously that year, Falwell's journey toward mass communication had started. From his own living room, as part of a radio show called *Old Time Gospel Hour*, Falwell began broadcasting his message of salvation and raising donations that helped him grow in wealth and influence. Falwell was a pioneer in understanding the importance of conveying the message through mass media and using trends to do so before they even become such. An understanding of and recognition in mass communications would characterize his life from the beginning of his path within the Thomas Road Baptist Church. However, that was only the first step in a series of leadership steps that would characterize his life thereafter. About the beginning of his path on the radio, he wrote: "Immediately after the church was founded, I started a radio show out of faith that if I was positively influenced, I could also influence others. I went to the radio station at 6:30 am, seven days a week, and broadcasted live from the radio station. The broadcast cost was $7 for every half-hour. I struggled to raise these funds, but I felt it was worth every penny."[12]

In the 1950s, further steps were taken beyond radio/television broadcasts, such as establishing a clinic to treat alcoholism and opening a free summer

---

10 Ibid., Liberty University Archive, Fal 1: Falwell Family Materials. FAL 1:1-2 Box 1. Pingry, *Jerry Falwell: Man of Vision*, 33.
11 Ibid., Liberty University Archive, Fal 1: Falwell Family Materials. FAL 1:1-2 Box 1. Pingry, *Jerry Falwell: Man of Vision*, 33.
12 Ibid., *Jerry Falwell: Man of Vision*, 23.

camp for children in Virginia.[13] Falwell worked to promote various social issues in the early years of his social activism. In a 1958 public address entitled "Segregation or Integration: Which?" Falwell criticized the Supreme Court's 1954 *Brown v. Board of Education of Topeka* decision, which invalidated segregation in public schools, saying, "If Chief Justice Earl Warren and his associates had known GOD's Word and had desired to do the Lord's will, I am quite confident that the 1954 decision would never have been made."[14]

In 1957, Falwell turned to his friend, Frank Pratt, owner of Lynchburg Oil Company, and requested a loan to purchase a building that could accommodate the growing number of participants in the Sunday services held in the old building. Pratt secured a loan of $5,000, and for the next five years, the church served the growing congregation. In 1962, a new church was built in its stead, in the shape of a cross, with event halls, seminar and prayer rooms inspired by Thomas Jefferson's summer home in Poplar Forest.[15]

1959 marked the first time that Falwell began expanding beyond his original circle in Lynchburg, Virginia, as he recounts in his autobiography: "In 1959, we added a second station in the nearby city of Roanoke, Virginia. In the 1960s, we added ten more stations throughout Virginia, West Virginia, Tennessee, North Carolina, and Washington, D.C. GOD trained me and my people to make wise use of this modern communication miracle. Step by step, slowly and gradually, it helped us expand our sphere of influence from 'Jerusalem, to Judea, and Samaria.' Thank GOD, one day we will use television to broadcast the good news 'to all parts of the earth' as Jesus Himself commissioned us."[16]

In the family aspect, the late 1950s and early 1960s were when Falwell established his own family. In 1958, Falwell married Macel Pate. The couple had three children: Jerry Falwell Jr. (who became president of Liberty University and was expelled in 2021 following a sex scandal), Jonathan (a senior religious leader at Thomas Road Baptist Church), and their daughter, Jenny, a surgeon.

---

13 "Moral Majority Founder Jerry Falwell Dies," *nbcnews.com*, May 15, 2007, available at: https://www.nbcnews.com/id/wbna18679412, accessed June 19, 2021.
14 Adelle M. Banks, "Jerry Falwell Marks 50 Years in the Pulpit," Religion News Service, July 8, 2006, available at: http://archive.naplesnews.com/community/jerry-falwell-marks-50-years-in-the-pulpit-ep-406161960-331426441.html/ , accessed June 19, 2021.
15 Dirk Smillie, *Falwell Inc.: Inside a Religious, Political, Educational, and Business Empire* (New York: St. Martin's Press, 2008), 61–62.
16 Ibid., *Strength for the Journey: An Autobiography*, 333.

The Formative 1960s

The early 1960s were primarily focused on expanding the congregation and fundraising toward constructing a larger structure that could accommodate the growing parish. Construction of the new, 1,000-seat church began in 1963 and was completed in 1964. It was named the Moody Building[17].

The first educational institution established during this time was the Lynchburg Christian Academy (LCA), founded in 1967 as an extension of Thomas Road Baptist Church to provide Christian education to children in central Virginia. The academy, established by Falwell as part of his educational and entrepreneurial development in the 1960s, became a fully accredited institution and a viable academic option for parents who wanted their children taught by a Christian worldview, with a curriculum based on the Bible.[18] The school was based on five principles that operate in the spirit of religion, offering the possibility of private tutoring in Lynchburg and its vicinity. The principles, as expressed in promotional pamphlets distributed to parents, were: Quality education, no drugs, Mandatory Bible reading and praying, No prejudices, and Patriotism.[19]

In the 1960s, Falwell toiled to deepen his interactions with the community and influence some of the most significant controversies of these years against the backdrop of the Civil Rights Act of 1965, which addressed the abolition of racial segregation between colored and white people. During 1964 and 1965, as the law was being enacted, Falwell delivered at least two sermons against the Civil Rights Movement, who had even protested outside his church.[20]

The most famous sermon in this context, which is significant mainly for understanding Dr. Falwell's worldview on mixing religion with politics, was the speech entitled "Ministries and Marches," held before an audience of over 1,000 listeners at his church on March 21, 1965. The speech addressed the racial tensions of the time, and Falwell responded to the role his church had taken upon itself to promote the issue of human rights legislation. Integration of colored individuals into his community transpired only in the late 1960s,

---

17 Liberty University Archive, Fal 1: Falwell Family Materials. FAL 1:1-2 Box 1. Pierre Guillermin, *Jerry Falwell: The People Business*, Selah Yearbook 1976–1977, 7.
18 LCA official website, About LCA, Academy folder (Liberty University archives, 1975), available at: https://www.lcabulldogs.com/about-lca/, accessed June 19, 2021.
19 "Five Things We Think You Will Like about Lynchburg Christian Academy," in Lynchburg Christian Academy folder (Liberty University archives, 1975).
20 Seth Dowland, *Family Values and the Rise of the Christian Right* (Philadelphia, PA: University of Pennsylvania Press, 2015), 23.

when Falwell allowed the first member of color to join his church in 1968, and the first African American student to attend LCA school in 1969.[21]

This speech received many criticisms, and Falwell even apologized later on for the way he chose to convey his messages. However, in the context of this work, and precisely because of the high media profile that this speech received, I shall focus on the crystal clear messages of Falwell against the political involvement of religious people from minutes of the speech distributed later throughout the United States.[22] And this is how Falwell opens, asking his believers: "Does the 'Church' [originally written with a capital C and within quotation marks for emphasis] have a divine command to intervene in marches, protests, and other actions, which a huge part of church leaders are doing today in the name of the civil rights movement?" Throughout the speech, interwoven into the text, as he relies on the scriptures, he answers why the church should not be part of the civic and managerial order of politics: "When we look at the writings of the Apostle Paul to Timothy, we find only the command Proclaim the Word of GOD' […] Nowhere do we find a mandate or external change. We are not commanded to wage wars against adults, liquor stores, people with prejudice, or institutions or any other evil deed."[23] He keeps explaining why active involvement in day-to-day politics should be avoided: "Right here, in Thomas Road Baptist Church, when I look at the faces of many of the people here on any given Sunday, some of whom were involved in the most heinous sins, they are now faithful, God-fearing servants of Jesus Christ. What changed them? Did we lead marches of adults to stop and sell alcohol? Did we go to Richmond, to try and pass laws to send such people to prison? No! In the name of Jesus the beloved, we went to them with the message of Christ, and they embraced Jesus as their Lord and Savior."[24] He mentions what message the church must convey: "When 2,000 members of the Thomas Road Baptist Church come to pray, they don't hear sermons about communism, civil rights, or any other topic except the gospel of Jesus."[25] But perhaps the most important part (which later became relevant to tax issues following the Supreme Court's ruling in 1973, as I explain later) is the lesson Falwell seeks to convey to his congregation regarding the

---

21 Blaine T. Browne, *Modern American Lives: Individuals and Issues in American History since 1945* (Armonk, NY: M.E. Sharpe, 2008), 283.
22 Jerry Falwell Library, *Falwell Family Papers, Ministers and Marches*, 3, available at: https://liberty.contentdm.oclc.org/digital/collection/p17184coll4/id/4092, accessed June 19, 2021.
23 Ibid., 5.
24 Ibid., 7.
25 Ibid., 9.

State-citizens relationship with regard to taxation. Falwell recounts Jesus's position on the tax imposed by the Roman emperor:

> *When Jesus was asked whether to pay the tax to Caesar or not, it was during a time when there was no government more oppressive or cruel than the Roman Empire. Christians were persecuted. Non-Romans were of little consequence, if at all. The tax system was unjust and unequal. The apostles assumed Jesus would take a political stance against the Roman government, but he decided not to. He asked for a coin, and before receiving it, he asked who was the figure depicted on it. They answered "Caesar," so he replied: "Repeat after me: Render unto Caesar the things which are Caesar's, and unto GOD the things that are GOD's." In other words, pay your taxes and forget about politics, "serve me faithfully with all your heart," thus, with his great wisdom, he managed to avoid a political debate. He did not come into the world to reform the Roman Empire.*[26]

Decades later, this vision of a strict divide between spiritual faith and political engagement would come under increasing scrutiny. In his influential 1984 book *The Naked Public Square*, Lutheran theologian and public intellectual Richard John Neuhaus warned that the erosion of religious voices in American civic life would have dire consequences. According to Neuhaus, excluding religious values from the public sphere would "almost certainly result in the death of democracy."[27] His critique resonated deeply within the Evangelical world, which felt increasingly marginalized by the secularizing trends of the late twentieth century. Neuhaus's work framed the return of Evangelical leaders like Falwell to political activism not as a betrayal of their faith's spiritual focus, but as a necessary corrective to restore moral clarity and religious presence in American democracy.

In 1965, Jerry Falwell devoted all his efforts to religious persuasion and did everything in his power to stay clear from significant political action, a policy that would change in the 1970s. In his book, Matthew Moen notes that in the context of this speech, Falwell's statement, "I believe that if we spent enough effort trying to clean up our churches, rather than trying to clean up state and national governments, we would do well" reflects a long history in which the church chose to remain outside the political game.[28] The dilemma of transi-

---

26 Ibid., 10.
27 Richard John Neuhaus, *The Naked Public Square: Religion and Democracy in America* (Grand Rapids, MI: William B. Eerdmans Publishing Company, 1984), 5.
28 Matthew C. Moen, *The Christian Right and Congress* (Tuscaloosa, AL: University of Alabama Press, 1989), 41.

tioning from religion to politics is exemplified in the article by Netanel Fisher and defined by him as the "Fundamentalist Dilemma."[29]

Its intensive activity during the 1960s led this school to become one of the ten most prominent in the country, even in its early years, with its Sunday school serving as the home of more than 10,000 students, from kindergarten through elementary school to high school.[30] The community's development and strength were expressed through a private Cessna 310 plane donated to the church by businessman Gene Dixon in the late 1960s. It facilitated Falwell's bridging capabilities between his different congregations, increasing his power base and his ability to quickly move from place to place.[31]

Israel's military victory in the Six-Day War (1967) was a turning point in the perception of Israel's importance in Falwell's worldview, which had previously spoken a lot about the People of Israel and the State of Israel in its sermons. For example, Shalom Goldman talks about Falwell's transformation and its transition to Christian Zionism: "For Falwell and others, the 'liberation' of Jerusalem was the fulfillment of a millennium-old vision."[32] He added that immediately after the military victory of the State of Israel in the Six-Day War, Falwell flew to Israel to witness the miracle. Stephen Haynes adds a social argument to the religious argument related to the zeitgeist and, according to him, it was such a vital point for Falwell, who, before 1967, was not concerned as much about the State of Israel, and noted that: "Prior to 1967, Falwell had not mixed religion and politics as much, and had not talked broadly about the modern State of Israel. However, Israel's victory in the Six-Day War left a considerable impression on Falwell, as it left on many Americans who lived during the US military entanglement in Vietnam, the hippies and the Civil Rights Movement, which left the community feeling helpless."[33] Michael Thomas further argues that, in fact, the Six-Day War locomoted Falwell from the realm of faith to that of political activism, which would become more evident about a decade later: "The Six-Day War helped shape the American Dispensationalist Movement. In 1964, Jerry Falwell said that nothing could be done except spreading the gospel; In 1967, he declared

---

29 Netanel Fisher, "The Fundamentalist Dilemma: Lessons From The Israeli Haredi Case," *International Journal of Middle East Studies* 48, no. 3 (2016): 531.
30 Falwell Macel, *Jerry Falwell: His Life and Legacy* (New York: Howard Books, 2008), 68.
31 Ibid.
32 Shalom Goldman, *Zeal for Zion: Christians, Jews, & the Idea of the Promised Land* (Chapel Hill, NC: University of North Carolina Press, 2009), 294.
33 Stephen R. Haynes, *Reluctant Witnesses: Jews and the Christian Imagination* (Louisville, KY: Presbyterian Publishing Corporation, 1995), 153.

that the war was won 'thanks to the intervention of the almighty,' and became a Zionist Christian activist."[34]

The Decision to Establish an Academic Institution

In his autobiography, Jerry Falwell recounts how he came to the decision to promote the establishment of a Christian academic institution. In 1968, he read a book by Dr. Elmer Towns called *The Ten Largest Sunday Schools and What Makes Them Grow*, which ranked Thomas Road Baptist School as the 9th largest Christian school in the United States. Inspired by Dr. Towns' work on church growth, he decided to invite the later to join his community in Lynchburg, Virginia. When he eventually called Dr. Towns, Falwell asked him to help him establish a Christian college in Lynchburg that would one day become a Christian university. Falwell asked Dr. Towns to help him establish an academic system, with a particular emphasis on planting churches and growing congregations. He promised Towns that that their graduates would be able to establish 5,000 new churches across America before the end of the century.[35]

Dr. Elmer Towns, an expert in church planting who has written dozens of books and articles on the methodology of church planting from a holistic perspective and who has academic accreditation from another institution, was chosen with great care. Steve Parr writes about Towns that "perhaps no one else is considered an expert in the cultivation of Sunday school in writing and speeches, like Elmer Towns. He is called by many 'Mr. Sunday School' and within this movement, he is also probably the most deserving of the title. All his life, he has promoted the Sunday School movement."[36] Towns, formerly the president of a Christian college in Winnipeg, Canada, received from Falwell what he describes in his book as a request to "establish the largest and best college for Christians."[37] According to Towns, the college should have three important components, like a three-legged stool. The first component would be academic excellence, where the college would be greater than other Bible colleges and offer degrees in various sciences, preparing individuals for careers as educators, businesspeople, engineers, and more. The second

---

34 Michael Thomas, *American Policy toward Israel: The Power and Limits of Beliefs* (New York: Taylor & Francis, 2007), 45.
35 Jerry Falwell, *Falwell an Autobiography: The Inside Story* (Lynchburg, VA: Liberty House Publishers, 1997), 328–329.
36 Steve R. Parr, *Sunday School that Really Excels* (Grand Rapids, MI: Kergel Publications, 2013), 20.
37 Elmer L. Towns, *Walking with Giants* (Ventura, CA: Regal Books, 2012), 167.

component would focus on creativity and innovation in communication and computers. The third component would focus on developing the community around the local church. They believed that a Christian college should work closely with the local church and be an extension of it. They suggested that the college be located near Thomas Road Baptist Church, where students can worship and be spiritually influenced by the church.[38]

In his book, Falwell testifies that the change that has proven his popular broadcast program went beyond Sunday frameworks, and the simultaneous establishment of a university that includes a communication department helped to "evangelize the nation."[39] According to him, until that time, most TV stations opposed selling airtime for broadcasts. They sold everything from cars to toothpaste ... but GOD remained in the Sunday morning broadcast "ghetto" with a panel of priests and rabbis talking about topics that no one was interested in ... Falwell talks about his motivations to establish the college: "We had an amazing opportunity to spread the words of Christ to nationwide television stations by creating a Christian university that would help students return home excited and trained to build churches and evangelize the nation."[40] Falwell continues to define his objectives, and writes in his book that In 1971, the land for the university was purchased with an aim use the media to spread the message of Jesus to the world. The team, including television personnel and industry professionals, discussed an opportunity to launch the Old Time Gospel Hour program, which would require a hefty financial investment of five to six million dollars for a nationwide color TV broadcasting station. The annual budget allocated for the college was one million dollars, requiring additional fundraising efforts. Therefore, debentures were issued with a commitment to repay them with interest within ten years. The college's establishment team sent hundreds of envelopes to supporters, offering them to purchase these debentures, successfully raising the money to build a Christian university with a national broadcasting station. Once the funding was secured, a TV studio was established in 1971, and the message was broadcasted to more than 300 stations across the United States. The decision to resonate the message through the media was an important catalyst for the headline given by *Newsweek* in the early 1970s, declaring Thomas Road Baptist Church as the "fastest-growing church in the country."[41] In the

---

38 Ibid.
39 J. Falwell, *Strength for the Journey: An Autobiography* (New York: Simon and Schuster, 1987), 311.
40 Ibid., 312–313.
41 Ibid., 313.

aftermath, the debenture scandal led to criminal proceedings against the organization by the Securities and Exchange Commission (SEC) in August 1973, which ended with the organization's acquittal.[42]

To continue the college's capacity for growth in its early years, one could examine the thesis written by Betty Gail Flint in 1978, which provided access to Liberty University marketing materials and a glimpse into how the college marketed itself to prospective students and especially their parents, when the thesis was written, in the early years of the college. For example, quoted from the catalog sent that same year to those interested in studying at the college, in the words of Falwell: "Liberty Baptist College combines academic excellence with a Christian lifestyle designed to train young people through the working framework of the New Testament [...] We are committed to holy living and the winning of hearts." But he is not afraid to mark the role he intends for the candidates: "The strength of our students is represented in our real purpose for GOD's world, which is to help them shape the world."[43]

The initial goal set by Falwell and Towns before the establishment of the college was enrolling 5,000 students and creating an institution slightly larger than Bob Jones University and Tennessee Temple University, both of which had around 4,500 students on their respective campuses.[44] During the first week of June 1971, Falwell arrived at the large tract of land that was purchased and declared, "We are standing on Liberty Hill; we are standing on the ground that for more than three years we have prayed would be the site of the largest Christian school in the world. That's what we prayed for. We believe that GOD gave us this hill for a reason [...]"[45]

In 1971, Pastor Jerry Falwell Sr. and Elmer L. Towns co-founded a new Christian college in Lynchburg, Virginia, originally naming it Lynchburg Baptist College to reflect its origin as an extension of Falwell's local Baptist church. Falwell challenged his Thomas Road Baptist Church congregation to support this vision, envisioning a school whose students would "go out in all walks of life to impact this world for God."[46] Towns, who became the college's

---

42 Ibid., *Jerry Falwell, His Life and Legacy*, 93–94.
43 Betty Gail Flint, "Thomas Road Baptist Church: A Study of the New Fundamentalism" (PhD diss., and Master's Projects, 1978). Paper 1539625043. https://core.ac.uk/download/pdf/235407635.pdf.
44 Ibid., *Walking with Giants*, 172.
45 Dr. Jerry Falwell's Vision for Liberty University, available at: https://www.youtube.com/watch?v=TjZjB-UP3Q, accessed June 19, 2021.
46 "History of Liberty," *Liberty University*, available at:. https://www.liberty.edu/about/history-of-liberty/#:~:text=In%201971%2C%20Pastor%20Jerry%20Falwell,Baptist%20College%20became%20a%20reality, accessed June 12, 2025.

first dean, embraced the mission and reportedly called Thomas Road "the closest to a New Testament church that I have seen" when he joined the effort.⁴⁷ Lynchburg Baptist College opened in 1971 with an inaugural class of 141 students meeting in the church's facilities, and it was renamed Liberty Baptist College in 1975 as its mission and scope began to expand beyond Lynchburg.⁴⁸

About the Growth of Liberty University

According to an article published in June 1985 in Liberty University's newspaper, *The Fundamentalist*, these are the figures testifying to the growth rate of the university: in its founding year of 1971, 141 students studied at the college with no permanent buildings or classrooms.⁴⁹ In the year before the establishment of the college (1970), the church's budget was $1 million, and 80 staff members were employed in two educational buildings. Particular emphasis was placed on setting up a TV studio for which four color television cameras were already purchased. In 1971, the average number of participants in religious conferences was 4,587. Houses around the church were purchased and served as dormitories, with a total of 200 workers employed in the overall maintenance of the campus.⁵⁰ In 1972, the first university degrees were awarded, marking the growth of the university from 141 students to 484 in the second year. The show broadcasted by the university already reached 200 TV stations and 100 radio stations. By 1975, there were already 1,244 students and an additional building was acquired for the university. By 1977, there were already 2,000 students.⁵¹ In 1980, there were 2,970 students enrolled in

---

47 Brandon Showalter, "Dr. Falwell's Enrollment Vision Fulfilled: 50,000 Students," *The Christian Post*, March 31, 2021, available at: https://www.christianpost.com/news/dr-falwell-s-enrollment-vision-fulfilled-50-000-students.html#:~:text=It%20was%20in%201971%20that,had%20founded%2015%20years%20prior.
48 Elmer Towns and Jerry Falwell, *Church Aflame* (Lynchburg, VA: Liberty University), available at: https://facultyshare.liberty.edu/files/40261510/Church%20Aflame.pdf#:~:text=Thomas%20Road%20Baptist%20Church%20so,The%20authors%27%20prayer%20for, accessed June 12, 2025.
49 "Liberty University Reaches New High," *The Fundamentalist Journal* 4, no. 6 (1985): 57, available at: https://digitalcommons.liberty.edu/cgi/viewcontent.cgi?article=1005&context=fun_85, accessed June 19, 2021.
50 "Looking Back...1972–1977," in *The Fundamentalist Journal* 5, no. 5 (1986): 65, available at: https://digitalcommons.liberty.edu/cgi/viewcontent.cgi?article=1003&context=fun_86, accessed June 19, 2021.
51 *The Fundamentalist Journal* 5, no. 5 (1986): 65, available at: https://digitalcommons.liberty.edu/cgi/viewcontent.cgi?article=1003&context=fun_86, accessed June 19, 2021.

the university, and an average of 9,000 worshipers attended Sunday services. By 1981, there were over 11,000 students studying Bible (and academic credit programs), and the radio station operating from the campus, WRVL, went on the air for the first time.[52]

As mentioned earlier, spreading the gospel through mass media was essential to Falwell, and after establishing the TV station next to the university, it was only natural to continue and establish an independent radio station that would broadcast from campus. The name given to the station was WRVL or its full name, W. Radio Victory Liberty according to the Liberty University website. The radio station established by Jerry Falwell was part of his vision: "to reach every available person, at any available time, by every available means."[53]

Today, the radio channel whose name was changed to Journey FM is a faith-based radio station that supports listeners, broadcasting the message of life, hope, and music throughout Virginia and North Carolina combined with contemporary Christian music for adults, and is available on FM frequencies. Its programs are also broadcasted in national syndication by the K-LOVE and Air1 networks, reaching millions of listeners in America through radio stations across the 50 states on over 900 frequencies. The continued investment in communication infrastructure focused on further expanding TV infrastructures. In January 1986, the university newspaper, *The Fundamentalist*, reported on the completion of a TV infrastructure purchase. As part of this, the "Old Time Gospel Hour" broadcasting strip of the national Christian network was purchased, which decided to purchase a cable TV broadcasting channel from a Florida network. This purchase enabled the expansion of worldwide distribution through the broadcast of Christian programs 24/7, 365 days a year. The channel moved from Florida to the station broadcasting from Liberty University campus in Lynchburg, Virginia, with the aim of reaching millions of American homes.[54] In 1986, Liberty University became the largest private university in the state of Virginia, as the number of students

---

52 "Looking Back …1980–1981," in *The Fundamentalist Journal* 5, no. 7 (1986): 58, available at: https://digitalcommons.liberty.edu/cgi/viewcontent.cgi?article=1005&context=fun_86, accessed November 9, 2020.

53 "Journey FM Nominated for Marconi Award as Religious Station of the Year," *Liberty University News Service*, August 9, 2019, available at:https://www.liberty.edu/news/2019/08/09/journey-fm-nominated-for-marconi-award-as-religious-station-of-the-year/, accessed November 29, 2020.

54 Jınet Burlington, "Liberty Now Virginia's Largest Private College," *The Fundamentalist Journal* 5, no. 5 (1986): 66, available at: https://digitalcommons.liberty.edu/cgi/viewcontent.cgi?article=1003&context=fun_86, accessed November 9, 2020.

grew to 5,930 from around 4,600 in 1985. According to Liberty University's admission brochure in 1997, over 14,000 students were enrolled in the institution, with 6,000 of them residing in dormitories on a campus that comprised more than 64 buildings worth $200 million.[55]

Today, there are approximately 130,000 students at Liberty University, the second-largest Christian university, ranked 70th in the world.[56] The university is one of the largest private universities in the United States, with a campus that spans approximately 28,000 acres, and an endowment of roughly $1.6 billion.[57]

---

55 The data on Liberty University in 1997 can be found at: us-israel.org.il. The source link is: https://us-israel.org.il/2022/05/23/%D7%A0%D7%AA%D7%95%D7%A0 %D7%99-%D7%9C%D7%99%D7%91%D7%A8%D7%98%D7%99-%D7%A0 %D7%9B%D7%95%D7%9F-%D7%9C%D7%A9%D7%A0%D7%AA-1997/.
56 "Liberty U. Official Twitter Account," October 29, 2022, available at: https://twitter .com/LibertyU/status/1586166326388817921, accessed November 29, 2022.
57 "Liberty Official Website," available at: https://www.liberty.edu/aboutliberty/index .cfm?PID=6925, accessed November 29, 2021.

Chapter 3

THE GRASSROOTS PLANTING METHOD ON CAMPUSES

What Is the Church Planting Movement?

David Garrison defines the Church Planting Movement as "rapidly multiplying indigenous churches planting churches that sweep across a people group or population segment [...]"[1] Garrison argues that the key to the Church Planting Movement is that it occurs at high and recurring rates, with a known and identical pattern of action, accelerating the local growth rate and aiming to reach the maximum number of people in the community. The second significant part is replicating the founding of churches from the home camp to increase the number of believers, which is why churches set goals to add more churches in the same city, district, or state in which they operate. Finally, there are additional parameters, such as the internal duplication of congregation members who set out to establish new churches in the same community and the possibility that these churches will be able to convey the message, thus changing the lives of devotees.

Jonathan Edwards puts his finger down on Falwell's 1971 speech, called "The Church at Antioch," which was spoken before a group of fundamentalist church leaders, as the speech that advocated for the church planting methodology. In this speech, Falwell distinguished between two types of churches. On the one hand, ethereal, transparent, universal and intangible churches attempted to conquer the entire world but lacked any members. He referred to them as universal churches, belonging to the national umbrella organization of churches that dealt with universal issues. On the other hand, Falwell described his vision that every fundamentalist church should be a local church whose role and responsibility were to "saturate" its immediate congregation with the Christian gospel. The more locals connect, the more

---

[1] David V. Garrison, *Church Planting Movements: How God is Redeeming a Lost World* (Midlothian, VA: WIGTake Resources, 2004), 22.

the church will grow; the more believers are at its core, the more become missionaries of the gospel. Hence, the church would eventually become a "Local Super Church" that could raise money from devotees by establishing radio and TV stations facilitating missionary work around the world. This process will eventually lead, according to Falwell, to a vast network of these "Local Super Churches." Edwards explains that Falwell relied on the actions of the apostles for spiritual support, telling the story of the establishment of the early Christian communities all relying on local communities that spread through aggressive preachings.[2]

Falwell documented his position on how local churches should be planted as part of a larger global influence initiative:

> *I believe every local church should try to do this and take its city in the name of Jesus. Every church that believes in the Bible should do this. any attempt should be made to conquer its metropolitan area in the name of Christ. We must work within the right of every person to salvation, starting with his Jerusalem [in our case, Lynchburg], moving to Judea [the surrounding area around the college], and then to Samaria [the state of Virginia for him], and ultimately to the ends of the earth [worldwide mission]. Every local church should start in its Jerusalem and build a strong church that provides super-aggressive service, first to its parish, and then to the world. The light that shines farthest shines brightest at home. Every super-aggressive local church that takes on the task has one goal and one obsession: to conquer its city in the name of Jesus. If your church is in a rural area, you must work to win over every farmer in your area for GOD [...] You need to learn how to use the principle of preaching the gospel to any available person at any available time and in any available means.*[3]

Elmer Towns, who, as mentioned, co-founded Liberty University and is considered the father of the Church Planting Movement at Liberty University, describes in his book the necessary steps and methodology for successful church planting. He suggests several methods, including

1. planting a new church in an environment that allows for its growth; a mother church leading to the establishment of satellite churches;
2. one church leading to the planting of another independent church;

---

2 Jonathan J. Edwards, *Super Church: The Rhetoric and Politics of American Fundamentalism* (East Lansing, MI: MSU Press, 2015).
3 Jerry Falwell, "I Still Believe in Saturation Evangelism by Local Churches," *Journal of the American Society for Church Growth* 14, no. 1 (2004, 3), retrieved from https://digital-archives.apu.edu/jascg/vol14/iss1/2, accessed June 19, 2021.

3. a consortium of independent churches in a particular religious or shared framework;
4. each mother church having its own branches; and
5. one of these churches would serve as a communication-based church.[4]

On the Importance of Church Planting in Falwell's Vision

In September 1981, the first issue of a magazine called *Liberty Journal for Church Planting*, which (obviously) was dedicated entirely to the importance of church planting, was published. Under the main header, "We Will Plant 5,000 Churches," Falwell wrote:

> *Not only do we need to clean up sins and generate a life-changing experience in the United States, but we also need to establish between 10,000 and 20,000 new churches in North America by the end of the century. Our school alone has set a goal of training 5,000 new pastors to plant 5,000 new churches in the next 20 years [...] There are now over 18,000 fundamentalist Christian schools across America, and schools are the future of our movement, with three new Christian schools joining every day. We must train an 'army' of Christian leaders for generations to come [...] Church planting must be our key agenda. We must plant thousands of new churches of Bible-believing Christians so that we can engage in evangelism and activist politics. Our goal at the college is to grow pastors who are effectively able to spread the gospel and lead their community [...] We must turn America into a grassroots movement operated at the local church level and grow churches in the coming decades.[5]*

Falwell saw in his imagination the church planting pastor as an ingrained part of the community and believed that beyond the role of the pastor, there is enormous significance to the communal fabric of a religious person and providing a response to a plethora of needs, with education being an important complementary part for Liberty University graduates, in expanding the circles of devotees. University graduates are required to generate an educational framework around the church during its planting. By 1980, 200 Liberty University graduates had already opened churches and provided academic lessons twice or thrice a week. As Falwell conveyed in 1980, the idea was that:

> *We will start many schools in 1980, as we have done in the past two years. I believe that we will already have four times what we have done so far by next year. I estimate*

---

4 Elmer Towns, *Planting Reproducing Churches* (Shippensburg, PA: Destiny Image Publishers, 2018), 23.
5 Jerry Falwell, "We will Plant 5,000 Churches," *Liberty Journal for Church Planting* 1, no. 1 (September 1981, 1).

> that by the end of this decade, we will start about 5,000 new churches in North America. In 1988, the true impact will come, as we will educate our children almost every town, county, and state. These will be our next leaders, as schools are pastors' way to have a daily presence in our lives. The schools I see in my mind will lift up and turn the nation. These are the leaders. These are the people who graduate from Liberty University, educating the next generation, and we already have those who have sent their children to study at the university. Christian schools are the best way to cultivate Christian leadership.[6]

Falwell nicknamed those young religious leaders "Young Timothy's," meaning young boys who grew up in a supportive atmosphere that reinforced the importance of GOD and His presence in their lives, named after Timothy, Paul's disciple. Falwell extensively considered nurturing these students, training them and sending them back to enable the continued growth and development of the community.

In 1984, Falwell published his vision to spread Christian schools, resulting in church planting in America, in the *Fundamentalist Journal*. Titled "The Master Plan That Can Change the Course of History," Falwell addressed high school graduates and presented his vision in the 66 fields of expertise offered by the university: "Liberty University will realize this vision within a decade. This unique Christian university will train America's future leaders. Our 25-year work plan calls for full-scale Christian fundamentalist training, with 50,000 undergraduate students on a 4,400-acre campus called Liberty. We will train journalists, tomorrow's politicians, educators, coaches, business people, scientists, lawyers, engineers, doctors, and other professionals. Every designation shall be employed to train future generation who must enter society as devout Christians and young people who love America. Already, Liberty University is the fastest-growing institution in America," and he continued talking about the vision of graduates spreading across the country: "By A.D. 2000, we will operate around 5,000 churches that will be either established or upgraded by our graduates, when already about 700 of our graduates are building the fastest-growing churches. Our students use their four years in college to realize their vision of establishing a mission headquarters for our global network. Around 5,000 Christian schools will be established in North America, where our graduates will be responsible for educating the next generation [...]"[7]

---

6 Ibid., *Jerry Falwell: Man of Vision*, 48.

7 *The Fundamentalist Journal*, Volume 3, No. 7, 1984. Page 25, available at: https://digital-commons.liberty.edu/cgi/viewcontent.cgi?article=1000&context=fun_84, accessed November 9, 2020.

Falwell refers to the political power created by establishing a school and expresses his vision for how the school serves as a gateway to realizing his vision in other areas.

> *We have established a conservative Christian advertising and distribution network that reaches millions of Americans. We publish newspapers, books, reports, and other materials for people everywhere. We work to spread the gospel through media channels. The "Old Time Gospel Hour" is currently watched on 392 television stations. We are working toward establishing a satellite TV that will reach 230 million Americans. We educate, teach, and train 25 million political activists. As private citizens, we founded an organization with 50 chapter leaders in every state and millions of Americans committed to moral values. We work to register voters and mobilize the conservative religious community to participate in their civic responsibilities.*[8]

Church Planting: Supportive and Motivational Activities

Falwell highlights the importance and necessity of cultivating and motivating churches at the beginning of their path and how to carry out the activity that will help in the church planting stage. The most important and significant way to support a graduate who wishes to plant a church is by establishing a support fund. To accompany graduates on their new church planting venture, Falwell declared the establishment of an organization called LBF (Liberty Baptist Found) in 1981 (which exists to date) and serves as a tool to assist and fulfill the establishment of those 5,000 new churches in the United States of America. The said organization assists pastors in planting churches through education, advertising, loans, concentrated procurement of equipment and lecturers, facilitated by seminars, national conferences, national newspapers, and organizational systems through central control. In an interview for the first issue of *Liberty Journal for Church Planting*, Falwell said: "We stand together because many can do more together than one can do alone" [further along this paper, I demonstrate the principle of proximity to other graduates through a heat map, as it had been explained to the graduates. K.B.]. Falwell continues to discuss the vision of establishing the organization: "Besides the graduates and former students involved in the LBF, this organization will include former team members who have already received financial aid for planting churches and joined out of a desire for aggressive marketing. The fund will promote the establishment of churches that operate through education, advertising and marketing. This will happen via seminars,

---

8 Ibid.

national conferences, national newspapers and organizational efforts."[9] In a 1985 issue of the *Fundamentalist*, the magazine tracked the LBF's progress. The article reported the progress in supporting 54 pastors so they could focus on full-time ministry instead of part-time jobs. The support ranged from $100 to $600 of monthly salary, for a period of up to six months.[10]

One of the manners by which the church succeeded in growing and bringing in new congregants was buses. The topic has been so significant for the growth of the Evangelical Movement that special conferences were held, where people from all over the United States met for seminars, conferences, and discussions. The importance of buses in the service of religion can be seen in an article written before the 12th National Conference in 1987 on "Bus and Children's Church." Bob Gray, the pastor of the hosting church, TRBC, and editor of the journal *National Bus Ministry Magazine*, said, "The goal of the conference is to challenge churches to implement plans to grow their congregations and to encourage them go out and expand their ministries." The interviewer asked if the peak era of buses had passed, and Gray responded: "Indeed, the peak of the era of buses occurred between 1971 and 1973, and toward the end of the 70s, many churches began selling their buses and convert the funds to support Christian school movements. Their excuse was incorrect from the beginning. In the 80s, churches returned to the subject of buses and have remained there. Most of them cannot afford a TV or radio station and they see the bus as a tool for spreading evangelism to win hearts."[11]

Falwell greatly desired to plant communities in the heart of America's distressed neighborhoods [as can be further deduced from Ken Richter's narrative, K.B.]. In 1987, a conference entitled "How Does Liberty Take a Noteworthy Role in Distressed Neighborhoods?" was held as part of the first conference of the Urban Affairs Association. The conference included pastors already involved in urban churches and university students planning to establish churches in large cities. Resolutions derived from the conference included creating a support envelope based on geographical distribution, including the Northern gathering for cities such as Chicago and Detroit and

---

9 "New Fellowship Will Plant Churches," *Liberty Journal for Church Planting* 1, no. 1 (September 1981): 1.

10 *The Fundamentalist Journal*, Volume 4, No. 10 (1985). 1985. Paper 9, Page 66, available at: https://digitalcommons.liberty.edu/fun_85/9/?utm_source=digitalcommons.liberty.edu%2Ffun_85%2F9&utmmedium=PDF&utm_campaign=PDFCoverPages, accessed November 9, 2020.

11 "The 12th National Bus & Children's Church Conference," *The Fundamentalist Journal* 1, no. 1 (1987): 42, available at: https://digitalcommons.liberty.edu/cgi/viewcontent.cgi?article=1012&context=fun_86, accessed November 9, 2020.

the Eastern gathering that included New York, Philadelphia, and the capital—Washington DC. Another resolution was to devise an apprenticeship program whereby students can specialize in these churches for half a year to gain considerable experience in community life in big city neighborhoods. Yet another resolution was to establish a support organization called "The Institute for Urban Involvement" to assist and accompany graduates through their referral to early placement activities in distressed neighborhoods.[12]

One of the activities defined as "most beloved" by Dr. Jerry Falwell was participating in the prayers organized by pastors who had recently graduated from Liberty University during the early days of establishing their new churches. Falwell considered this guidance an important educational goal of the highest degree, as described in the book written about him, *Man of Vision*: "There is nothing Dr. Jerry Falwell loves more than participating in the ceremony of a church just founded by a 'Young Timothy.' He will do everything in his power, with great effort, to be able to deliver the welcoming speech at the opening ceremony. Falwell would then sit in his chair and watch how someone who recently was a student of Liberty University now serves as the pastor of a church he had founded, proud of the creation of a young pastor who serves as a living testament to Falwell's doctrine of 'producing producers'." For example, the story of a graduate who founded a church in Lansing, Michigan, recounts Falwell's behavior during the opening ceremony: 'Dr. Falwell listened to his former student's opening remarks, joined the congregation in singing, received the keys to the city, and, generally, behaved like a proud father at his son's graduation ceremony.' Actually, that's exactly what it is because, at that moment, the 'student' evolves into an adult, embodying all the theories and education he received at Liberty University. This scene is repeated almost weekly by Dr. Falwell, who serves as a loving father and a religious mentor to his graduates. He shares their disappointments and takes pride in their successes; they are, in fact, a part of who he is, and they are Jerry Falwell's legacy to serve the world in a spiritual way.[13]

Competition "The Fastest-Growing Church"

One of the topics that Falwell intensively dealt with was the growth and expansion of the Evangelical Movement across America. One of the devices used to propel that movement forward was the "Fastest-Growing Church"

---

12 Liberty University Archive, LU 18-1, Series 6; *The Shepherd's Journal*, Vol. 5, No. 4 (December–January 1987): 1.
13 Ibid., *Jerry Falwell: Man of Vision*, 56.

competition, held in each state of the Union, which awarded the church and its pastor with a diploma at the international conference of pastors held in Lynchburg, Virginia. The model according to which the certificate was granted was how fast a church was growing compared to the previous year, according to its records. The 1985 to 1986 Fastest-Growing Church award was granted to Phoenix First Assembly of GOD church in Phoenix, Arizona, now called Dream City Church, for growing from a community of 5,381 participants in 1985 to 7,688 participants in the following year—a growth of 42.87 percent (today, according to the church's website, the community serves about 40,000 worshipers—almost a 420 percent growth over the years).[14] Pastor Tony Barnett noted that the impressive growth was "not only because we built a hall for 7,000 worshipers, but also due to an aggressive marketing policy that sent buses from Sunday Schools to fetch community members. According to him, 1,200 additional worshipers come every Saturday, thanks to these transportation services."[15]

In 1986, the largest church in America was First Baptist Church in Hammond, Indiana, with 19,320 worshippers in 1984, up from 18,700 worshippers in 1983—a growth of about 3.32 percent. The First Baptist Church also used buses as a recruiting method, especially in the greater Chicago area, physically bringing worshippers into the church. The article notes there were eight churches that doubled their number of participants in one year. It focused on the Atlantic Shores Baptist Church in Virginia Beach, which grew from 468 worshippers in 1984 to 1017 in 1985, a 117.31 percent growth in one year. The church was founded in 1981 by Pastor George Sweet, a Liberty University graduate.[16] At its peak in 1996, the church's parish numbered 4,000 devotees. However, due to the scandal, where the founding pastor was accused of embezzling hundreds of thousands of dollars from an older woman, the church now welcomes around 1,000 worshippers each week, on average.[17]

---

14 "Our Story," dreamcitychurch.us, available at: https://dreamcitychurch.us/about-us/our-history/, accessed November 9, 2020.

15 "Fastest Growing Churches," *The Fundamentalist Journal* 5, no. 6 (1986): 42, available at: https://digitalcommons.liberty.edu/cgi/viewcontent.cgi?article=1012&context=fun_86, accessed November 29, 2020.

16 Tony Wharton, "Atlantic Shores Pastor Unexpectedly Resigns Sweet Apologizes for Unnamed 'Mistake,'" Virginian-Pilot, Saturday, August 16, 1997, available at: https://scholar.lib.vt.edu/VA-news/VA-Pilot/issues/1997/vp970816/08160255.htm, accessed November 9, 2021.

17 "Atlantic Shores Baptist Church," churchstaffing.com, available at:https://www.churchstaffing.com/church/176077/atlantic-shores-baptist-church, accessed May 9, 2021.

It would be interesting to look at one such church's growth story, of Liberty Baptist Church in West Nottingham, New Hampshire, awarded the title "The Growing Little Church" in 1986. Its story is documented in the book *The Little Country Church on Freeman's Hall Road*. It was planted by its founder and a Liberty University graduate, Pastor John Ehrlich. An article in the *Fundamentalist* in 1986, described how the church grew from 9 worshippers to 90—a 900 percent growth—in one year.

John Ehrlich was born in Baltimore in 1946 and grew up in Delmar, Maryland. After graduating from high school in 1964, he joined the Navy. After working in various jobs for several years, he followed a calling and became a pastor. He attended Liberty Baptist College, the International Bible Seminar, and the Covington Seminar. He then served at the Liberty Baptist Church in West Nottingham, New Hampshire, and succeeded in making it the fastest-growing church in the state in 1985, for which he was awarded by Liberty University. In the introduction to his book, *The Little Country Church on Freeman's Hall Road*, he writes, "This is the true story of the Liberty Baptist Church in West Nottingham, New Hampshire, from its uncertain beginnings with a handful of worshippers in 1978 to its peak in the mid-80s as the fastest-growing church in New Hampshire, to the departure of Pastor John in December 1990. Even Jerry Falwell was fascinated by the story and how it unfolded, as well as many other pastors and laymen throughout the country."[18]

Did Falwell Succeed in His Vision to Plant 5,000 Churches?

As mentioned earlier, Falwell's original intention was to strive to plant 5,000 churches from the day the college was founded in 1971 until the end of the twentieth century. Several sources documented the growth rate of church planting over time. According to a report in the 1982–1983 alumni cycle book of Liberty University, up until that point in time, 136 new churches had been planted throughout the United States, and 152 additional churches worldwide, which were operated by Liberty alumni.[19] In October 1986, *Shepherd* magazine reported that graduates of Liberty University established 152 churches; 634 Liberty graduates worked as pastors in existing churches, and about 230 went on mission trips..[20] In his 2009 book, Elmer Towns wrote

---

18 "John Ehrlich Amazon page," https://www.amazon.com/-/he/John-Ehrlich/e/B004ZNV81S?ref_=dbs_p_ebk_r00_abau_000000, accessed May 9, 2021.
19 "Liberty University 1982–83 Yearbook," available at: https://issuu.com/luyearbook/docs/lu_1983/273, accessed February 9, 2022.
20 Liberty University Archive, LU 18-1, Series 6, *The Shepherd's Journal*, Vol. 5, No. 2, October 1986, 4.

that "according to a survey, graduates of the university planted around 2,000 churches."²¹ The following details are published on LCN website:

> The Thomas Road Worldwide Church network actively implements the planting of churches according to the New Testament method, to win over the next generation of believers for Christ through assessment, training, guidance, and funding of qualified pastors and new churches. Over the past 30 years, more than 1,100 churches have been planted throughout the United States, and around 4,800 international churches through our Liberty Church Network (LCN) training organization. Each of these churches is committed to further establishing new churches, thereby exponentially multiplying the spread of GOD's word worldwide. The network set itself a mission to have a significant impact by 2025. Through a network of 50 regional centers, 500 local centers, and 10,000 churches of the LCN network, it will be possible to bring a new generation home to Jesus. Church planting will continue to be a central method for this church. Our goal is one million new students by 2025.²²

Status Report on Falwell's Economic Empire in the Mid-1980s and How the Grassroots Movement Operation Was Supported from Lynchburg

A 1984 article in the *Washington Post* trying to decipher the secret of Falwell's success provided the following data: "~20,000 of Lynchburg, Virginia residents (a quarter of its population) were employed by the Little Thomas Road Baptist Church. 392 TV stations broadcasted the 'Old Time Gospel Hour,' as well as Ted Turner's cable TV stations and others. Total donations collected for the Church exceeded $72 million (with an additional $12 million for Falwell's political lobby campaigning for the Moral Majority)." Falwell was quoted in this article, saying that a large part of the organization's expenses, amounting to $65 million, was intended for missionary assignments in 65 countries, highlighting helping graduates establish churches after completing their studies. The rest of the budget, amounting to $10 million per year, went to subsidizing the college; $18 million for TV and radio broadcasting; and $15 million for the annual salaries of 2,200 employees. In 1984, there were 4,566 students enrolled in Liberty College, and Falwell's goal was set on reaching 50,000 students. The article described how the information and

---

21 Elmer Towns, *What's Right with the Church: A Manifesto of Hope Destiny Image Publishers* (Shippensburg, PA: Bethany House Publishers, 2009), 102.
22 "One Million by 2025," www.thomasroadworldwide.org, available at: https://www.thomasroadworldwide.org/ministries/church-planting/, accessed February 9, 2022.

revenue generation factory operated: The "Old Time Gospel Hour" warehouse stretches for several hundred meters and is manned 24/7. Employees working in this heavily guarded facility open 60 million envelopes sent there each year. Other employees are stationed at the 80 phone posts at all hours. The article further describes the sophisticated operation of phone banks, the object of envy for every politician—receiving donations through toll-free numbers provided on the TV screen. The fundraising of each "Old Time Gospel Hour" broadcast ranges from as low as $100,000 a day to $1 million a day around Christmas. One floor holds the books, Bibles, records, tapes, and "Jesus First" buttons sent to worshipers. Every week, the computers generate "personalized" fundraising letters that are being sent to 7.5 million households on Falwell's distribution list. In the "Management and Development" department, hone operators are employed who take requests and applications to give property to the church or include the church and its college in people's wills. From an unmarked old warehouse in Lynchburg, the Moral Majority's headquarters sends its recruitment reports to 1 million donors. According to Falwell, there is an overlap of about 18 percent of Moral Majority supporters and the "Old Time Gospel Hour" followers. Although being a separate and taxable political campaign, its critics claim that politics are so intertwined with the "Old Time Gospel Hour" that the latter faces a danger of losing its legal status as a recognized tax-deductible donation. Falwell responded as follows: "It seems that my diverse roles are mixed together, which happens when you're a public figure. As a private individual, I support Ronald Reagan openly. As a pastor, I do not force my flock to do the same. However, my critics are wrong when they say everything is murky." In response to the question about tax exemption, he said: "That's a tough question. Our constitutional teams examine this issue once a month for the past five years. If the church does not use its resources for political purposes, it's okay."[23]

---

23 Myra MacPherson, "The Rise of the Falwell Empire," www.washingtonpost.com September 26, 1984, available at: https://www.washingtonpost.com/archive/lifestyle/1984/09/26/the-rise-of-the-falwell-empire/9dda636e-3475-4b64-899a-650a1d6dbb89/, accessed June 9, 2021.

Chapter 4

THE CENTRALITY AND IMPORTANCE OF ISRAEL IN THE VISION OF FALWELL IN PROMOTING POLITICAL ACTION FROM LIBERTY UNIVERSITY

The Religious Context of Falwell's Connection with the State of Israel

In his book, Falwell talks about the first time he understood the importance of Israel to a believing Christian, which occurred during his religious studies at college.[1] "Chapter after chapter, book after book, the scriptures tell the story of those whom GOD chose and how He helped to bring about their creation. He made a covenant with the fathers: Abraham, Isaac, and Jacob. He promised them a great nation in the promised land. 'And from My people of Israel,' GOD promised, 'will come a Messiah who will save all people from their sins.'" The understanding that the Israelites are GOD's chosen people recurs throughout Falwell's writings, speeches, and declarations as a cornerstone of his faith. Falwell expected every believing Christian to understand that the Israelites are GOD's chosen people and that they need and are obligated to live in peace in the land promised to them by GOD almighty himself.

In his book, *Listen, America*, Falwell discusses the prophecy of the attack that would befall Israel at the end of days. Falwell's interpretation describes the attack by Israel's enemies, the primary enemy being the Soviet army with its Arab allies. He quotes chapters 38 and 39 from Ezekiel's prophecy describing the battle against Israel and interprets: "Russia will be defeated, and Israel will succeed for the second time to be saved by the hand of GOD. If the Russians just read the word of GOD and believe in it, they may not find themselves falling on their knees and begging the GOD of Israel for forgiveness. No, GOD has not yet finished his relationship with Israel. But he may

---

1 Ibid., *Falwell: An Autobiography*, 163.

end up with those nations who pursue it, as quoted in Genesis 12:3, 'I will bless those who bless you, and whoever curses you I will curse; and all peoples on earth will be blessed through you.'" He summarizes with this verse, recurring many times in the religious motivation of those who believe that non-Jews are commanded to bless the People of Israel, and this is the only religious motivation to support the Jewish people and Israel. Falwell takes the written Torah literally: whoever blesses the People of Israel shall be blessed himself. He continues his theological explanation and says that throughout history, every nation that persecuted the Jews felt the arm of GOD. On the other hand, anyone who stood by the Jews received GOD's blessing. Falwell states that if we want America to remain blessed ...[2]

In the chapter "The Miracle Called Israel," Falwell further pursues the prophetic part, explaining that GOD continues blessing the small country of Israel as this book is being written, in 1980. He proves the existence of GOD by saying: "Despite all the efforts of its neighbors to destroy that nation and the problems that ensue in the operation of the Knesset, Israel continues to shine and be a testimony to GOD's commitment. Israel remains free thanks to Divine Intervention."[3] Falwell further details in a historical narrative interspersed with biblical quotes the Jewish history since the Israelites left the promised land, including the dispersion of the Jews in exile, until their return to the Land of Israel, through the Balfour Declaration, the establishment of the State of Israel, the wars Israel had to face, and the miraculous Divine Providence, given GOD's commitment to safeguard the people of Israel. Falwell discusses the contemporary situation where the influence of the oil embargo on U.S. relations with Israel: "There is an increasing tendency to allow our need for oil to blind us to our greater need for God's continued blessing. If America allows herself to be blackmailed by the oil cartel and trades her allegiance to Israel for a petroleum 'mess of pottage,' she will also trade her position of world leadership for a place in the history books alongside of Rome. We cannot allow that to happen."[4]

One of the noteworthy issues in the context of Falwell's religious attitude toward Israel revolves around his reaction to the theory of Armageddon: a renewed version of Jesus's Second Coming, and the battle of Gog and Magog that is supposed to bring the destruction of most of the Jewish people and the Christianization of the other part, also known as Darby's theory. Falwell made numerous comments about that theory, claiming that he does not

---

[2] Jerry Falwell, *Listen, America!* (New York: Bantam Books, 1981), 98.
[3] Ibid., 93.
[4] Ibid.

promote that belief and that his support for the Jews in general and Israel in particular derives only from what is attributed to the chosen people in the Old Testament. For example, when asked about the subject during a tour in Israel in 1985, Falwell said that he does not share the same point of reference embraced by many Christian Zionists, that Armageddon must occur in the Holy Land to bring the Second Coming of Christ. He also added that "the holy scriptures speak only of the battle in the Valley of Jezreel and not of the destruction of humanity." When asked if he believed that President Reagan held the position of the theory of Armageddon, he replied, "I do not know anyone who believes or seriously accepts that anything that happens in Israel will hasten or delay the coming of the Messiah."[5]

How Does Falwell Convey the Importance of Israel to Students and Future Pastors?

In various opportunities, Falwell talks about establishing the "Young Pastors Movement," whose role is to educate their community to love Israel and the Jewish people. For example, David Brog notes in his book, "I personally feel a heavy responsibility to educate the American people on the importance of supporting the State of Israel and the Jewish people everywhere. I train thousands of pastors to do the same. At Liberty University, where I serve as a mentor, and in our seminary, we teach 6,000 students about the importance of this topic and how they can do their part in the future to eliminate anti-Semitism."[6]

As part of the training in an academic institution, an explanation and emphasis were provided [as mentioned later in the research testimonies, K.B] regarding the importance of Israel for fulfilling the commandments and spreading the gospel. On the Thomas Road Baptist Church's website, where Falwell began his journey, under "History," the connection is further described as follows:

> To equip champions for Jesus to enter all areas of life, Thomas Road Baptist Church established the Christian Academy in Lynchburg in 1967 and Liberty University in 1971. Since its inception, this unique educational system has underscored academic excellence and its local church. The curriculum is focused on the return of Christ. In the early 1970s, Thomas Road Baptist Church received national recognition as one of the fastest-growing churches in America. A Christian counseling office

---

5 Steve Rodan, "Falwell Affirms Support of Israel Despite Cool Hello," *Arizona Republic*, March 9, 1985, F3-1.
6 Ibid., *Standing with Israel: Why Christians Support the Jewish State*, 143.

was established during this time to assist families with problems and help them build homes in the spirit of biblical principles. The vision for curricular programs and international missions became increasingly aggressive each year, resulting in the addition of new missionaries and special projects.[7]

The website further refers to the Book of Deuteronomy 6: 4–9: "Hear, O Israel: The Lord is our GOD, the Lord is one. And you shall love the Lord, your GOD, with all your heart and with all your soul, and with all your means. And these words, which I command you this day, shall be upon your heart. And you shall teach them to your sons and speak of them when you sit in your house, and when you walk on the way, and when you lie down and when you rise up. And you shall bind them for a sign upon your hand, and they shall be for ornaments between your eyes. and you shall inscribe them upon the doorposts of your house and upon your gates," as a commandment given by GOD to the children of Israel for the education and the instruction of faith.

The Importance of Jerry Falwell's Organized Excursions to the Holy Land, with Students and Graduates

One of the most significant courses Falwell took to deepen the relationship between pastors and the community was through organized expeditions to Israel, even during the Intifada when the State Department warned American tourists against it. Falwell believed that a trip to Israel was an essential genealogical journey for strengthening the faith of university students, pastors" roles in their communities, or mere congregation members. Falwell spoke about his first trip to Israel, back in the 1960s, and described to author Merrill Simon the religious experience of entering Jerusalem for the first time: "It would be impossible to describe my feelings […] In my opinion, every Christian must take that journey at least once in their lifetime. I have never taken a group to Israel without the feeling that after this journey they would become friends of the people and the Holy Land."[8] Elsewhere, Jerry Falwell is quoted in the context of that first trip to Israel after the Six-Day War: "My first trip was after the '67 War. It was really an eye-opener. I was

---

7 "Thomas Road Baptist Church Official Website," available at https://old.trbc.org/history/, accessed January 3, 2021.
8 Ibid., *Jerry Falwell and the Jews*, 60–61.

previously convinced that Israel was huge, and its minimal size and independence impressed me."⁹

Macel Falwell, Jerry Falwell's wife, spoke about the immense importance her husband saw in touring Israel, starting after the establishment of the college. She recounted a conversation in the living room between Dr. Townes and Falwell where Townes said there was no way to recruit students because all the magazines had closed their publications, and it was impossible to purchase more advertisements. Falwell responded, "We will have to build the college like they build a church, thinking outside the box," and continued, "I am traveling to Israel with a delegation of pastors. Why don't we offer each pastor who sends us five students a free trip, and maybe even to any pastor who brings me just one student?" Townes was excited and said, "Let's give a free trip to our students."[10] Thus, the college, which had not yet been founded, developed an aggressive recruiting strategy combining marketing with a love for Israel.

These excursions are described in detail in the book by Timothy Weber. Alongside his actions for Israeli objectives, Falwell continued to promote journeys to Israel to form a popular support base for the Jewish state. In 1982, Falwell brought 40 English-speaking religious leaders to Israel on an introductory tour, hoping that they would bring their large constituencies to Israel in the future. During the 80s and 90s, he used his wide-ranging church and political contacts to sponsor many more such tours. Falwell even made the establishment of strong ties with Israel an essential part of his educational mission at Liberty University in Lynchburg, Virginia.[11] According to Weber, in 1983, Falwell brought 630 participants on his excursions to the Holy Land; by 1985, there were already 850 participants who met with various Israeli government officials. During those journeys, Falwell held a noteworthy event for Israel in the presence of ministers Ariel Sharon and Moshe Arens. Later on, in 1998, with a donation of $4 million, Falwell brought thousands of first-year Liberty students on an organized trip to the Holy Land.[12] According to a summary document of the Israeli Pilgrimage Committee dated May 22, 1985, a Moral Majority delegation led by Falwell brought around 2,800 participants earlier that year.[13] These expeditions had a significant economic

---

9 Deborah H. Strober, *Israel at Sixty: An Oral History of a Nation Reborn* (Independence, KY: John Wiley & Sons, 2008), 250.
10 Macel Falwell, *Jerry Falwell, His Life and Legacy* (New York: Howard Books, 2008), 139.
11 Timothy P. Weber, *On the Road to Armageddon: How Evangelicals Became Israel's Best Friend* (Ada, MI: Baker Academic, 2005), 219
12 Ibid., 219–220.
13 Archive of the Israeli State, ISA-MFA-Religion-R0003a9a, 78.

impact on the Israeli tourism industry; as Michael Thomas writes in his book: "There was an economic reason why Likud needed to strengthen ties with the Christian right. Evangelical pastors led influential groups of pilgrims to the Holy Land. Religious tourism became a substantial asset in the Israeli economy at a time when part of the American Jewry canceled visits to the Holy Land, but Christian pilgrims did not." [14]

Lynchburg's local community followed Dr. Falwell's expeditions with great enthusiasm, as can be seen, for example, from the front and back covers of the *Thomas Road Family Journal Champion for Truth* dedicated to Falwell's tour of Israel in 1978. The journal reports about "Falwell's November tour of the Holy Land, accompanied by 480 American Christians," and mentions his words that "Christians are asked to pray for the peace of Jerusalem." Falwell is quoted saying: "The continued blessing of God upon America is in a real way conditional by America's treatment of Israel [...] It is very important that America in these crucial days reaffirm her loyalty to the people of GOD. It is especially important that Born Again Christians are obedient to Scriptures in this respect." During that tour, Israeli prime minister Menachem Begin has granted Dr. Jerry Falwell an exclusive interview which was later aired during the Old-Time Gospel Hour. This interview, held against the backdrop of the peace agreement between Israel and Egypt, was also leveraged by Begin to thank Falwell for his support. Begin was quoted saying that "he was willing to record a broadcast for Falwell's television program on the Camp David agreement and was happy to issue permits for the stay of Evangelicals in Israel, 'beyond the standard quotas that allowed for the construction of new communities,'" thus, increasing the number of tourists entering Israel for religious tourism.[15]

There are several examples of the impact of Liberty students" visits to the Holy Land. Evidence of the significance of opinion leaders" tours of Israel can be found in the 1981 yearbook of Liberty University. In the chapter about the group of representatives, one of its members speaks about his tour with Jerry Falwell to the Holy Land: "Our public relations team went on a journey to Israel with hosts, Dr. Jerry Falwell and Rev Don Norman. 'The journey made the Bible come alive.' One of the band members concluded: 'Now I can see the places I read about in the Bible.'"[16]

---

14 Ibid., *American Policy toward Israel: The Power and Limits of Beliefs*, 18.

15 *The Journal Champion* Vol. 1, Issue 16 (1978): P-1, available at: https://digitalcommons.liberty.edu/paper_78_80/23, accessed November 9, 2020.

16 "Liberty University 1980–81 Yearbook," 137, available at: https://issuu.com/luyearbook/docs/lu_1981?fbclid=IwAR1HCevxXu2Sphe-A5n9lWf88DJfj83CzsG0tuchsUmz7_Cl38bWBI8ySXE, accessed November 9, 2020.

Another example of students" impressions after visiting the Holy Land is given by a group of singers. As part of Liberty University's activities, a student group was formed to spread the word of GOD and love for Israel through song. The group, named LBC Singers, was the university's representative group. An article prepared with the students for the 1980 yearbook, titled "Members of the Group Express Patriotism as Representatives of Liberty," depicts the experience for which the group was formed. The group, which completed six years at the university, appeared before thousands and even visited Israel. The show the group brought forward was called "I Love America," and according to one of the singers, it was "a positive Christian patriotic angle that left its mark on us."[17]

Converting Support into Politics Influencing U.S.-Israel Relations

Daniel Hummel's book describes the years 1976–1984 as a period when the special relationship between Evangelicals and the State of Israel was shaped. Within less than one generation, Zionist Christianity became a lobby of the Christian Right as an organized political grassroots movement.[18] Israel succeeded in finding loyal Zionist Christians who became part of the grassroots movement of the Republican Party. In 1978, Falwell first quoted the verse from Genesis as an important basis of the faith for supporting Israel: "I will bless those who bless you, and whoever curses you I will curse," to warn Americans against forsaking Israel. This verse would become the "cornerstone" of the explanation, both for believers and for opponents who claim that Falwell's commitment to Israel stems from his fascination with Reversal Theories. Falwell sees that verse as a Divine commandment intended for every believing American to support the State of Israel and its survival, from religious motivations, as part of the work of GOD.

Jerry Falwell develops his theory on the importance of Israel to Christianity, based on the Zechariah prophecy: "And in that day I will make Jerusalem a burdensome stone for all people: all that burden themselves with it shall be cut in pieces, though all the people of the earth be gathered together against it" (Zechariah 12:3). According to Falwell's interpretation, failing to defend

---

17 "Singers Stress Patriotism while Representing LBC," Liberty University 1980–81 Yearbook, 169, available at: https://issuu.com/luyearbook/docs/lu_1981, accessed November 9, 2020.
18 Daniel G. Hummel, *Covenant Brothers: Evangelicals, Jews, and U.S.-Israeli Relations* (Philadelphia, PA: University of Pennsylvania Press, 2019), 160–161.

Israel is an existential threat to America. Beyond the religious aspect by which Falwell explains the importance of Israel to Americans, Falwell sees himself as a man on a mission to bring peace to the Middle East, justifying his regional tours and meetings with Anwar Sadat and other Middle Eastern leaders to promote this mission. He is also quoted during the 1980s as repeatedly saying: "To stand against Israel is to stand against GOD." Even more directly, he defended Begin's West Bank settlement policy. He invited Orthodox Jews to join the Moral Majority and truly believed Armageddon would begin with a Soviet attack on Israel.[19]

In Merrill Simon's book, the interviewer asks Falwell about a wide range of topics, among other things, about where Evangelical Christian faith is headed in relation to Israel. Falwell replied in 1984:

> *In the last twenty years, fundamentalists and evangelicals have undergone a rapid process of conversion toward supporting Israel. This was not the traditional position. It is a position most evangelicals and fundamentalists in our country now adopt. Leading pastors and teachers throughout the land have taken a strong stand that they believe theologically but were reluctant to take active steps to show for it. Every day, the number of supporters of Israel grows in the evangelical Christian community, surpassing the opponents. This is my position because today, Israel's best friends come from among the evangelical and fundamentalist Christians. I believe that in five years from now, the consensus around Israel will be a unified voice.*[20]

Falwell was also asked about the future impact of the Israel issue on the electoral system. "The day will come when to be elected as a candidate in the United States, one will have to be pro-Israel," he said at a Jerusalem press conference in 1983. Paul Findley, who represented Illinois's 20th congressional district in the United States House of Representatives from 1961 to 1983 as a member of the Republican Party, then lost his seat to Democrat Dick Durbin in a closely contested race, cited the quote in his book. Findley, who was a critic of Israel, argues that the pro-Israel lobby in Washington was the one that ousted him from his seat. In his book, written in the 1980s during the peak of its influence, he continues to describe the impact of pro-Israel and the Moral Majority on the Republican Party: "Although the Moral Majority's attempts to elect its preferred candidates were not 100% successful,

---

19 Frances FitzGerald, "A Disciplined, Charging Army," *The New Yorker Magazine*, May 18, 1981, 53–141, available at: https://www.newyorker.com/magazine/1981/05/18/a-disciplined-charging-army, accessed July 7, 2021.
20 Merrill Simon, *Jerry Falwell and the Jews* (New York: Jonathan David Publishers, 1984), 88.

many candidates, disconnected from their religious beliefs, are now committed to these issues [referring to support for Israel, Ed.] which have now become the evangelical political agenda." He claims, "The prophecy's argument is embraced by most of the fundamentalist conservative groups, like the 'Moral Majority' who receive wider media coverage, but this alliance is likely held by a larger audience of around 40 million Christian believers."[21] Perhaps Falwell's most significant quote, that explains the importance of planting churches and promoting the political agenda concerning Israel is found in Brog's book: "I personally feel a heavy responsibility to educate the American people on the importance of supporting the state of Israel and the Jewish people everywhere. I train thousands of pastors to do the same. At Liberty University, where I serve as a mentor, and in our seminary, we teach 6,000 students about the importance of this topic and how they can do their part in the future to eliminate anti-Semitism."[22] In his book, Stephen Sizer mentions Falwell's stance on motivating and activating advocates of the State of Israel, where the former comments on a 1985 Rabbinic conference in Miami where Falwell spoke and said his goal is to "mobilize 70 million conservative Christians to support Israel" and against antisemitism. Stephen Sizer also quotes Falwell concerning the topic of mobilizing and activating the loyal crowd in support of the State of Israel. Sizer comments on a 1985 Rabbinical Conference in Miami, where Falwell delivered a speech and said that his goal, through his public mission, is: "To mobilize and move about 70 million conservative Christians to action in favor of Israel and against anti-Semitism."[23]

The Vision to Move the American Embassy to Jerusalem

Moving the American embassy to Jerusalem was an important part of Falwell's doctrine, and many efforts were invested over the years to promote that agenda until it finally became the Jerusalem Embassy Act on November 8, 1995. This effort culminated in the actual move of the U.S. Embassy to Jerusalem on May 14, 2018, during Donald Trump's presidency.

---

21 Paul Findley, *They Dare to Speak Out: People and Institutions Confront Israel's Lobby* (Toronto: Lawrence Hill Books, 1985), 259–260.
22 Ibid., *Standing with Israel: Why Christians Support the Jewish State*, 143.
23 Stephen Sizer, *Christian Zionism: Road-Map to Armageddon?* (London: Inter-Varsity Press (IVP), 2021), 91.

Falwell appeared before the Subcommittee on International Relations of the U.S. House of Representatives on May 1, 1984, and gave his testimony in favor of the said move:

> *Thank you, Mr. Chairman. My name is Reverend Jerry Falwell. I am the pastor of Thomas Road Baptist Church in Lynchburg, Virginia, the Chancellor of Liberty College, and, as a part-time extra-curricular activity, I sometimes participate in the Moral Majority. One of the issues we have addressed from the outset of Moral Majority in 1979 and from the beginning of my ministry nearly twenty-eight years ago is support for the nation of Israel, born in our lifetimes, and for the Jewish people everywhere [...] The question before this joint hearing today, however, is not the support of Israel (though it is in a sense), but rather whether a sovereign nation has the right to declare its capital where it wishes and have that capital recognized by other sovereign nations. As all of you are aware, the United States recently granted full diplomatic recognition to The Vatican, a religious entity that, despite this recognition, still does not recognize Israel as a nation, much less Jerusalem as its capital [...] Jerusalem is not only the capital of the nation of Israel, it is also the capital of the three great religions. Why did Jesus come to Jerusalem? Because he recognized it as the capital of His country.*[24]

Beforehand, on February 23, 1984, Mr. Cal Thomas, Vice President of the "Moral Majority" movement, testified before the foreign committee of the Senate in the context of the Jerusalem Embassy Act. From the outset of his address, Thomas uses a religious argument, to represent the Evangelical community and oppose the Catholic Church. To justify the move, he argues: "The United States recently granted full diplomatic status to The Vatican, clearly a religious entity whose political affiliation stems from its religious status. Jerusalem, on the other hand, is revered not by one religion, but by three, and even by those who hold secular faith. It has always been the historic capital of Israel. It is ironic that a representative of the Roman Catholic Church is here, opposing this proposal, especially since The Vatican, despite its recognition by the United States, still refuses to recognize Israel as a sovereign nation, much less Jerusalem as its capital." He continued justifying the move in the name of freedom and progress: "From the very beginning, Israel, and

---

[24] Legislation Calling for a Move of the U.S. Embassy in Israel to Jerusalem, United States. Congress. House. "Committee on Foreign Affairs. Subcommittee on Europe and the Middle East," 82–84, available at: https://books.google.co.il/books?id=HiIRYGLSY80C&pg=PA263&dq=Falwell+EMBASSY+JERUSALEM&hl=iw&sa=X&ved=2ahUKEwii7b739_z1AhU4if0HHUZSCfEQ6AF6BAgHEAI#v=onepage&q=Falwell%20EMBASSY%20JERUSALEM&f=false, accessed July 7, 2021.

particularly the city administration of Jerusalem Mayor Teddy Kolleck, have meticulously maintained access for Jews, Christians and Moslems. Compare Israel's treatment of the holy places to Jordan's when that nation was in control of East Jerusalem. I might mention that the United States, which does not recognize Berlin as the capital of East Germany, still maintains its embassy in Berlin. Israel is the only nation on earth which is denied the right to place its capital where it wishes. It is not right. It is not fair," and he concludes:

> *Certainly Israel has a greater claim to national identity and to its own capital of Jerusalem, than, let us say, the Hashemite Kingdom of Jordan, which was created by government decree. Israel's heritage and history of Israel are much older. There are hundreds of references to Jerusalem in both the Old and New Testaments. In Psalm 128:5, the king of ancient Israel, David, said, "The Lord shall bless thee out of Zion, and thou shalt see the good of Jerusalem all the days of thy life." He had no reference to Tel Aviv. Mr. Chairman, fairness, equity, and morality argue in favor of the United States moving its embassy to Jerusalem, the past, present, and future capital of Israel. I respectfully urge you to pass this important bill.*[25]

Falwell's activity to move the embassy did not only go through writing position papers and attending hearings before Congress but also through actual political involvement in the seats of power handling U.S. foreign relations. One of the interesting stories related to the Evangelical lobby's ability to influence Congress members and senators is documented in Morris Bowers' book on Reagan's first presidency: "He [Falwell] also takes credit for converting Senator Jesse Helms (R., N.C.) into one of Israel's staunchest allies. Helms soon became chair of the Senate Foreign Relations Committee."[26] At the beginning of his career in the 1970s, Helms was a colonial opponent of the State of Israel. Falwell personally toiled to ensure the election of Republican Senator Jesse Helms in the 1984 elections. Falwell's involvement was particularly significant due to the efforts of the Democratic Party in Helms' district, and the personal involvement of African American pastor Jesse Jackson in enrolling black voters for the Democratic Party. At a special awakening conference held in Charlotte on July 8, 1983, before 250 ministers and lay leaders, Falwell said, "Jesse Helms is a national treasure" and added, "Jesse Helms is the most important man in Washington, besides the president, in the cause of leading this nation back to moral sanity. Can you imagine if we had

---

25 Documents and Articles Concerning Christians and Evangelicals Who Support Israel 1981–1984, Menachem Begin Heritage Center, P5-31.
26 Morris Glen Bowers, *Israel: The 51st State: The Unspoken Foreign Policy of the United States of America* (Bloomington, IN: iUniverse, 2005), 184.

100 Jesse Helms in the U.S. Senate." The event was the last stop on a two-day tour to enroll new Republican voters in the cities of Asheville, Wilmington, Raleigh, and Charlotte, North Carolina. Falwell announced at the event that, "We plan, minimum, to enroll 200,000 new voters in the state by next year [...] And we're talking about the kind of people who make a difference." It should be emphasized that the event was held at a time when polls in the state indicated a Democratic advantage, with then-governor Jim Hunt leading on Senator Helms 50:31. In the mid-term elections of 1982, two Republican members of Congress were replaced by Democrats.[27]

Falwell's speech became one of the key issues in the election campaign, despite the relatively small Jewish community in North Carolina. The Democratic candidate, Jim Hunt, accused Helms during the 1984 Senate campaign of having "the worst anti-Israel record of any member of the American Senate."[28] In an open letter sent to a national network of donors, the industrialist Arthur Cassell, a significant supporter of Hunt's campaign, wrote that "Helms voted against Israel in 25 votes held on significant issues for Israel, including opposing the Camp David Accords and the air package portion tied to it, and even proposed in 1982 to suspend diplomatic relations between the United States and Israel." He signed the letter with a personal appeal to donors that "we cannot rely on the extreme right on issues that are important to you and me."[29] According to Alex Brock, who served at the time as the government-appointed election supervisor, the article reported that "we know that both pastors [Jerry Falwell and Jesse Jackson, K.B.] visited North Carolina, and according to our estimates, both of them did very well." Brock reported that by the set enrollment deadline of October 8, 1984, "about 75% of those eligible to vote had undergone an early enrollment

---

27 Martin Tolchin, "Helms and Anti-Helms Campaigns Going Strong," *New York Times*, July 9, 1983, Section 1, Page 5, redirected May 20, 2021, https://www.nytimes.com/1983/07/09/us/helms-and-anti-helms-campaigns-going-strong.html.

28 William A. Link, *Righteous Warrior: Jesse Helms and the Rise of Modern Conservatism* (New York: St. Martin's Press, 2008), 319, available at: https://ebin.pub/righteous-warrior-jesse-helms-and-the-rise-of-modern-conservatism-0312356005-9780312356002.html.

29 William D. Snider, *Helms and Hunt: The North Carolina Senate Race* (Chapel Hill, NC: UNC Press, 1984), available at: https://books.google.co.il/books?id=yus2DwAAQBAJ&pg=PT135&lpg=PT135&dq=%22anti-Israel+record+of+any+member+of+the+U.S.+Senate%22&source=bl&ots=ms1U32L62J&sig=ACfU3U3Cp4YE-5tfq9dmTTnyeY_1nFRYbA&hl=iw&sa=X&ved=2ahUKEwjp2pm5hb30AhUuB2MBHUwuBvUQ6AF6BAgCEAM#v=onepage&q=%22anti-Israel%20record%20of%20any%20member%20of%20the%20U.S.%20Senate%22&f=false, accessed July 7, 2021.

process."[30] Apparently, Falwell's personal commitment for Helms" campaign changed the latter's position not only with regard to Israel in general, but especially in the context of the Jewish settlements at the West Bank. Being the chairman of the Foreign Relations Committee, Helms' change of heart could have promoted the legislation of the embassy bill. In Senator Helms' archive, there is an entire chapter dedicated to Israel, including letters, photos, and materials related to Israel-U.S. relations. For example, in May 1984, Senator Helms wrote a letter to the president of the United States about moving the U.S. embassy to Jerusalem, as a first step toward full recognition of Israel's sovereignty over Jerusalem. The following is the wording of the letter sent to President Reagan:

> *As you know, the bill proposing the move of the embassy from Tel Aviv to Jerusalem is gaining more and more supporters both in the Senate and in the House of Representatives. The growing number of supporters of the bill testify to the desire to solve the problem in the Middle East. Jerusalem is the capital of one country, but is the center of the three religions—Christianity, Judaism, and Islam. As such, it must serve as a symbol and landmark for anyone looking at the biblical land of Israel as the Holy Land. A united Jerusalem must be the central goal of our policy. We must not in any way bring pressure that would lead to the separation of the West Bank from Israel. The people in the Holy Land must live together under one roof, and the Jordan River must also be secure. Due to Israel's deep sentiments for Judea and Samaria, which are among the deepest spiritual motives, there must be free access to the biblical lands.*
>
> *However, the Palestinians also have a long history with these lands. Therefore, the Palestinians need to choose between accepting political, economic, and civil rights through representation in the Knesset, where Hebrew and Arabic will serve as the official languages of the country, or accepting autonomy within a conservative state, where Jerusalem serves as a shared capital. What we cannot accept is a Soviet-backed PLO state, established in the heart of the Holy Land. An undivided Jerusalem is the basis for a comprehensive solution to the problem in the Middle East [...] I urge you to recognize Jerusalem in the context I have proposed, where the move of the embassy will be the first step in the process.*

---

30 "Senate Race Gives Churches a Chance to Try political Clout," *The Arizona Republic*, October 27, 1984, F2.

This letter was first read at a conference organized by Falwell the following day (May 17, 1984) as part of his keynote speech before over 300 participants at the "Israel is Safe Now" rally.[31]

Falwell continued to support the transfer of the embassy to Jerusalem vigorously, and on March 8, 1984, he visited the Herzl Institute and spoke before an audience of 200, reiterating his strong and well-known support for Israel, saying, "I thought every American should be fully committed to the welfare of the State of Israel." In his lecture, he spoke about the efforts being made by the administration to move the U.S. embassy to Jerusalem, saying, "I and the Moral Majority supported the proposed bill in Congress calling on the Reagan Administration to move the US embassy from Tel Aviv to Jerusalem."[32]

To summarize this chapter, we have witnessed Falwell intertwining his political and religious positions regarding the importance of Israel in the relationships of the community he led, vis-a-vis the significance and time he devoted to the political promotion of this goal concerning Israel as a whole, and the efforts to move the embassy to Jerusalem in particular. In the next chapter, I will try to connect the ability to augment power through the planting of communities from the 1970s until the move of the embassy to Jerusalem, as a major part of the Christian-Zionist community agenda.

---

31 "Helms Urges Reagan to Recognize Jerusalem as Israel's Capital; First Step Would Be to Move U.S. Embassy," *JTA*, May 17, 1984, available at: https://www.jta.org/1984/05/22/archive/helms-urges-reagan-to-recognize-jerusalem-as-israels-capital-first-step-would-be-to-move-u-s-emba, accessed July 7, 2021.

32 "Falwell Seeks to Alleviate Concern Among Jews about Reasons for Fundamentalists' Support for Israel," *JTA*, March 9, 1984, available at: https://www.jta.org/archive/falwell-seeks-to-alleviate-concern-among-jews-about-reasons-for-fundamentalists-support-for-israel?fireglass_rsn=true#fireglass_params&tabid=a885fcc27f4b5504&application_server_address=tie2.fg.gov.il&popup=true&is_right_side_popup=false&start_with_session_counter=1, accessed July 7, 2021.

Chapter 5

THE RELATIONSHIP WITH MENACHEM BEGIN AND THE POLITICAL ALLIANCE WITH ISRAEL

Introduction to Falwell's Relationship with Menachem Begin

The first-ever documented meeting between Menachem Begin and Falwell dates back to 1975. During Begin's meeting with a group of Evangelical leaders, Jerry Falwell pledged to support Israel. Jan Pieterse wrote about that meeting in his book: "During the meeting in Washington D.C. in 1975 between evangelical leaders and Menachem Begin, the evangelicals pledged full support for Israel. Jerry Falwell stated during the meeting that 'we proclaim that the Land of Israel encompasses Judea and Samaria, as integral parts of the Jewish patrimony, with Jerusalem as its indivisible capital. Israel stands as bulwark of strength and determination against those who by terror and blackmail threaten our democratic way of life.'"[1] However, the close relationship between Begin and Falwell commenced only after the political upheaval of 1977 and the formation of government by Menachem Begin.

Before exploring the personal rapport between Falwell and Menachem Begin, it is important to briefly introduce Begin's background to readers unfamiliar with his trajectory. Born in 1913 in Brest-Litovsk (then Poland), Begin rose to prominence as the leader of the Revisionist Zionist youth movement Betar, and later as commander of the Irgun, a Jewish underground organization that fought the British Mandate in Palestine.[2] After Israel's independence, Begin founded the Herut party, remaining in the political opposition for nearly three decades. His rhetoric—shaped by his personal history as a Holocaust survivor and Soviet prisoner—was marked by passionate appeals

---

1 Jan Nederveen Pieterse, *The History of a Metaphor: Christian Zionism and the Politics of Apocalypse* (Archives de Sciences Sociales des Religions, Annie 1991), 92.
2 Avi Shilon, *Menachem Begin: A Life* (New Haven: Yale University Press, 2012), 13–35.

to Jewish history and biblical destiny.³ In 1977, Begin led the Likud Party to a dramatic electoral victory, becoming Israel's first right-wing prime minister.⁴ A skilled orator with deep ideological convictions, Begin appealed to religious and nationalist audiences in both Israel and abroad. This biographical context helps explain why Begin would soon find a natural ally in Jerry Falwell, as described in the following section.

In his book, historian Daniel Hummel describes the outset of the relationship between Israel and the Evangelical movement: "In 1976, a well-connected group of Evangelical leaders began working to promote relations between Israel and the United States, but in less than a decade, this popular movement became a conservative force active in the Republican party."⁵ He continues: "Begin's victory and the revisionists in 1977 helped to change Zionist Christianity. Begin, as a revisionist, saw the importance of Jewish sovereignty in Judea, which he insisted on calling by names from the Bible, such as Judea and Samaria [...] Between 1976 and 1984, right-wing Christian evangelicals became an integral part of the 'special relationship' with Israel, also known as the 'lobby for Israel.' Within less than a decade, Zionist Christianity became an organized political movement." Hummel notes in this context the key role Menachem Begin played in establishing Israel's alliance with Evangelicals: "To use the power of the evangelical movement, Begin directly approached those leaders, especially those who held political power. The Christian right established cultural-conservative, anti-Communist, and pro-Israel frameworks that helped create groups with a common interest [...] Begin, who was aware of how these groups operated, worked directly with these leaders. Israel under Begin valued those pastors as the best force to work for Israel."⁶

In his article, Donald Wagner examines the trends that led to the Evangelical movement's growth in the mid-1970s. He counts at least five trends that contributed to the rise of Christian Zionism: First, Evangelical and charismatic movements became the fastest-growing branch of North American Christianity. The major Protestant and Roman Catholic churches shrank both in budgets and in attendance. Second, Jimmy Carter's election to the presidency in 1976 increased the visibility and legitimacy of the Evangelical movement that had been relatively marginal until then. Third, *Time* magazine's declaration of 1976 as "The Year of the Evangelicals."

---

3 Anita Shapira, *Israel: A History* (Waltham, MA: Brandeis University Press, 2012), 334–336.
4 Ofer Kenig and Gideon Rahat, "The Electoral Rise of the Israeli Right," *Israel Studies* 14, no. 3 (2009): 116–118.
5 Ibid., *Covenant Brothers: Evangelicals, Jews, and U.S.-Israeli Relations*, 160.
6 Ibid., 163.

Fourth, the closeness of some Jewish organizations and the desire for cooperation resulted directly from the occupation of parts of Arab countries after 1967. This occupation created tension between many Jewish organizations and Protestant, Orthodox, and Catholic communities, as will be further detailed later. Therefore, many Jewish organizations, especially lobbying groups like AIPAC, turned to support the growing Evangelical community. As Rabbi Marc Tanenbaum of the American Jewish Committee said, "The Evangelical community is the largest and fastest-growing block of pro-Israeli, Pro-Jewish sentiment in this country." AIPAC and the Anti-Defamation League (ADL) added a special team in the 1970s to focus on relations with Evangelicals. The fifth factor that sparked the political agenda of the emerging Christian Zionist movement was the election of Menachem Begin as prime minister of Israel in 1977. Before Begin's election, Israeli politics was dominated by the secular Labor Party.

Begin's Likud Party was supported by an increasingly powerful settler movement and small Orthodox religious parties. Likud leaders used the biblical names "Judea and Samaria" for the West Bank and a religious argument to justify the settlement of the land: Because GOD gave the land exclusively to the Jews, they have a Divine right to settle anywhere in the Land of Israel. This politically exploitative perception, rooted in biblical entitlement, found a receptive audience and open arms among Evangelical leadership. Evangelicals took every opportunity to bless the Likud leaders and vocally support their political and religious agenda. The final development that brought about the alliance between the Likud Party and the religious Right was Jimmy Carter's statement in March 1977 that he supported Palestinian human rights, including "the right to a homeland." Two months after the Likud came to power, it reached out immediately to the Christian Evangelicals. The Likud's strategy was simple: To tear the Evangelicals from Carter's political base and support opposition from conservative Evangelicals to the UN's proposed Peace Conference in the Middle East. The Israeli government also sought to strengthen ties with the Evangelicals when the Israeli Tourism Ministry saw them as a new and vital market for tours of the Holy Land and a major source of income from both the Christian and pro-Israeli camps.[7]

---

7 Donald Wagner, "Evangelicals and Israel: Theological Roots of a Political Alliance," *The Christian Century*, November 4, 1998, 1020–1026, available at: https://www.religion-online.org/article/evangelicals-and-israel-theological-roots-of-a-political-alliance, accessed July 7, 2021.

The importance that Menachem Begin placed on the association with the land and the Evangelical movement can be seen in the guidelines he provided for the establishment of a pilgrimage center in Judea and Samaria, covering an area of about 49 acres.[8] Another example of Begin's unique attitude can be found in a letter written by Matityahu Shmulevitz, CEO of the Prime Minister's Office during Begin and Shamir's tenure, to Mr. Nevo, the appointed official for tourism in the Judea and Samaria region, on October 23, 1983: "Following your request and our telephone conversation, I confirm that the former Prime Minister, Mr. Menachem Begin, gave his blessing to the plan to establish a tourist center for pilgrims at the Inn of the Good Samaritan site."[9]

In September 1981, Prime Minister Menachem Begin took an official tour to Washington, DC. The prime minister's schedule included a planned meeting with Rev. Jerry Falwell. Falwell was accompanied by the governor of the State of Virginia at the time, John Dalton, and two senators from Virginia, the more senior Harry Byrd Jr., who served as an independent Democrat, and Senator John Warner, elected on behalf of the Republican Party in 1979. Falwell's ability to bring senators from both sides of the aisle, alongside the governor of Virginia as his entourage, is an indication of his power and influence in the American political system. The participants' remarks were quoted in the *Washington Post*: "He told me, 'Reverend Falwell, there are those who are working very hard to separate us. But we are not going to be separated.' He said, 'There is a special relationship with Christians and Jews that is very dear to me,'" Falwell recounted. Falwell continued, "I believe history supports the premise that GOD deals with nations as they deal with Israel." He added that the Bible explicitly warns against "rulers and potentates who dare touch the apple of GOD's eye."[10] The United Press International news agency also reported on the same meeting, which lasted about an hour, on September 11, 1981. Begin praised the support of the fundamentalist and Evangelical community in Israel. Falwell said that "the Christian coalition reaffirmed its support for Israel's right to exist," and stated that the fundamentalist and Evangelical community will provide "unwavering support for the state of Israel and the Jewish people everywhere." He concluded in a statement: "I am glad that we have a

---

8 Ibid.
9 The State of Israel Archives, ISA-moag-DeputyMinister-0013xtg.
10 Martin Schram, John M. Goshko, and Valarie Thomas, "Jerry Falwell Vows Amity with Israel," *Washingtonpost.com*, September 12, 1981, available at: https://www.washingtonpost.com/archive/politics/1981/09/12/jerry-falwell-vows-amity-with-israel/282947d1-47ff-4851-8884-495506fe1773/, accessed June 9, 2021.

president who stands with Israel."[11] On the other hand, Begin responded to the meeting with Falwell by saying: "They [the Evangelicals, K.B.] are sincere and devoted friends. We are very grateful to them. They have proven it," and added: "There are some who object to it. But if a man or group will stretch out his hand and say 'I am a friend of Israel', I say, 'Israel has very strong enemies and needs friends.' Reverend Falwell is a very strong friend."[12]

According to David Brog, the deeply rooted acquaintance between Begin and the Evangelicals began shortly after Menachem Begin's election in 1977, when he came for medical treatment at the Hadassah hospital and met Dr. Larry Samuels, a nuclear medicine specialist. After speaking to him in Hebrew with an American accent, Begin asked him when he had made Aliyah to Israel. In response, Dr. Samuels told him that he was not Jewish, but an Evangelical Christian from Illinois "whom GOD had called to come to Jerusalem and practice medicine here."[13] In an interview to the *Daily Dispatch*, Dr. Samuels spoke about the circumstances that brought him to Jerusalem, following a car accident he met with earlier in his life: "I heard a very clear calling to come to Jerusalem. I felt afraid and wondered if I was hallucinating […] Finally, I said, 'Dear GOD, I can't do this, I don't have the money. If the voice I heard in my head is real, you need to make it happen yourself.' When I got home, I found an envelope (with compensation money for the disability I suffered) that I didn't expect. It covered the cost of my trip and my wife's to Jerusalem […] Menachem Begin came to me to treat his heart problems."[14] Begin wanted to learn more about Samuels' background, and the latter told him: "You know, I think you have more supporters among Christian Evangelicals in North America than you have Jews supporting Israel."[15] When Begin left that day, he asked his aides to check

---

11 David E. Anderson, "Israeli Prime Minister Menachem Begin is Pleased with the Support U.S. Fundamentalists and Evangelicals have Given Israel," upi.com, September 11, 1981, available at: https://www.upi.com/Archives/1981/09/11/Israeli-Prime-Minister-Menachem-Begin-is-pleased-with-the/2313369028800/, accessed June 7, 2021.
12 "Begin Reportedly to Meet Moral Majority Leaders," *Washington Post*, August 31, 1981, A5.
13 Ibid., *Standing with Israel Why Christians Support the Jewish State*, 140.
14 "Samuels Rebuilds Life after Accident," *The Daily Dispatch*, Moline, Illinois, November 30, 1981, 5, available at: https://www.newspapers.com/image/?clipping_id=15269&fcfToken=eyJhbGciOiJIUzI1NiIsInR5cCI6IkpXVCJ9.eyJmcmVlLXZpZXctaWQiOjM0MDAwMTc2MywiaWF0IjoxNjQ5NzU3OTA5LCJleHAiOjE2NDk4NDQzMDl9.hwDXL0I649F-2B-Nz759fo1RNSdnzChzf1LP_1MkcA4, accessed March 1, 2022.
15 Ibid., *Standing with Israel Why Christians Support the Jewish State*, 140.

what was said. According to Brog, this was the point where the historical connection between Begin and Falwell was created. It was a starting point for a special relationship between Begin and Evangelicals in general, and the personal relationship that was formed between him and Jerry Falwell in particular. Yehiel Kadishai, who was the Chief of Staff of the Prime Minister's Office, spoke in an interview about Begin's relationship with Evangelicals: "The Prime Minister said that a person who holds the Bible in his home, reads it, and believes in it, cannot be a bad person." He added: "He said that Evangelicals know that we are deeply rooted in this land, and hence, there is understanding between us and them."[16]

In an opinion column written by David Parsons, Deputy VP of the Christian Embassy in Jerusalem, to mark the 100th anniversary of Menachem Begin's birth in 2014, he discussed Begin's significant role in establishing connections with Christianity: "Indeed, of all the successive prime ministers of Israel following the nation's rebirth in 1948, Begin stands out as the first premier to publicly welcome Christian-Zionist support and to seek to harness it in defense of the Jewish state. Others before him may have had connections to individual Christian figures, but the story of the Israeli-Evangelical partnership as we know it today starts with Begin." He adds: "But Menachem Begin holds the unique distinction of being the first Israeli Prime Minister to warmly embrace Zionist Christian support. He, too, had developed personal friendships with individual Christian leaders like author Dr. David A. Lewis. But Begin went further than his predecessors by actively seeking Christian support and acknowledging its value in public." And he explains and specifies the reasons for this:

> *First, Begin came to realize that he shared a certain biblical worldview with Evangelical Christians. Although Begin saw much of the world through the prism of the Holocaust and thus was fully aware of the long, tragic history of Christian anti-Semitism, he also had a strong biblical worldview and knew this gave him much in common with Bible-believing Christians today. In particular, he looked on the Bible as Israel's title deed to the land and saw the Jewish return to the land as fulfillment of the vision of the Hebrew prophets, just as many Christians did. Second, Begin was surrounded by several close advisers who shared his friendly spirit toward pro-Israel Christians. This included the late Harry Hurwitz, the founder and long-serving president of the Begin Heritage Center [...] His good friend Harry Hurwitz was thus the key official within Begin's inner circle who convinced Begin to endorse the founding of a Christian Embassy in Jerusalem in 1980.[17]*

---

16 Craig Unger, *The Fall of the House of Bush* (New York: Scribner, 2007), 109.
17 David Parsons, "Menachem Begin and the Evangelicals," www.israel365news.com, April 2, 2014, available at: https://www.israel365news.com/13071/menachem-begin-evangelicals/, accessed March 9, 2021.

Indeed, Menachem Begin saw the alliance with the conservative wing of politics as a covenant that could unite under a common flag. That flag was the Bible, and the man who served as the liaison to this world was Jerry Falwell.

In his book, Stephan Rock argues that it was a deliberate strategy by Menachem Begin and the Likud to sow discord within the Evangelical camp: "Jimmy Carter announced in March 1977 that he supported granting rights to Palestinians, including 'the right to a homeland.' When the Likud took power in May 1977, a decision was made to 'split' the fundamentalist Evangelical voice from Carter's political base and generate support among conservative Christians for Israel's opposition in the UN to a peace initiative."[18]

Carter, the Palestinian Issue, and the Beginning of the Alliance Between the American Right-Wing and Menachem Begin

On May 22, 1977, during a policy speech at the University of Notre Dame (prior to signing the peace accord with Egypt), President Carter became the first American president to argue that "the Palestinians have the right to a national homeland." The following is the important part of his political vision regarding Israel and its relations with neighboring countries: "We are taking deliberate steps to improve the chances of lasting peace in the Middle East. Through wide-ranging consultation with leaders of the countries involved—Israel, Syria, Jordan, and Egypt—we have found some areas of agreement and some movement toward consensus. The d negotiations must continue" […] I've also tried to suggest a more flexible frameworks for the discussion of the three key issues which have so far been so intractable: the nature of a comprehensive peace—what is peace; what does it mean to the Israelis; what does it mean to their Arab neighbors; secondly, the relationship between security and borders—how can the dispute over border delineations be established and settled with a feeling of security on both sides; and the issue of the Palestinian homeland. The historic friendship that the United States has with Israel is not dependent on domestic politics in either nation; it's derived from our common respect for human freedom and from a common search for permanent peace. We will continue to promote a settlement which all of us need. Our own policy will not be affected by changes in leadership in any of the countries in the Middle East. Therefore, we expect Israel and her neighbors to continue to be bound by United Nations resolutions 242 and 338, which they have previously accepted. This may be the most propitious time for a

---

18 Stephen R. Rock, *Faith and Foreign Policy: The Views and Influence of U.S. Christians and Christian Organizations* (New York: Bloomsbury Publishing USA, 2011), 106.

genuine settlement since the beginning of the Arab-Israeli conflict almost 30 years ago. To let this opportunity pass could mean disaster not only for the Middle East but, perhaps, for the international political and economic order as well.[19] It wasn't the first time President Carter used the term "Palestinian Homeland." The first time was months earlier, in a speech he gave on March 16, 1977, in Clinton, Massachusetts, but the speech did not receive the same media attention as his speech at the university. This statement was the first significant trigger for Evangelical action in this context. Full-page advertisements in U.S. newspapers were published by Evangelical religious figures who said: "It is time that Evangelicals affirm their belief in biblical prophecy and the divine right of Israel to the land," and they ended their remarks with a direct attack on Carter's statement: "We as Evangelicals affirm our belief in the Promised Land for the Jewish people [...] We view with heavy concern any effort to extricate from the Jewish homeland or to establish with another political entity."[20]

According to Richard Kyle, the body that assisted in funding and coordination was an Evangelical organization with a Christian Zionist orientation called the Jerusalem Institute for Holy Land Studies. The publication of this campaign marked the first indication of the beginning of the alliance between the Evangelicals and Menachem Begin's Likud Party, which came to power in the elections held that same month.[21]

The speech given by Carter, which included the first acknowledgment by an American government regarding the Palestinian homeland, received particular analysis by Theodore Windt at the annual conference of the National Communication Association in 1989: "The part that dealt with the Middle East, for example, received a significant meaning as just a week earlier, a new prime minister was elected in Israel, Menachem Begin from the Likud party. When describing the settlements in Israel in the West Bank, Begin saw these territories as 'liberated' rather than 'occupied.' During his election campaign, Begin committed not to return the territories captured in the 1967 war under any circumstances. Therefore, Carter's mention of a Palestinian homeland and his call for Israel to comply with UN Resolution 242, which recommended the return of the occupied territories as an essential part of a peace settlement,

---

19 Jimmy Carter, "President's Commencement Address at the University of Notre Dame," *Notre Dame Law Review* 53 (1977): 9, available at: https://scholarship.law.nd.edu/ndlr/vol53/iss1/2.

20 Irvine H. Anderson, *Biblical Interpretation and Middle East Policy: The Promised Land America, and Israel, 1917–2002* (Gainesville, FL: University Press of Florida, 2005), 113.

21 Richard G. Kyle, *Apocalyptic Fever: End-Time Prophecies in Modern America* (Eugene, OR: Wipf and Stock Publishers, 2012), 222.

received significant attention and regretful learning in Israel's press."[22] The Irish theologian and colonial critic of Israel and Zionism, Michael Prior, argued in a discussion held at a Palestinian think tank in Washington in 2002 that "the Evangelical community was the main reason for Jimmy Carter's election in 1976. However, Carter's call for a 'Palestinian homeland' in 1977 ultimately led to his downfall, and the shift of the Evangelical right to vote for Ronald Reagan in 1980 was the main cause of Carter's defeat."[23] Kathleen Stewart also claims in her article that Carter's declaration and other actions taken in recognition of the Palestinian people led to

> *significant criticism from Jews and Evangelical Protestants, especially Jerry Falwell. The decision to mobilize political forces in the name of Israel began following the rejection of Carter's recognition of the Palestinians' right to a state in exchange for peace. The Evangelicals declared that such a stance was contrary to the biblical mandate and Israel's right to the Holy Land. Although there were other significant factors in Carter's defeat against Reagan, exit polls showed that Carter lost both among Jewish voters and a substantial segment of the Evangelical vote, who were a considerable part of his base [in the 1976 election K.B]. While he was willing to ignore Carter's religious foundations for the interests of the Israeli right wing, Falwell hastened his supporters to vote for Reagan.*[24]

Half a year before the elections, in April 1980, Menachem Begin arrived in Washington for a tour. The prime minister began his stay in Washington with a reception from a delegation of Christian and Evangelical leaders led by Falwell, who gave him a letter expressing "warm and enduring love" for Israel. This letter of support is revealed by what Wolf Blitzer describes in an article that claims, according to American and Israeli sources, that Prime Minister Begin refused to discuss two key issues related to the Palestinian self-definition that President Carter requested of him: the question of East Jerusalem Arabs who voted for the proposed Palestinian Authority as a self-governing entity, and whether to expand the legislative or judicial functions of this council. Israel's position, as presented by Begin, was that the council

---

22 Theodore Otto, Jr. Windt, "A New Foreign Policy: President Jimmy Carter's Speech at Notre Dame," May 22, 1977. A Paper Presented in Honor of Everett Lee Hunt, eric.ed.gov, November 20, 1989.19, available at: https://files.eric.ed.gov/fulltext/ED314767.pdf, accessed June 9, 2021.
23 George S. Hishmeh, "'ChristZion Alliance' Takes Grip on Bush's Foreign Policy," http://www.miftah.org, October 29, 2002, available at: http://www.miftah.org/PrinterF.cfm?DocId=1254, accessed June 9, 2021.
24 Caitlin Stewart, *Patriotism, National Identity, and Foreign Policy, United States Foreign Policy and National Identity in the 21st Century* (Oxfordshire: Taylor & Francis, 2009), 54–55.

should only be administrative in these two matters. The prime minister rejected all of Egypt's demands. The Christian leaders, led by Falwell, were essentially Carter's opposing weight and his demand to allow the establishment of a national home for the Palestinians.[25]

Falwell as Mediator Between Menachem Begin and Anwar Sadat

The relationship between Prime Minister Begin and Falwell was intimate, and Falwell regularly visited Begin's office whenever he came on tours in the region. During his visits to the area, Falwell served as a messenger for transferring messages between Israel and the people of the region. The scholarly literature did not delve much into the subject of Falwell's mission and his attempts to bring about a peace agreement. Falwell served as a special envoy between Begin and Sadat during their tours of the Middle East in 1978 in Cairo, Oman, and Jerusalem, as stated in Darren Dochuk's book, which claimed that Falwell "served as Sadat's envoy to Begin."[26] The topic of Falwell's mission is also discussed in an article by Colin Shindler, who wrote that "Begin was pleased to use Falwell and his Evangelical supporters as interlocutors with Cairo and Oman."[27] This work will further attempt to examine the additional contexts surrounding the claim that Falwell acted as mediator between the parties and someone who could and has contributed, to the extent possible, to the peace accord between Israel and Egypt. For example, the Jewish Telegraphic Agency reported during a tour organized by Falwell in the area in April 1978: "Egyptian President Anwar Sadat is concerned about Israeli settlements in Sinai. He told a group of American evangelical leaders he met with a few days ago. They met today with Prime Minister Menachem Begin in Jerusalem. Sadat warned that Israel could not continue to establish itself in Sinai, to which he referred as 'his land,' and violate his 'sovereignty'."[28] However, the pastors noted that Sadat was a "very warm

---

25 Wolf Blitzer, "Firm on Rights, Begin Flexible on Procedure in Talks with Carter," *The New York Jewish Week*, April 27, 1980, available at https://www.proquest.com/newspapers/firm-on-rights-begin-flexible-procedure-talks/docview/371566805/se-2?accountid=12084, accessed January 3, 2021.
26 Darren Dochuk, *From Bible Belt to Sunbelt: Plain-Folk Religion, Grassroots Politics, and the Rise of Evangelical Conservatism* (New York: W. W. Norton, 2011), 404.
27 Colin Shindler, "Likud and the Christian Dispensationalists: A Symbiotic Relationship," *Israel Studies* 5, no. 1, The Americanization of Israel (Spring, 2000): 165.
28 "Sadat Concerned over Settlements in Sinai but Is Refraining from Hardline Demands, Ministers Tell Begin," Jewish Telegraphic Agency, April 19, 1978, accessed July 28, 2025, https://www.jta.org/archive/sadat-concerned-over-settlements-in-sinai-but-is-refraining-from-hardline-demands-ministers-tell-be.

and polite man." The delegation of 10 friends serving as ambassadors of Goodwill arrived in Jerusalem yesterday via the Allenby Bridge over the Jordan River after visiting Amman and Cairo. Led by Jerry Falwell, the delegation met with Sadat on Saturday and with Crown Prince Hassan and government officials in the Jordanian government on Sunday. The representatives delivered a special message from Sadat written by himself to Falwell. After the meeting with Falwell, Sadat told reporters that Israeli settlements in Sinai would not be acceptable "because it was a violation of his land and sovereignty." Sadat also said, "There must be a solution to the Palestinian problem before there can be peace in the Middle East," Falwell said. However, the delegation members noted that Sadat insisted on not making demands that could be perceived as harsh or "something Israel cannot live with." Personally, Falwell said, "I was impressed that Sadat was a warm and generous man, and after listening to him, I am convinced that a peace settlement is attainable." The delegation conveyed another request expressed by Sadat to build a "church, synagogue, and mosque" on Mount Sinai. In response, Falwell promised his guests that "everything is subject to negotiation." According to the pastors, Begin said, "If we want to achieve peace, we cannot say that nothing is negotiable. Let's keep talking, let's keep the doors open." Begin and they noted: "Just like Sadat did—we want peace—and we believe in both of them."[29] In the Israeli newspaper *Ma'ariv* that came out on the same day, under the headline "Tell Sadat that I call him to return to the talks," it was written that "Prime Minister [Begin, K.B] in response to President Sadat's request to establish a mosque, a church, and a synagogue on Mount Sinai [...] and asked to convey a message to President Sadat to return to the talks without limiting conditions, as was the case in Jerusalem and Ismailia. 'Please tell President Sadat that I want to renew the talks in an atmosphere that prevailed in Jerusalem and Ismailia, when we called each other friends.'"[30]

President Sadat promoted the idea of establishing sacred prayer sites for all religions as part of the message exchange he facilitated through his visit to bring peace on the wings of religion. The *Washington Post* extensively reported on the ceremony in 1979:

---

29 "Sadat Concerned over Settlements in Sinai but Is Refraining from Hardline Demands, Ministers Tell Begin," JTA-Jewish News Bulletin, April 19, 1978, available at https://www.jta.org/1978/04/19/archive/sadat-concerned-over-settlements-in-sinai-but-is-refraining-from-hardline-demands-ministers-tell-be, accessed January 3, 2022.
30 Yosef Waxman, "'Regarding the Evangelical Delegation: 'Tell Sadat that I am Calling on Him to Return to the Negotiating Table,'" *Maariv*, April 19, 1978. Page 4.

> *Egyptian President Anwar Sadat fulfilled the vow he made after his historic visit to Jerusalem exactly two years ago. He prayed for peace today on the mountain, where it is said that Moses received the Ten Commandments 3,500 years ago. In a ceremony rich in symbolism and combining religious harmony, Sadat declared unequivocally that 'this place will now be open to the followers of the three religions without any restrictions or formalities.' Israeli Prime Minister, Menachem Begin, was absent from the ceremony, although he was invited by Sadat, he refused, saying he had a busy schedule. His aides said that Begin felt the ceremony should be Sadat's day and that his presence would be inappropriate. Carter's campaign manager, Alfred Atherton, U.S. ambassador to Egypt, Harold Saunders, Middle East Assistant Secretary, and twelve other Americans invited by Strauss, and some well-known Democratic Party contributors, attended the ceremony. Religious figures from all corners of the world participated in the event, including Muslims, Greek Orthodox, Egyptian Copts, Episcopalians, Jews from Cairo, Buddhist monks, and Shintoists from Japan.*[31]

Sadat was supposed to lay a cornerstone for a $60 million building planned to include worship houses for Islam, Judaism, and Christianity, but, apparently, due to time constraints in raising the required funding, this part of the ceremony was postponed. In his speech, Sadat appealed to the people of the world to abide by the will of GOD and act "to promote brotherhood, friendship, and the elimination of bloodshed, violence, and hatred." He further added "today, peace has already become a bright reality" in a reference to the peace accord between Egypt and Israel and added "no one can change everything."[32]

The event hosted by President Anwar Sadat of Egypt, which took place in the remote desert at the foot of Mount Sinai, was covered by the *New York Post*. Before the ceremony, political moves had been made to enable it, including Israel's return of the area—part of the fifth stage of Israel's withdrawal from Sinai—to Egypt. The ceremony marked the second anniversary of Sadat's journey to Jerusalem, which kick-started his peace policy. A diverse crowd of approximately 600 guests gathered at the site, believed by some researchers to be where the ancient Israelites camped while waiting for Moses to bring down the Ten Commandments.

---

31 William Claiborne, "Sadat, Praying at Mt. Sinai, Vows Shrine Will Be Open to All Faiths," *Washington Post*, November 20, 1979, available at: https://www.washingtonpost.com/archive/politics/1979/11/20/sadat-praying-at-mt-sinai-vows-shrine-will-be-open-to-all-faiths/8b5448cf-1bcd-4963-b803-b83bda80c9e1/, accessed March 9, 2021.

32 Ibid.

A review of Carter's archive shows that the president knew that Falwell was working at the behest of religious leaders to advance the peace accord based on religious motivations. The following was written in a letter issued by the Melodyland Christian Center organization, based in California, which was part of Falwell's Middle East tour:

> *Six weeks ago, 13 evangelical leaders traveled to meetings in Jordan, Egypt, and Israel. The group, AKA the Evangelical Fact-Finding Mission, was led by Dr. Jerry Falwell and Dr. John Montgomery, and had the opportunity to pray personally with President Sadat, King Hussein of Jordan, and Menachem Begin. Each was given a sign with a quote from Isaiah 15: 23-25, showing how Israel, Egypt, and Syria can live together. They all seemed very responsive to the message conveyed through the Bible. Mr. Sadat asked us to pass a message to Mr. Begin that he intends to build a mosque, synagogue and church on Mount Sinai in October. We felt that if there were a day of prayer where the three religions could be called upon and perhaps President Carter, Sadat and Begin could pray together, this could possibly bring relief to the problems of the Middle East.*[33]

According to Brooks Flippen, Falwell sent a report to Carter, saying: "After returning from the Middle East we formulated all our findings and sent them to the White House, but no response nor a request for us to convey and discuss them was received."[34]

The first simulation of the religious centers planned to be built on Mount Sinai was presented in 1981 by *The Plain Truth* magazine, a free magazine founded in the 1930s by Herbert Armstrong, founder of the Worldwide Church of GOD. At the height of its distribution, the magazine reached over eight million copies in seven languages. Armstrong developed the British-Israelite doctrine, which claimed that the origin of the British is in the lost tribes of Israel and the true heirs of the Israelite tradition at the end of days.[35] The magazine elaborates on the activity took place to promote the prayer centers:

---

33 Carter Archives, Folder Citation: Collection: Office of Staff Secretary; Series: Presidential Files; Folder: 5/12/78 [2]; Container 75, available at: http://www.jimmycarterlibrary.gov/library/findingaids/Staff_Secretary.pdf, accessed March 9, 2021.

34 J. Brooks Flippen, *Jimmy Carter, the Politics of Family, and the Rise of the Religious Right* (Athens, GA: The University of Georgia Press, 2011), 195.

35 Ralph Orr, "How Anglo-Israelism Entered Seventh-day Churches of God: A History of the Doctrine from John Wilson to Joseph W. Tkach, 1999," retrieved March 19, 2023: https://archive.gci.org/articles/anglo-israelism-and-the-united-states-britain-in-prophecy/.

The model presents a triangular compound with walls along the side of the mountain with a mosque, a church, and a synagogue at its three corners—representing the three major religions that recognize Moses as a prophet [...] The architects are Dr. Abdel Halim El Rimali, an Egyptian Muslim; Pierre Vago, from France; and Professor Al Mansfeld, from Israel. Mr. Sadat told them he wanted to lay the cornerstone on November 19, 1981—the third anniversary of his historic peace journey to Jerusalem. According to reports, Mr. Sadat intends to invite Pope John Paul II and the President of the United States, among others, to the cornerstone ceremony. The architects estimate that completing the building will take up to three years from the day the cornerstone is laid.

One can learn about the importance that Sadat saw in the project from the article, as it states:

To emphasize the great importance Sadat gives to the project, he expressed his desire to be buried there when he dies, and wrote it in his will. The tomb would most likely be next to the mosque. "There is one GOD," Sadat explained in an interview to *People* magazine last October, and there is one shared mission: the Ten Commandments that GOD gave to Moses on Mount Sinai. Sinai is part of my country and I am very proud of it. These commandments are the basis for all three religions. Therefore, I will build a temple for all three religions on Mount Sinai—one compound that will include a mosque, a church, and a synagogue.[36]

According to the estimates provided by the author of the article, the projected cost of building the religious Peace Complex was around 70 million dollars. Since the mountain is sacred to all religions, the choice of President Sadat of Mount Sinai as a symbol of peace and unity among faiths and countries was appropriate for the creation of a common denominator that could be accepted by all three religions. Unfortunately, Egyptian president Anwar Sadat was assassinated by a terrorist on October 6, 1981, and the plans for constructing the religious complex were never realized.

The task Jerry Falwell took upon himself was to link political agendas through religion, which is clearly manifested in the minutes from his special meeting with Menachem Begin on April 18, 1978, at 11:00 a.m., immediately after Falwell arrived with a delegation of religious dignitaries on a tour of the Middle East that included meetings with Sadat in Egypt and the Jordanian cabinet. It is imperative to note that the Egyptian and Israeli governments funded this trip, as both sides viewed the delegation as potential

---

36 Keith W. Stump, "The Amazing Story Behind the Mount Sinai World Peace Centre," *The Plain Truth*, March, 1981, P-5, available at: https://www.hwalibrary.com/cgi-bin/get/hwa.cgi?action=getmagazine&InfoID=1341055169, accessed March 9, 2021.

intermediaries between them. The minutes, found in Falwell's archive, provide a rare glimpse into the discussion, with Falwell serving as an emissary, carrying messages between the sides, which, as far as is known, have never been fully presented in scientific research [the annotations do not appear in the original text and were added by the author]. Due to the importance of the transcript, it is attached in full as Appendix B to this work. Here are its key points:

Falwell was introduced to Begin and described the group as "Evangelicals" who "accept the Bible to be the inspired, infallible Word of GOD." He announced that "there are some 46 million professing Evangelicals in America who are of like mind and faith." He stated that they "came at the invitation of **the Egyptian and Israeli governments**, sponsored by those governments," to offer their support and prayers to promote the peace process. During their visit to Egypt, the group met with President Sadat and were influenced by his warmth and commitment to peace. Falwell continued by saying that "our first visit was to Egypt, and the President was in Aswan. We were flown down to Aswan, where we met President Sadat on the veranda of the rest home there. We had a very delightful time with him and I must say that we were very impressed with his warmness […] his sincerity—and his very expressed desire for peace, all of which you two have talked about in detail." **In the course of our conversation, he asked us to convey to you three basic things**, and he did so very graciously and very respectfully. He asked us to reaffirm to you that he still very earnestly desires peace, and his efforts will continue in that direction. However, he, in expressing his concern over the Sinai matter, was very rigid in his statement regarding the settlements and the security. He was pleased, he said, when you expressed to him that you were willing to give back the Sinai. He was displeased when he learned that the Israelis were going to provide the security. His words were, "this is a violation of my soil and my sovereignty." He seemed to indicate that he would not negotiate that point. Secondly, he said that he felt that there could be no peace unless the Palestinian problem was resolved. However, on a positive note, he offered no prescription for the solution. He made no demands. He simply said, "The situation must be solved," but he made no demands or prescriptive requests of you. Finally, he advised us that he planned to build, on Mount Sinai, where Moses received the Law, three buildings: a church, a synagogue, and a mosque. And he asked us to ask your cooperation. "And that is the message from President Sadat to Prime Minister Begin."

Begin thanked Falwell warmly, invoking their shared spiritual foundation: "I am very grateful to you for the words you uttered in recognition for the book of books which we all believe. It is the source of our life, it's eternity."

He then emphasized the role of Christian supporters of Israel, stating: "I have met many times people of good will—Christians who understand our cause, support it wholeheartedly, and therefore, I want to express my gratitude." Yet even as he expressed thanks, Begin also used the meeting with Falwell to deliver a political message. Referring to President Sadat, Begin stated: "If you would go now to Cairo, I would give you also a message to President Sadat." Begin recalled their historic meetings in Jerusalem and Ismailia, which he described as moments of profound diplomatic understanding, resulting in joint peace proposals and the formation of Israeli-Egyptian political and military committees.

However, Begin admitted the peace process had stalled. Sadat, he claimed, had taken a rigid stance on Israeli settlements in Sinai. Begin asked Falwell to convey that while Israel was willing to dismantle some settlements in southern Sinai, others—particularly in the north—were strategically vital. Begin proposed placing those areas under international oversight to guarantee freedom of navigation and prevent future conflict. Turning to the broader context of peace, Begin insisted that "after all the wars we won't have real peace; this is our striving, and we want it with all our hearts."

Begin's tone shifted when discussing Judea and Samaria. He led Falwell to a map in his office, pointing to the biblical regions of Samaria and Judea and warning that any Israeli withdrawal would jeopardize national security. "From the Bible. As you can see [...] if this mountain [...] by Mr. Arafat, then we face immortal danger," he warned, citing past bloodshed and the indefensibility of the pre-1967 borders.

To resolve the Palestinian issue, Begin advocated for municipal autonomy in the West Bank and Gaza. Palestinians would elect their own administrative councils, while Israeli security needs would be safeguarded. "Such was our peace plan. Such it is. It wasn't yet negotiated," he told Falwell. Begin closed with a plea: "Let us renew the spirit of the days of Jerusalem and Ismailia [...] I am the same man. I didn't change. And this is the same peace plan."

The message exchanges, as revealed in these minutes, the way Jerry Falwell spoke to Menachem Begin and the delegation, and the joint funding of the trip alongside Sadat's desire (which was eventually thwarted due to his assassination) to establish a mosque, a church, and a synagogue on Mount Sinai, all attest to the intimacy and trust both sides shared with Falwell as a special peace envoy. Patricia A. Pingry elaborates on the relationship of these three individuals, in her book about Falwell's life:

> *The emergence of the Moral Majority movement and political power brought Jerry Falwell to become a guest of such leaders as Prime Minister Begin and President Sadat and a speaker for a large part of the American public. Falwell befriended these*

leaders and considered them his personal friends. Falwell builds the logical context for the importance of Israel to Americans: 'If America can return to its biblical and moral values, which brought her to be the greatest nation in the world, GOD will then be able to return and bless America; and then the churches of America will draw the spiritual and physical values to care for the whole world. Only in an atmosphere of freedom can the churches of America evangelize the world. America has a responsibility to defend Israel, and the Moral Majority has a significant role in assisting America to fulfill her part.'[37]

Caitlin Carenen quotes Michael Farhi, Begin's advisor on church affairs, in her book as saying that "the invitation of the religious delegation was made so that we could hear about the situation from an Evangelical perspective." In other words, Begin invited the Pastors' delegation, funded by Israeli (and Egyptian) money, to negotiate the peace treaties, and serve as religious envoys and mediators between the two States! The significant and honorable role Menachem Begin granted Falwell brought their relationship closer and laid the foundation for the tight relationship between the two countries after the Ronald Reagan was elected president of the United States.[38]

Menachem Begin's Decision to Award Falwell with the Jabotinsky Medal and the Rift vis-a-vis the Jewish World

During Menachem Begin's tour of the United States in September 1980, he decided to award the "Jabotinsky Medal" in a grand ceremony to mark Jabotinsky's 100th anniversary to individuals who made outstanding contributions to the Jewish people. The award was presented on behalf of the Israeli government to 100 Jews and non-Jews at the Waldorf Astoria Hotel in New York.[39] Among the dignitaries who received the medal, one can find writer Elie Wiesel, Judge Esther Antin Untermeyer, designer and artist Nathan George Horwitt, lawyer Paul S. Riebenfeld, singer Roberta Peters, writer Leon Uris, Rabbi Herzel Kranz, Dr. William R. Perl, and more. According to a report by Yitzhak Rabi, of the Jewish Telegraphic Agency (JTA), more than 2,000 guests listened to the 13-page speech delivered by Menachem

---

37 Ibid., *Jerry Falwell: Man of Vision*, 70.
38 Ibid., *The Fervent Embrace: Liberal Protestants, Evangelicals, and Israel*, 182.
39 Noach Zevuloni, "Organ Transplants on Behalf of the Kingdom," *Davar*, November 25, 1980. Page 15, available at: https://ranaz.co.il/articles/article2230_19125.asp, Accessed July 11, 2021. Hebrew Source.

Begin to mark the event, organized by the Jabotinsky Association as part of the government's decision to commemorate Jabotinsky's centennial.[40]

The ceremony is also described in Hart N. Hasten's memoirs, which sheds light on the process itself and his experiences as someone who sat close to Jerry Falwell: "I arrived at the ceremony with 99 other recipients. Since we were seated alphabetically, I found myself placed next to the televangelist Jerry Falwell, who also received the award from Prime Minister Begin. I remember how proud I felt after shaking the hands of the guests, including Jerry Falwell's."[41]

However, not all medal recipients agreed to accept it and share the honor with Rev. Jerry Falwell. Democratic Senator from Idaho Frank Church refused to accept the Jabotinsky Medal with Falwell. Church, considered a big supporter of Israel, declined the honor and was quoted as saying, "While I appreciate very much the award granted to me," he said to honor the sponsors of the event, "I am sorry that I cannot accept the honor at the same time you invite Jerry Falwell. Mr. Falwell has attempted to distort the American political process by making his moral views a test of an individual's fitness for office. Our political and religious liberties are the cornerstone of our system and cannot be compromised. The security of Israel and the freedom of America are inextricably linked. I will continue to fight for both." Jewish Mayor of New York City at the time, Ed Koch, and Democratic Governor of New York, Hugh Carey, also refused to accept the medal.[42]

The decision to award the prize to Jerry Falwell brought about a deep rift vis-a-vis the leadership of the Jewish world. The gesture was perceived as a direct hit at the Jewish community by the prime minister of Israel. For example, Rabbi Alexander M. Schindler expressed his opinion at the semi-annual conference held in San Francisco, by saying, "this is madness and suicide [...] when Jews show respect to right-wing Evangelicals for their support of Israel, even though those same people pose a threat to Jews in the United States," and concluded, "The Free Congress Foundation is talking about turning America into a Christian nation. If the Christian fundamentalist doctrine becomes a litmus test for political opinion, then the Jewish community is lost."[43] In concert with the award ceremony, a large protest was held against

---

40 Yitzhack Rabi, "Begin Cites Jabotinsky's Visions as an Architect of Jewish State," *New Jersey Jewish News*, November 20, 1980: 4, available at: https://www.jta.org/archive/begin-cites-jabotinskys-vision-as-architect-of-jewish-state, accessed June 9, 2021.
41 Hart Hasten, *I, Shall Not Die!: A Personal Memoir* (Jerusalem: Geffen Books, 2003), 300.
42 Ibid., Zevuloni, "Organ Transplants on Behalf of the Kingdom."
43 "The Jewish Community is Lost," *Davar* Newspaper, November 24, 1980, https://www.nli.org.il/he/newspapers/dav/1980/11/24/01/article/31/?srpos=11

granting that honor to Jerry Falwell, who was also asked to address the issue before some journalists and said that he is a Zionist and a friend of Israel for 25 years. According to him, support for Israel is one of the core principles of the moral majority.[44]

The arm-twisting and suspicion of the American Jewish community toward Falwell began several years before the decision to award him the Jabotinsky Medal and related to statements like the one written in his book *Listen, America!* where he described the Jewish people as "spiritually blind and desperately in need of their Messiah and Savior."[45] Falwell posed a cause for concern among American Jews. For example, Rabbi Yechiel Eckstein, who in recent years was the man who connected Evangelicals to donations to Israel through the Friendship Fund, expressed his views after Falwell's death: "I remember that almost 30 years ago, I invited him to speak in my synagogue and I received criticism from many in the Jewish community who cast doubt on his motives."[46] There were also those in the Jewish community who claimed that Falwell was antisemitic due to his comment about Jewish money: "A Jew can make more money accidentally than you can on purpose."[47]

Additional criticism by Jewish leadership refers to Falwell's ties with the Christian Right in America was expressed in an article by Murray Friedman: "Support from fundamentalist Christians for Israel continued until September. Following the massacre in Beirut, Jerry Falwell, leader of the moral majority, called on Christians in the United States to rally around the Jewish state. Begin was scheduled to meet fundamentalist leaders, during a visit to the United States that was cut short by the death of his wife, Aliza. That schedule meeting was criticized by Avraham Hirschson, president of the American Jewish Congress, who argued that Israel, by chasing the

---

&e=———198-he-20-1-img-txIN%7ctxTI-%22%d7%a4%d7%90%d7%9c%d7%95%d7%95%d7%9c%22———-%d7%a2%d7%91%d7%a8%d7%99%d7%aa———1, accessed July 11, 2021, Hebrew Source.

44 "Begin Cites Jabotinsky's 'vision' As Architect of Jewish State," jta.com, November 23, 1980, available at: https://www.jta.org/1980/11/13/archive/begin-cites-jabotinskys-vision-as-architect-of-jewish-state, accessed June 9, 2021.

45 Michael Brenner, *In Search of Israel: The History of an Idea* (Princeton, NJ: Princeton University Press, 2018), 222.

46 Ami Eden, "Reflecting on Falwell," forward.com, May 15, 2007.

47 Sheldon Kirshner, "Evangelists' Support of Israel Outdone Only by Jews Themselves," *The Canadian Jewish News*, December 10, 1981: page 2, available at: https://newspapers.lib.sfu.ca/cjn2-28378/page-2, accessed May 9, 2021.

Christian Right, risks losing those members of the Jewish community who were opposed to the politics of the Christian Right."[48]

But criticism of Falwell's ties to Israel did not come only from American Jewish leaders. The Israeli Left also voiced strong opposition to his growing influence. In a 1984 article published in the Israeli magazine *HaOlam HaZeh* under the title "Uzi and the Belt of the Bible," Falwell was described in particularly harsh terms. He was labeled a "neo-fascist," and the alliance between Prime Minister Menachem Begin and the Moral Majority leader was referred to as a "Christian-Zionist Hunnic coalition." The magazine's editor, Uri Avnery, portrayed the Evangelical worldview as believing that God created the United States to defend Jews and Israel, but only as a prelude to the Second Coming of Christ—at which point, according to this belief, Jews would have to convert or face damnation. Avnery concluded: "This is the most active and the darkest form of the Christian Right as far as the Jews are concerned."[49]

The relationship between Ronald Reagan and Jerry Falwell was the subject of a series of election ads by the Carter-Mondale campaign that aired for 30 seconds on 252 radio stations with a large Jewish audience. The ad stated that "Dr. Jerry Falwell said that GOD does not listen to the prayers of Jews and if Reagan enters the White House, Falwell will come with him and they will purify the earth as someone else did not long ago."[50] The ad was taken off the air after a lawsuit threat, implying that Falwell was compared to Hitler in the broadcast.

Falwell, who was all too aware of the antagonism that had developed over the years toward the Jewish community, attempted to appear before various forums of the Jewish community. For example, from the private archive of Rabbi Marc H. Tenenbaum, who held the unique distinction of being the only Rabbi present at the Vatican Council and participating in the creation of "Nostra Aetate." This groundbreaking document, advocating for a fraternal dialogue between Christians and Jews, earned him the title "the Human

---

48 Murray Friedman, "Intergroup Relations," *The American Jewish Year Book* 83 (1983): 127.

49 "*Uzi and the Belt of the Bible,*" *HaOlam HaZeh*, February 29, 1984, p. 23 (Hebrew), available online at: https://us-israel.org.il/2020/08/09/%d7%92%d7%9c%d7%99d7%95d7%9f-2426-29-%d7%91d7%a4%d7%91d7%a8%d7%95d7%90d7%a8-1984-%d7%a2%d7%9e%d7%95d7%93d7%99d7%9d-22-23/, accessed June 9, 2025.

50 "An Interview with Rev. Jerry Falwell," in *The Jewish Veteran*, Vol. 32.17, available at: https://books.google.co.il/books?id=TETjAAAAMAAJ&pg=RA6-PA18&dq=jews+falwell&hl=iw&sa=X&ved=2ahUKEwjapfGnqr73AhXWgVwKHYIMCTA4HhDoAXoECAUQAg#v=onepage&q=jews%20falwell&f=false, accessed May 9, 2021.

Rights Rabbi." We can learn about Falwell's attempts to deal with the wall of hostility among American Jewry from his address at the annual meeting of the CCAR (Central Conference of American Rabbis); he spoke about the importance of honesty and patience when building relationships, and stated that "every meaningful and continuing relationship must be based on several principles; the first being complete honesty." He emphasized that his commitment to the relationship between Jews and Christians was not based on bad qualities or a desire to hasten the coming of the Messiah, but rather on "faith in the Abrahamic Covenant [Genesis, chapter 22] where GOD deals with nations as they deal with Israel. We believe in the choice of the Jewish people, and we believe that what GOD said to Abraham is true today as it was when he said it, 4,000 years ago." He went on to bless those who bless the Jewish people and curse those who curse them, stating that "there is no amount of wickedness, from your camp or ours, that will break this commitment."[51]

The Jewish world's attitude toward Jerry Falwell can also be found in reports and status updates sent by Israeli diplomats to the Ministry of Foreign Affairs, which, on the one hand, present Falwell's commitment to Israel but, on the other hand, express the concern of the liberal Jewish community, which sees the promotion of Christian values as a direct threat to the way it operates in America. For example, a detailed review by G. Shomron from the Consulate in New York, published on the eve of the 1980 elections, titled "Israel and the Evangelical Political Awakening in the United States," maps out the key players in Christian politics and describes them as follows: "Reluctance [to evangelicals. K.B.] is perhaps too mild a word. Therefore, when you hear people referring to evangelicals twice, you can only conclude that it is outright aversion and even contempt [...] This is how the large liberal camp, of which most American Jews are a part, views him." He goes on to describe the complexity of the Jewish community: "As an example of Jewish dislike, I am attaching a copy of a letter from Rabbi D. Polish, the interfaith coordinator for the Council of Synagogues, to the Ambassador, written in response to meetings between the Prime Minister and Jerry Falwell and his group. Similar responses were received verbally from the ADL and various dignitaries."[52] Even messages delivered from the Ministry of Foreign Affairs to general consuls in the United States request to consider the sensitivity of

---

51 The Jacob Rader Marcus Center of the American Jewish Archives, MS-603: Rabbi Marc H. Tanenbaum Collection, 1945-1992. Series A: Writings and Addresses. 1947-1991 Box 4, Folder 26, Rabbinical Assembly session with Marc H. Tanenbaum and Jerry Falwell [tape transcription], March 19, 1985. 9-10.
52 Israel State Archives, ISA-MFA-Religion-R0003e6i, 286.

the relationship between the Jewish community and the Christian fundamentalist one. For example, the importance of balance in all matters related to religion and the State within the United States is mentioned, which positions the fundamentalist, pro-Israeli conservatives versus the liberals, who make up the majority of the American Jewish population. Therefore, the Ministry of Foreign Affairs recommends that its representative should be "sensitive to the ongoing polemic in the American public on matters related to religion and State, a polemic that generally splits the public into two camps: liberal and conservative," and he concludes, "I am not ignoring the current reality, in which the conservative camp and its Evangelical proxies are more open to our explanations and to cooperating with us [...] Against this backdrop, our representatives have a natural tendency (perhaps more in Southern states) to act almost exclusively with the Evangelicals and fundamentalists, at the expense of the other camp."[53] This sample heavily leans toward Evangelicals and fundamentalists, neglecting the other side. This creates a dilemma for the diplomatic corps, caught between the existing hostility within the Jewish community (primarily affiliated with the liberal camp) and the increasingly vocal grassroots movement that emerged during Reagan's first term.

Falwell remained a controversial figure in relation to the Jewish establishment even into the 1980s. For example, Abe (Abraham) Foxman, who served as the national director of the ADL (Anti-Defamation League), claimed that Falwell "infuses anti-Semitism" with regard to the controversy surrounding the movie *The Last Temptation of Christ* (directed by Martin Scorsese in 1988), insinuating that Jewish studios in Hollywood were responsible for Jesus's crucifixion.[54]

The Israeli government also offered diverse approaches with regard to Falwell's relationship with the Jewish community. Unlike Menachem Begin and Yitzhak Shamir, Shimon Peres chose to keep a low profile in his association with Falwell. In March 1985, when Peres was prime minister of the Unity Government, Falwell toured Israel and the two had a brief and modest meeting. No photo ops were allowed during that meeting.[55]

Akiva Eldar, a *Haaretz* reporter, wrote on the efforts made by Falwell to meet with Shimon Peres two weeks before his arrival in Israel: "Haaretz reporter was informed that in the past, Peres had rejected a request from Reverend Falwell, who is considered a close associate of President Reagan, to

---

53 Israel State Archives, ISA-MFA-Religion-R000375j, 164.
54 Editorial, *The Jewish Voice*, September 2, 1988. 4.
55 Israel National Archives, File: "Evangelicals Friends of Israel." ISA-MFA-Religion-R0003e6i, 120.

meet with him. It is almost certain that Peres will try to avoid the meeting with Falwell."[56] Behind the scenes, Falwell employed his connections in the White House to secure a meeting with Prime Minister Peres. In a letter sent from the embassy on February 11, 1985, Ambassador Meir Rosenne described the situation regarding Peres's refusal to meet with Falwell: "Following our telephone conversation—I met with Falwell at a social event, and the person in charge of his visit to Israel informed me that there is no approval for a meeting with the Prime Minister. Needless to say, how politically significant Falwell is in the United States today. I hope the proposal we formulated in our conversation—i.e., a meeting of the Prime Minister with a small group, and a senior Minister appearing before the entire group—will indeed be implemented." At this point, he signs the letter with a statement affirming the commitment of the president of the United States to Falwell, stating that not only is he intervening on his behalf, but he also expects to hear what has been decided: "Please inform me, as we must reply to the White House on this matter."[57]

What marks Falwell's influence on the White House the most is evident in the special interest that the Reagan administration showed in this meeting. Marshall Berger, President Reagan's advisor to the Jewish community, directly contacted the Foreign Ministry in Jerusalem and asked to clarify the importance the Administration sees in Shimon Peres's agreement to meet with Falwell.[58] The pressure bore fruit and a telegram from the Ministry of Foreign Affairs stated that "The Prime Minister, accompanied by a small entourage will receive Falwell and his delegation for a brief conversation."[59] Falwell conveniently presented to the outside world that Shimon Peres did not meet with him, given the "pressure from American Jewish groups that caused Peres' advisors to doubt whether it was worth meeting him at all."[60] Falwell, who headed a delegation of 830 pilgrims, expressed his attitude toward the new government: "The change in government is unrelated to his

---

56 Akiva Eldar, "Peres Agreed to Meet with the Right-Wing Pastor Falwell," *Haaretz*, January 31, 1985 (in the National Archives file: ISA-MFA-Religion-R0003e6i, page 175). Hebrew text.
57 Israel National Archives, File: "Evangelicals Friends of Israel." ISA-MFA-Religion-R0003e6i, 159. Hebrew text.
58 Israel National Archives, File: "Evangelicals Friends of Israel." ISA-MFA-Religion-R0003e6i, 160. Hebrew text.
59 Israel National Archives, File: "Evangelicals Friends of Israel." ISA-MFA-Religion-R0003e6i, 158. Hebrew text.
60 Haim Shapiro, "Falwell Meets with Peres and Speaks with Begin," *Jerusalem Post*, February 4, 1985 (from the State Archives file: ISA-MFA-Religion-R0003e6i, page 164)." Hebrew text.

unconditional support for Israel. His relationship with the State of Israel was forged even before the Likud's political revolution in 1977." The newspaper directly quotes Falwell: "We support the State of Israel and the Jewish people without reservation."[61] It further reports that "Falwell accuses Jewish liberals of cold reception and that no minister of the establishment met him on that trip except for Shimon Peres." Avraham Burg, then advisor to the Prime Minister on Diaspora affairs, was also quoted in the article: "We are very concerned about the positions of American Jewry on this matter." *Haaretz* report was titled: "Short and Modest Meeting Between Peres and Falwell" as no photos of the meeting were allowed.[62] However, others in the Israeli media criticized Shimon Peres's decision as "primitive and unwise." After the tour, Mordechai Horowitz wrote in *Hadashot* newspaper that

> ministers do not think. They do not have time to think even in those rare cases when they have the ability to do so. They take advisers who think for them. Recently, it seems that a person must present an Imbecile Certificate in order to be accepted into the inner circle of advisers of Israeli ministers. The primitiveness and lack of wisdom reflected in Peres's decision to boycott the Moral Majority Conference, the movement of Reverend Jerry Falwell, is not what we would expect from him. That's not how we know him. Whoever advised the prime minister to act this way has severely hampered him [...] Jerry Falwell is an American pastor and patriot. American Jews are so entrenched in their positions; they abide by their traditional alliance with secular progressive groups and hostility toward conventional conservative groups to the point where they do not recognize recent changes [...] The State of Israel is not overflowing with friends and is not authorized to reject true friends like Jerry Falwell and his movement. American Jews must understand, and it is Mr. Peres's role to explain to them, that there are things that we cannot see eye to eye on.[63]

In a letter to the Israeli Ministry of Foreign Affairs, dated April 21, 1985, Revital Poleg, an Israeli diplomat, draws attention to an article in the *Washington Post* about Jerry Falwell and the differences in perspective between American Jews and Israeli leaders. The article, titled "Falwell Attempts to Mend Interfaith Fences" was written by Cathy Sawyer and revealed that Falwell was perceived as representing religious intolerance of right-wing

---

61 Steve Rodan, Arizona Republic, March 9, 1985, F3.
62 Israel National Archives, ISA-MFA-Religion-R0003e6i, 120.
63 Mordechai Horowitz, "Jerry Falwell, a True and Powerful Friend," *Hadashot* newspaper, March 7, 1985, p. 14, available at: https://www.nli.org.il/he/newspapers/hadashot/1985/03/07/01/article/69/?srpos=6&e=-------he-20--1img-txIN%7ctxTI-%d7%94d7%a8d7%95d7%91+%d7%94d7%9e%d7%95d7%a1%d7%a8d7%99--------------1, accessed March 11, 2022. Hebrew Text.

tendencies, who objects to American Jewish religious pluralism. Nevertheless, Israeli leaders received Falwell as an unofficial ambassador of American right-wing Christians given his loyalty and support. Falwell's efforts to align with the Jewish community in the United States were seen by critics as driven by frightening theological motivations. At a conference held in Miami, Falwell introduced his inspiration as stemming from the spirit of pluralism that exists today, which was not present in the past, and promised to bring 70 million conservative Christians to support Israel and oppose antisemitism. He was also ready to acknowledge his previous positions regarding human rights and apologize for them ... According to a senior Israeli political observer, the love story of Falwell with Israel began in 1977 with Begin's election for prime minister, who embraced every friend of Israel. Prime Minister Peres toned down publicity of the issue within Israel.[64]

Not only did Shimon Peres avoided Falwell's presence. In her speech of December 13, 1983, Knesset Member Ora Namir from Peres's party—the Labor Party—targeted missionary activities "operated by the Moral Majority in Israel" and dissociated herself from its activities: "I spoke with several people who are familiar with the missionary activities up close, and I was alarmed to hear from one of them that the activities are carried out in close connection with the guidance of the Christian embassy, which is accepted in Israeli government circles as a pro-Israeli body, and with the assistance of the 'Moral Majority' in the United States, whose leader had recently visited Israel, and Minister of Defense, Professor Arens, spoke before him and his delegation. These missionaries, guided by the Christian Embassy, operate in kibbutzim, in IDF bases, in absorption centers, in youth hostels, in schools, and in universities."[65]

The differences in Falwell's perception between the Begin administration and the Peres administration, from the perspective of the connection between the Israeli government and American Jews, are summarized by Cathy Sawyer's article in the *Washington Post*: "According to a senior political observer in Israel, Falwell's 'love affair with Israel' began in 1977 when Menachem Begin came to power. 'Falwell's people always sought audience with Begin, and were always granted,' he said. 'Begin didn't care. He felt that every friend of Israel is more than welcome,' regardless of how some Jews

---

64 State Archives File: "Evangelicals Friends of Israel," ISA-MFA-Religion-R0003e6i, a letter from Revital Poleg to the Consuls. Hebrew Text.
65 Knesset archive, "Proposal for the Agenda – Overcoming Missionary Activities in the North of the Country," Tuesday, 7 Tevet 5744, December 13, 1983. 606, available on the website: https://fs.knesset.gov.il/10/Plenum/10_ptm_530117.PDF, accessed March 11, 2022.

felt about Falwell." That sources also mentioned that while the Israeli press presented "PR photos" of Falwell with Likud leaders under Begin, Peres mitigated such publicity in Israel pertaining to his relations with Falwell. Peres's Labor Party was more sensitive to the emotions of the liberal Jewish community than the Likud, but as prime minister, Peres could not have taken the intellectual liberties of refusing to see Falwell … "We have a friend in him, let his motives be what they may."[66]

Bombing Iraq's Nuclear Reactor and the Phone Call from Begin to Falwell

First, a brief background on the establishment of the Iraqi reactor with French assistance, the Israeli perspective, and the American response after the bombing. During the 1970s, Iraq began to build a nuclear reactor to advance toward assembling a bomb. In August 1978, the issue was brought to the attention of Begin's administration. According to estimates, the Tammuz 1 and 2 reactors were capable of producing four plutonium bombs per year.[67] The Israeli government, in collaboration with the United States, attempted to act against France to stop their aid in establishing the reactor, but despite the Mossad's sabotage of a reactor core cooling equipment before being shipped from France, the works continued according to schedule.[68] Reagan's administration was not in the know, and archived documents indicate that the U.S. government did not know the intended use of American weapons that Israel had committed not to use offensively, when it was caught off-guard after the bombing.[69] Immediately after the bombing, the United Nations General Assembly and the Security Council took a very harsh condemnation resolution against Israel. Contrary to its usual friendly position, this time the United States not only did not veto or abstain, but supported Security

---

66 State of Israel Archives, ISA-MFA-Religion-R0003e6i, 322.
67 Shelomoh Nakdimon, "Tamuz in Flames: The Iraqi Nuclear Reactor Explosion – The Story of the Operation," *Yedioth Ahronoth* – Hemed Books, 2007, on the website of the digital library for the history and heritage of the Israeli Air Force, 134. Hebrew Text.
68 Yossi Melman, "The Scientific Hand of the Mossad on the Way to Attack the Iraqi Nuclear Reactor," *Haaretz* website, June 10, 2021, https://www.haaretz.co.il/blogs/yossimelman/2021-06-10/ty-article/.premium/0000017f-f8d5-d887-a7ff-f8f5a2b60000, accessed March 27, 2023. Hebrew Text.
69 Or Rabinowitz and Giordana Pulcini, "The Israeli Raid Against the Iraqi Reactor – 40 Years Later: New Insights from the Archives," wilsoncenter.org, June 3, 2021, available at: https://www.wilsoncenter.org/blog-post/israeli-raid-against-iraqi-reactor-40-years-later-new-insights-archives, accessed March 9, 2023.

Council Resolution 487 condemning the attack on the Iraqi nuclear reactor.[70] The operation led to a temporary freeze in the delivery of American military equipment to Israel, including additional F-16 aircraft, but the freeze was lifted immediately after the Israeli elections.[71]

Shortly before the Israeli Air Force bombed the nuclear reactor in Iraq, the prime minister contacted Falwell to tell him about the operation, how it was carried out, and to ask for his assistance in explaining and mediating the Israeli position to the American government and public. Falwell, at a conference he attended at the Landmark Church in Cincinnati in early July 1981, told an audience of about 2,000 worshippers who came to Sunday worship, that Menachem Begin called him two days after the reactor was bombed in June 1981. Falwell is quoted as saying, "I am a friend of Israel for many years and a friend of Begin for several years. He just wanted me to tell the American people why the reactor was bombed. They [the Israelis. K.B.] did not try to start a war. They just tried to defend themselves," and added: "They carefully chose a time when Baghdad would not be endangered by radioactive decay." In the context of Menachem Begin's request, Falwell emphasized and said that he responded to Begin's wishes and found America open to the prime minister's explanation of the bombing: "I think the American people wholeheartedly support what happened," he said during that speech.[72] In his book, David New describes what Falwell said to Begin in that conversation: "Mr. Prime Minister, I want to congratulate you on a job well done. I was very pleased to hear that it was done with the F-16s we manufactured."[73] Joe Kincheloe and George Staley explain in their article that both Falwell and Begin had good reasons for that conversation. According to them, Prime

---

70 Resolution 487 Iraq-Israel, http://unscr.com, http://unscr.com/en/resolutions/doc/487, accessed March 9, 2023.
71 Mordechai Bar-On, "The White House Officially Announces the Renewal of the 'F-16' Shipments," *Davar*, July 2, 1981, https://www.nli.org.il/he/newspapers/dav/1981/07/02/01/article/3?&dliv=none&e=-------he-20--1img-txIN%7ctxTI----------1&utm_source=he.wikipedia.org&utm_medium=referral&utm_campaign=%2D7%AA%D7%A7%D7%99D7%A4%D7%AA+%D7%94D7%9B%D7%95D7%A8+%D7%94D7%92D7%A8%D7%A2%D7%99D7%A0%D7%99+%D7%91D7%A2%D7%99D7%A8%D7%90D7%A7%22&utm_content=itonut, retrieved March 28, 2023. Hebrew Source.
72 "Moral Majority Leader Jerry Falwell Says Israeli Prime Minister…," upi.com, July 6, 1981, available at: https://www.upi.com/Archives/1981/07/06/Moral-Majority-leader-Jerry-Falwell-says-Israeli-Prime-Minister/7833363240000/, accessed May 9, 2021.
73 David S. New, *Holy War: The Rise of Militant Christian, Jewish and Islamic Fundamentalism* (Jefferson, NC: McFarland, 2002), 42.

Minister Begin knew there were many political reasons to strengthen and continue the alliance with Falwell. The traditional basis of Israeli support in America had generally come from the political Left. With the decline of liberalism in America in the late 1970s and early 1980s, along with the parallel growth in the political system of the Evangelical Right, Prime Minister Begin saw the need to renew and shape the pro-Israeli power base in American politics. This need was particularly acute given the negative reactions of traditional liberal supporters to Israel's bombing of the reactor in Iraq and the raid on the PLO headquarters in Beirut. Furthermore, there was also concern about the "oil factor" that could lead to a possible change in America's attitude toward Israel. The concern was that American public opinion might shift toward the oil-rich Arab countries, as global supply began to decline in those years. Thus, Begin realized the need to emphasize and promote a new source of American support—the Conservative Movement in general, and especially in the Christian fundamentalist context, which relies on faithful support, by gaining the support of the "Moral Majority" movement and the Evangelicals, which translated into support among America's conservative audience.[74]

Falwell also had his own reasons for taking part and promoting the idea that was first reported by him, with regard to that phone conversation. When Falwell takes a call with the prime minister of an important foreign country to the United States, such as the State of Israel, which was presented as an important ally during a dramatic security event, such conversation places the relationship beyond mere friendship for Falwell. When, at Begin's request, Falwell engages in clarification, explanation, and mainly in supporting the Evangelical response to the bombing of the nuclear reactor in Iraq, he puts Israel in a position of future commitment. Moreover, the conversation itself places Falwell in the category of international leadership, helping to boost his prestige and, certainly, his ego.

According to journalist Craig Unger, on the eve of the bombing of the reactor, it was Begin who contacted Falwell and reported to him about exceptional events that might occur in the immediate future: "Tomorrow you will read some strange things about what we are going to do. But our security is on the line. I wanted you, my good friend, to know what we are going to do," referring to Israel's use of F-16 aircraft supplied by the United States

---

74 Joe L. Kincheloe and George Staley, "The Menachem Begin-Jerry Falwell Connection: A Revolution in Fundamentalism," *Journal of Thought* 17, no. 2 (summer 1982): 37.

to destroy the nuclear reactor in Osirak, Iraq.[75] Begin apparently did this because of the military procurement agreement and out of concern that the United States would oppose Israel's use of aircraft for non-defensive purposes. This concern indeed became apparent in congressional discussions about the possibility of selling AWACS planes to Saudi Arabia.[76]

In response, Falwell said to Begin: "I want to congratulate you on the mission that makes us very proud of producing these F-16 planes." According to Begin's own testimony, the conversation between him and Falwell was reported in the government meeting, highlighting the immense importance that Begin gave to Falwell as someone who was supposed to provide him with the dual value of the government's pledge not to impose sanctions against Israel and public support. On the day after the bombing, Falwell said in an interview with Unger: "Quite definitely, they managed to insert the bomb through the chimney." According to the same report, Begin even reported to the Cabinet on the conversation and support he received from Falwell, which testified to the importance that Begin gave to the relationship and Falwell's significance.[77]

About a month after the bombing, Falwell held a religious conference with 4,000 people and provided more details about his conversation with Begin. Falwell said that Begin told him, "I decided to bomb the reactor to protect our children from annihilation," and added that Begin told him about a case of a seven-year-old boy who held onto his leg on the street a few weeks before the bombing and left a considerable impression on him. Begin asked Falwell to "tell the Christian believers in America that we are not a warmongering nation. All of our actions are to protect our little children from annihilation." Falwell also told Begin that he and his followers support Israel steadfastly and that "GOD deals with nations according to their treatment of Israel." Begin also conveyed to Falwell that according to Israeli intelligence estimates, the

---

75 Craig Unger, *The Fall of the House of Bush: The Untold Story of How a Band of True Believers Seized the Executive Branch, Started the Iraq War, and Still Imperils America's Future* (New York: Scribner, 2007), 109–110.
76 "Arms Sales Package to Saudi Arabia: Hearings before the Committee on Foreign Relations," United States Senate, Ninety-seventh Congress, First Session, on the AWACS and F-15 Enhancements Arms, Sales Package to Saudi Arabia, October 1, 5, 6, 14, and 15, 1981, available at: https://books.google.co.il/books/about/Arms_Sales _Package_to_Saudi_Arabia.html?id=RdgRAAAAIAAJ&redir_esc=y, accessed March 1, 2022.
77 "Israel's Laborites Aid Critics, Begin's Cabinet Says," *Arizona Republic,* June 15, 1981, available at: https://www.proquest.com/historical-newspapers/june-15-1981-page-3 -99/docview/1930952891/se-2?accountid=12084, accessed September 9, 2021.

reactor was supposed to be ready within three years, and "the intention was to bomb Tel Aviv, Jerusalem, and Haifa."[78]

In his book, Sean Durbin highlights the significance of Begin's strategic priorities, particularly in his initial conversation with Falwell. Durbin notes, "In 1981, Menachem Begin, aware of potential repercussions in America after bombing the Osirak nuclear reactor, strategically sought support. He did not call a Jewish Senator or Rabbi; he called Falwell. Begin was concerned that he used the bombs and F16s given to Israel for defensive purposes—in an offensive attack. Begin told Falwell, "You'd do the work for me," and Falwell, in turn, pledged to do just that."

In conclusion, the close relationship that developed between Menachem Begin and Jerry Falwell was manifested in the special closeness that prompted Begin to turn to Falwell for support both in lobbying vis-à-vis Reagan's administration and Congress and as a persuasive promoter of the importance of the bombing vis-a-vis the media and the public.

Begin's Decision to Annex the Golan Heights and Falwell's Support of That Move

On Monday, December 14, 1981, Menachem Begin shocked the Knesset when he presented the proposed bill to annex the Golan Heights, without any prior notice. Journalist Gil Littman describes: "Early evening on Monday, December 14, 1981: Prime Minister Menachem Begin has just finished his speech where he presented the proposed bill to apply the Israeli law to the Golan Heights and full annex this region to the State of Israel, and asked the Knesset to approve the proposal in three calls on that same day [...] The proposed bill was approved by a large majority in the first call and was sent two floors down to the Foreign Affairs and Defense Committee, to prepare it for the second and third calls [...] The ultra-Orthodox [Haredi] Knesset members, surprise by the intensity of the argument, fell silent. They understood all too well the rebuke turned against them: It was precisely them, members of the Agudath Israel party, loyal partners of the coalition, who decided not to participate in the vote on that bill. After learning at noon that day about the prime minister's initiative to go ahead with the bill, they turned to Rabbi Shach and asked for his advice." The 87-year-old rabbi, who was considered a political dove, instructed the ultra-Orthodox Knesset members not to support the Golan Heights bill, but also not to oppose it out of respect for the Prime Minister. "We are going to quarrel with the whole world over nonsense, just

---

[78] "Falwell Says Begin Telephoned Him after Israel Attacked Iraqi A-plant," *Washington Post,* July 6, 1981, A12.

to provoke the nations of the world," the ultra-Orthodox leader was quoted in one of the newspapers ... In retrospect, it turned out that the elderly rabbi's estimate of the wrath that erupted worldwide after the approval of this law was quite accurate. The prime minister got a pretty good idea as to that future wrath, already during the first stages of the legislation. While the debate in the Knesset persisted, a handwritten note was handed to Begin stating that: "The annexation of the Golan Heights violates UN Resolution 242, which is the basis for the Camp David Accords." The note was signed by one of the American delegation's leaders for the autonomy talks. ... The Americans took matters into their own hands. The day after the Knesset passed the bill, and the State of Israel's sovereignty on the Golan Heights was published, the official response of the American Administration was unusually harsh: "President Reagan and his senior aide's express astonishment, concern, and anger at the steps taken by the government of Israel," the statement said. The president of the United States was not only overwhelmed with anger over the annexation, but also—perhaps primarily—felt a searing insult: "The President is deeply angry and disappointed personally that the Prime Minister did not bother to consult with the United States in advance," the statement continued. The practical responses came shortly after: the United States announced the freezing of the strategic understanding memorandum signed between the two countries at a ceremony in Washington just a few weeks earlier. The planned visit of the American military commander to Israel was canceled. The Department of Defense announced that it was holding back the shipment of F-16 aircraft to Israel. The Administration emphasized that the United States does not acknowledge the Israeli sovereignty over the Golan Heights and even encouraged the Security Council to present an ultimatum to Israel that it must cancel the annexation of the Golan within two weeks. ... A few days after the Knesset approved the Golan Heights Law, Begin summoned the U.S. ambassador to Israel, Samuel Lewis, to his office in Rehavia, and played for him the famous "Are we a Banana Republic?" speech, also known as the "Vassals' Speech." But Begin was not going to settle for mere rhetoric. The Americans announced the suspension of the understanding memorandum with Israel? He would take one step further and declare—no more or no less—a unilateral cancellation of the memorandum: "Are you trying to hold Israel hostage by the understanding memorandum?" Begin asked rhetorically, and immediately replied: "I perceive your announcement of suspending the discussion of the memorandum as its utter cancellation."[79]

---

79 Gilad Littman, "Against the World: Not Afraid to Annex the Golan Heights, but No Ideological Motives'," *Makor Rishon*, January 16, 2022, available at: https://www.makorrishon.co.il/news/446861, accessed April 11, 2022.

Begin's decision, as described above, was made without prior coordination with the local political system, and certainly not with the global one. It was subject to a steamroller pressure of the American Administration, but not only them. The decision was also met with astonishment in Congress. For example, Republican Representative from California, Paul McCloskey, condemned Israel's annexation of the Golan Heights as an "aggressive and imperialistic action" and urged Congress to withhold the $2.2 billion in foreign aid that Israel was supposed to receive in 1982–1983, "unless the action is reversed [...]" He added: "Until Congress is willing to stand up to Israel, every time we give them F-16 planes, we will get the bombing of Beirut city center, we will agree to whatever they want to do. Israel's annexation of the Golan Heights was a further step that could ultimately lead the United States to a nuclear war."[80]

Falwell included his visits to the Golan Heights as part of his journeys to the Holy Land. For example, during his visit to Israel in 1978, he filmed scenic views of the Golan Heights: "Falwell was joined by the Old Time Gospel Hour TV crew, director Bruce Brown and a team of photographers and recorders for the special broadcast that will include many scenic views of beautiful Israel from the Golan Heights in the North to Masada in the South. The show will focus on prophecy against the backdrop of nature," said Dr. Falwell, "in addition to proclaiming the gospel of Jesus Christ."[81] In a later response, after he had received the Jabotinsky medal from Begin, Falwell said that "there is no question about Judea and Samaria. They must be part of Israel" and added: "I believe that the Golan Heights must be annexed as part of the State of Israel." Following the dramatic decision in the Knesset and in light of the broad criticism by the United States and the world, Falwell appeared before a breakfast club of 500 Christian and Jewish opinion leaders in February 1983, and discussed the demand to relinquish territories which he considered to be Israeli territory, comparing it to in the United States: "It's like asking the United States to give up all its land between the Blue Ridge Mountains and the Rocky Mountains to a country that wants to destroy it."[82]

---

80 "McCloskey Urges Congress to Reject Foreign Aid Israel is Due to Receive," jta.org, December 16, 1981, available at: https://www.jta.org/archive/mccloskey-urges-congress-to-reject-foreign-aid-israel-is-due-to-receive, accessed March 1, 2022.
81 "Falwell, Begin Tape TV Special," *The Journal Champion* 1, no. 16 (August 12, 1978): 1, available at: https://digitalcommons.liberty.edu/cgi/viewcontent.cgi?referer=&httpsredir=1&article=1018&context=paper_78_80, accessed March 1, 2022.
82 "Some 500 Christians and Jews Express Solidarity with Israel at National Prayer Breakfast," jta.org, February 3, 1983, available at: https://www.jta.org/archive/some

Falwell Endorses Menachem Begin and the Israeli Government with Regard to the Lebanon War

Jerry Falwell was one of the greatest advocates of Menachem Begin and the State of Israel in connection with the Lebanon War. In many aspects, he chose to publicly endorse Menachem Begin and defend the government's decisions to establish a demarcation zone, or a "Security Strip" in Southern Lebanon. For example, in his speech dated October 9, 1982, Falwell said: "It is hypocrisy on the part of world leaders who demand the resignations of Begin and Sharon. No one demanded the resignation of the President of the United States after the My Lai massacre in Vietnam."[83] Falwell adopted the Israeli narrative for the invasion into Southern Lebanon and said: "The Peace for the Galilee Campaign is imperative, with the hope it shall restore Lebanon to its previous role as a democratic, freedom-loving nation."[84] First-hand testimony of Falwell's commitment to Israeli interests can be found in the book *In Their Shoes*, which describes a social event in Washington where Falwell presented Ariel Sharon as a historical figure: "At the conference I attended, Falwell presented Sharon and said that in the annals of history there are only a few outstanding individuals who have made such a resonating impact. Falwell named George Washington, Abraham Lincoln, and Ariel Sharon."[85]

Menachem Begin needed all the help he could get in Washington, given how the international community and the American public perceived the invasion. Public opinion data, as cited in Richard Bonney's book, shows the predicament Begin found himself in: "After the Six-Day War, there was a peak of support for Israel with 64% support, a figure that would stand as the peak until the outbreak of the First Gulf War. The American public support for Israel hit rock bottom after the invasion of Lebanon in 1982, with American support for the Palestinians reaching an all-time high of 28%."[86] According to Hummel's book, Falwell organized a trip to Lebanon: "After a conversation

---

-500-christians-and-jews-express-solidarity-with-israel-at-national-prayer-breakfast, accessed March 1, 2022.
83 Raphael Mann, "Reagan is about to Invite Begin for Talks," *Maariv*, October 10, 1982, p. 12, available at: https://www.nli.org.il/he/newspapers/mar/1982/10/10/01/, accessed July 11, 2021.
84 Stephen Zunes, "Review of the Book Jerry Falwell and the Jews by Merrill Simon," *Journal of Palestine Studies* 14, no. 3 (Spring, 1985): 137.
85 Grace Halsell, H. Halsell, and Allen Kathleen Hamilton, *In Their Shoes* (Fort Worth, TX: TCU Press, 1996), 216.
86 Richard Bonney, *False Prophets: The "Clash of Civilizations" and the Global War on Terror* (Bristol: Peter Lang, 2008), 117.

with Begin and at the height of the siege on Beirut, Falwell organized a delegation of 50 religious people to visit the battlefields and witness firsthand what was happening there. Upon their return, Falwell assured journalists that after being there, he was convinced that 'indeed, it was surgical warfare and out of concern for innocent civilians.' When asked about the issue of the massacre in Sabra and Shatila, he responded that it was an 'Israeli mistake,' summarizing Falwell's trip to Lebanon as a "HASBARA" (P.R in Hebrew) trip."[87] Jeffry Haynes also refers to Falwell's briefing upon his return to America and a press conference he held, where he said that the media has an anti-Israel bias and is insisting on pushing it. Therefore, every Christian in America plays an important role in building the Israeli message and the image of the Israeli State.[88] And indeed, Falwell served as a sort of "explainer-in-chief" of Israel to the American public, as Allan Brownfeld writes in his article: "When the massacre took place in the Palestinian camps, Falwell simply parroted the Israeli line: 'The Israelis were not involved.' And even when the *New York Times* reported eyewitness accounts of Israeli firepower sent to help the Phalangists enter the camp, Falwell said 'it was only a ploy'."[89]

Another participant in the same journey was Pastor Lamar Mooneyham, who at the time served as the field director of Liberty University, and summarized the trip they made in 1983: "The Israelis freed Lebanon from the claws of the PLO. I was one of 45 people whom the Israelis decided to give full access to and allowed us to film. They also gave us recordings that we could broadcast on stations in America. They took us to the border, and we saw with our own eyes how the mortar shells were falling. It was really wonderful."[90]

Falwell's commitment to Begin was so deep that at the end of the trip, he told him: "Mr. Begin, I'm just praying that you won't leave Lebanon until you finish the job."[91] In response, Menachem Begin told him, "Dr. Jerry, please come back and explain the truth to the American people about our invasion of Lebanon."[92]

---

87 Ibid., *Covenant Brothers*, 172–173.
88 Jeffrey Haynes, *Handbook on Religion and International Relations* (London: Edward Elgar Publishing, 2021), 369.
89 Allan C. Brownfeld, *The Washington Report on Middle East Affairs*; Vol. XVIII, Issue 4 (June 30, 1999): 82.
90 Ibid., *Allies for Armageddon: The Rise of Christian Zionism*, 193.
91 Dinesh D'Souza Falwell, *Before the Millennium: A Critical Biography* (Washington, DC: Regnery Gateway, 1984), 163.
92 Alan J. Steinberg, *American Jewry and Conservative Politics: A New Direction* (Ann Arbor, MI: The University of Michigan Press, 1988), 35.

Journalists Roland Evans and Robert Novak reported on Falwell's reason for denying a meeting with a delegation of Arab Christian priests who wanted to convey to him the messages they believed in, in the context of the war in Lebanon. According to the newspaper, "the reason Pastor Falwell refused to meet with the group that sought to convey its anti-Israeli agenda to him was his personal commitment to Prime Minister Menachem Begin not to hold such meetings," adding that "in prolonged phone conversations with Begin, Falwell agreed to check the status of those who requested a meeting with him through the Israeli embassy. When a friend recently asked Falwell to meet a priest from the Middle East, Falwell refused on the grounds that the embassy in Washington advised him not to meet."[93]

Cal Thomas, a conservative columnist and Deputy Chairman of the Moral Majority, in his column in the August 1982 issue of the "Moral Majority Report," wrote that the PLO, not Israel, was responsible for the killing of civilians, as the PLO forced Israeli forces into areas where there were many local civilians. Thomas wrote that "the PLO is nothing but a terrorist organization whose main goal was, and probably still is, the elimination of Israel and the Jewish people in the region."[94]

What could have been Falwell's motivations for supporting Begin despite the relatively low popularity of the Lebanon War among the American public? Beyond the arguments previously presented by Falwell himself, researchers suggest other explanations. For example, an attempt to explain why Falwell supported Begin's invasion of Lebanon so strongly can be linked to a religious motivation described by V.C. Thomas in his book, which is based on the belief that one must actively help bring about Armageddon, and thus fulfill Darby's vision of "In one of the events that took place in Jerusalem, hundreds of Falwell's supporters shouted 'Hallelujah' and 'Amen' as Defense Secretary Caspar Weinberger described the combat maneuvers of the invasion of Beirut in 1982 that led to the deaths of around 20,000 Palestinians and Lebanese—in terms of striking enemies and communists. The death of the Lebanese earned applause and cheers from the feeling that it hastens the coming of Armageddon."[95] In contrast, Jeffrey Haynes argues that the Peace of the Galilee Operation represented a boost for both national and local politics in the United States: "The partnership [between Falwell and Begin K.B.]

---

93 Roland Evans and Robert Novak, "Falwell's Promise," *Cincinnati Enquirer,* July 27, 1981, 11.
94 Cal Thomas, "Lebanon: Infected by Hypocrisy," *MMR* 3, no. 6 (August 1982): 9.
95 V. C. Thomas, *The God Dilemma: To Believe or Not to Believe* (Bloomington, IN: Xlibris Publishing, 2009).

immediately and forcefully raised Falwell's local and national profile in the context of Israel's diplomatic low point following the invasion of Lebanon in 1982. The Falwell-Begin partnership offers a sneak peek into the critical role of religion in U.S.-Israel relations, even though it sits within a much larger and longer relationship between the United States and Israel as far as religion is concerned."[96]

The Sale of AWACS Planes to Saudi Arabia

One of the allegations raised by the American government was that Jerry Falwell, in an attempt to exert his influence in Washington, including over Evangelicals, was involved in trying to stop the sale of AWACS surveillance planes to Saudi Arabia. Menachem Begin, the Israeli prime minister, was interviewed by the *Yedioth Ahronoth* newspaper and responded to the allegations:

> *The Secretary of State told me in one of our meetings: 'The President received a report that you gave a list of senators to Dr. Falwell.' Falwell is a very talented man who heads a movement called 'The Moral Majority.' They are very staunch. He claims to have the support of 20 million such Christians, Catholics, and Protestants. They support Israel on every issue. They are truly loyal friends of ours. I met with Falwell and 20 of his pastor friends. It was a very pleasant meeting. He started, and then everyone there spoke for two to three hours about their warm feelings toward Israel. I thanked them and said, 'We know how to be grateful for friendship,' but it never occurred to me to give them a list of senators in connection with the AWACS. I told the Secretary of State that it was a complete fiction. I didn't want to say 'lie.' If the President receives such information, it's really not good.*[97]

Jerry Falwell himself responded to the issue of the sale of the planes and pressured the Reagan administration not to go through with the sale, claiming that: "If the United States does not stand with its only friend in the Middle East, we will pay a domestic price." He made this statement at a conference attended by about 300 pastors in Lynchburg, Virginia.[98]

---

96 Jeffrey Haynes, *Handbook on Religion and International Relations* (Northampton, MA: Edward Elgar Publishing Inc., 2021), 364.
97 Interview with Prime Minister Begin in *Yedioth Ahronoth*, September 28, 1981. Historical Documents of the IMF, available at: https://mfa.gov.il/MFA/ForeignPolicy/MFADocuments/Yearbook5/Pages/60%20Interview%20with%20Prime%20Minister%20Begin%20in%20Yedioth.aspx, accessed July 11, 2021.
98 Bruce Buursma, "Radar Deal Imperils Israel, Falwell Says," *Chicago Tribune*, April 23, 1981, A2.

According to Murray Friedman, there were indications that Falwell tried to exert his influence on lawmakers to prevent the AWACS sale to Saudi Arabia. "Falwell visited Israel in September, 1981 and announced his support of the Jewish State. However, when the debate over the issue of selling the planes reached its peak, there was some indication that many of the senators associated with the conservative right-wing had backed away from their opposition to the sale."⁹⁹ In Falwell's appearance on Phil Donahue's television show in April 1981, he asked the host to wait with his questions about prayer in schools and abortion, and said: "Ask me about the weapons sale to Saudi Arabia." When asked, he replied, "We must not negotiate."¹⁰⁰

Testimonies about the use of pressure at the grassroots level of the conservative right appear in an article by Ruth Mouly and Roland Robertson: "During the debate concerning the sale by the U.S. of AWACS to Saudi Arabia in the fall of 1981 an intriguing type of communication showed up in several Congressional offices. A number of letter writers identified themselves as Christians and based their opposition to the sale of planes and weapons to the Saudis on a Biblical ground, frequently citing Genesis 12:3," where GOD promised Israel:

> *I will bless them that bless you, and curse them that curse you. These letters reflect the interest in, and support for, Israel among certain sections of the Premillenarian, fundamentalist-evangelical community, based on theological conviction concerning Israel as the fulfillment of biblical prophecy. This concern has been presented in the positive relationship between the Rev. Falwell and the former Prime Minister Begin. The connection was clearly exhibited by the telephone call made by Begin to Falwell shortly after the Israeli destruction of the Iraqi nuclear facility in the summer of 1981. Begin urged Falwell to explain to American Christians Israel's reasons for the act. In response, Falwell gave a sermon from his pulpit in Lynchburg, made several public statements defending the Israeli action and consulted with Begin when the latter visited the United States in connection with the AWACS controversy.*¹⁰¹

Falwell operated in the realm of advocacy in an attempt to cancel the arms deal. On October 25, 1981, at the height of preparations for the Senate vote

---

99 Ibid., *Intergroup Relations*, 70.
100 Mary McGrory, "The Jews and AWACS: With All That 'Help,' They Couldn't Win," *washingtonpost.com*, October 29, 1981, available at: https://www.washingtonpost.com/archive/politics/1981/10/29/the-jews-and-awacs-with-all-that-help-they-couldnt-win/b68c8a7b-11a9-442c-898b-7c155795d41b/, accessed June 9, 2021.
101 Ruth Mouly and Roland Robertson, "Zionism in American Premillennial Fundamentalism," *American Journal of Theology & Philosophy* 4, no. 3, Millennialism and Eschatological Thought (September 1983): 97.

on the decision, while President Reagan was trying to persuade senators to join the government's wish to sell the planes, a coalition of religious leaders called "Christians for American Security" issued a full-page, signed advertisement in the *Washington Post* calling for the cancellation of the arms deal. The group, which included former Democratic congressman and pastor Robert Drinan from Massachusetts and Moral Majority leader Jerry Falwell, called the Saudi regime "anti-American" and said the sale would jeopardize Israel's security.[102]

There are conflicting testimonies about how Congress members supported by the Moral Majority acted when voting on the sale of the planes to Saudi Arabia. For example, Republican Senator Roger W. Jepsen of Iowa, a friend of Falwell's, initially declared that "I am a Christian and therefore I am for Israel. This sale must be stopped."[103] However, eventually, after heavy pressure from the government and at the request of President Reagan, Jepsen reversed his decision and withdrew his opposition to the approval of the deal.[104]

After the sale of the planes, Falwell was asked about its impact on his relationship with President Reagan. In a newspaper interview, he replied, "One of the positions of the Moral Majority is unconditional support for the State of Israel." When asked if the decision to sell the planes to the Saudis diminished his support for the president, he replied, "I would have been concerned if I did not know about Reagan's level of commitment to Israel. I disagreed with the sale of AWACS, but I know that the President's consideration was that it was good for Israel and the United States. Reagan's actions would not endanger Israel, so I am not disappointed with the government's decision in this regard."[105]

---

102 John M. Goshko, "AWACS Votes to Shift, Baker Says," *washingtonpost.com*, October 26, 1981, available at: https://www.washingtonpost.com/archive/politics/1981/10/26/awacs-votes-to-shift-baker-says/d8a8fd79-ec1b-4927-8386-0e51c4f8c3e1/, accessed June 9, 2021.

103 Ibid., *The Jews and AWACS: With all that 'Help,' They Couldn't Win.*

104 "Falwell," *The Arizona Republic,* November 14, 198, 147. available at: https://www.proquest.com/historical-newspapers/november-14-1981-page-147-155/docview/1931029884/se-2?accountid=12084, accessed March 1, 2022.

105 "Falwell," *The Arizona Republic,* November 14, 1981, 147, available at: https://www.proquest.com/historical-newspapers/november-14-1981-page-147-155/docview/1931029884/se-2?accountid=12084, accessed March 1, 2022.

Summary of the Special Relationship Between Begin and Falwell

On August 28, 1983, Begin announced his intention to resign from the office of prime minister and retire from public life. "I cannot continue," he said without elaborating. He submitted his resignation on September 15 of that year. In the years that followed, Begin secluded himself in his apartment on Tsemah Street in Jerusalem, rarely leaving except to visit the grave of his wife on the anniversary of her passing. Family members, close friends, and a handful of visitors continued to visit him. In the last year and a half of his life, he lived in Tel Aviv with his daughter, Leah.[106]

Although Menachem Begin met very few people from the outside world after his retirement, there are some testimonies that he made an effort to maintain his warm relationship with Jerry Falwell. On November 21, 1983, Menachem Begin spoke with Falwell over the phone. During their conversation, Falwell acknowledged the strong relationship between them, and Begin, in turn, thanked Falwell for the support of his movement in Israel.[107] Additional testimony was given in a news article on April 23, 1986, that attempted to understand why Begin became a recluse in his own home: "Dr. Jerry Falwell reported that he had met with him for a brief conversation at his home and that Begin seemed to be in good spirits. 'I was surprised by his good appearance,' he told reporters. 'Begin was alert, responsive, and had many questions.' It was later clarified that there was no meeting, only a telephone conversation."[108] Also, during his visit to Israel in February 1985, the *Jerusalem Post* reported that it was Menachem Begin who requested to speak with Falwell, in a 15-minute-long conversation, after which Falwell described Begin as sounding alert and vigorous, with the conversation revolving around general topics and not politics.[109]

These conversations, which took place after Begin's self-confinement to his home, testify to the intimacy that developed between the two men and Begin's willingness to continue and maintain the relationship despite his decision to

---

106 "The Resignation of Menachem Begin," website of the Menachem Begin Heritage Center, available at: https://www.begincenter.org.il/en/the-legacy-center/the-resignation-of-menachem-begin/, accessed July 11, 2021.
107 "Begin Spoke by Phone with Dr. Falwell," *Davar*, November 21, 1983, available at: https://www.nli.org.il/he/newspapers/dav/1983/11/21/01/.
108 Zvi Gilat, "Menachem Begin," *Hadashot*, April 23, 1986, available at: https://www.nli.org.il/he/newspapers/hadashot/1986/04/23/01/article/69/?srpos=1&e=------he-20--1img-txIN%7ctxTI-%d7%91d7%92d7%99d7%9f+%d7%a4%d7%9c%d7%95d7%95d7%9c-------------1, accessed July 11, 2021.
109 Israeli State Archive, ISA-MFA-Religion-R0003e6i, 164.

stay home and retire from political activities. However, it is undoubtful that this alliance, between people of such different backgrounds, born out of a shared political interest as described at the beginning of the chapter, was not devoid of interests. The special relationship formed between the two was one where each side used their power, influence, and prestige to advance their own agenda. For example, David Snowball, who wrote about the Moral Majority movement, explains the importance of the alliance with Begin to the movement: "The movement's support of Israel apparently resulted from two variables: One was that Menachem Begin warmly adopted the foreign policy of the Moral Majority movement, making him the first head of state to recognize the organization; the other was to deflect accusations that the movement was anti-Semitic."[110] However, for Menachem Begin, the support of a pastor representing tens of millions of Americans across the United States, with an open door at the White House, during a period he suffered international criticism for the destruction of the nuclear reactor, the invasion of Lebanon and the annexation of the Golan Heights, was a valuable asset, as Michael Brenner describes in his book: "For Menachem Begin, Falwell and his supporters were more than welcome to be part of Israel's supporters during a period of great international isolation [...] Falwell's statement that the return of Judea and Samaria to the Arabs would be like giving Texas back to the Mexicans, and similar remarks, made Falwell the first non-Jew to receive the Jabotinsky Legacy Award."[111]

To summarize this chapter, Begin was the first prime minister to publicly embrace Zionist Christianity, and from the end of the 1970s, the Prime Minister's Office became a focal point for the pilgrimage of pastors, priests, emissaries, and Christian figures. To those who doubted the Beginist embrace, whether given the memory of the history of Christian antisemitic persecution or the fear of missionary activity intended to convert Jews at the expense of the Jewish community in America, Begin used to say that Israel has many enemies and he does not intend to reject help from friends. "When the Messiah comes today, we will ask him, 'Have you been here before?' he added. Until then, I can live with the Evangelicals."[112]

---

110 David Snowball, *Continuity and Change in the Rhetoric of the Moral Majority* (Santa-Barbara, CA: ABC-CLIO, 1991), 82.
111 Ibid., *In Search of Israel: The History of an Idea*, 221.
112 Tal Shalev, "The Birth of the Great Hug of Evangelical Christians to Right-wing Israel," *The Liberal*, November 16, 2014, available at http://theliberal.co.il/%D7%9B%D7%9A-%D7%A0%D7%95%D7%9C%D7%93-%D7%94D7%97D7%99D7%91D7%95D7%A7-%D7%94D7%92D7%93D7%95D7%9C-%D7%A9%D7%9C-%D7%94D7%A0%D7%95D7%A6D7%A8D7%99D7%9D-%D7%94D7%90D7%95D7%95D7%A0D7%92/, accessed July 11, 2021.

One cannot but wonder what the relationship between Falwell and the State of Israel would have looked like if Menachem Begin had not come to power in 1977, especially given the ambivalent attitude of Shimon Peres, as revealed in the earlier correspondence cited in this chapter. The natural inclination of the Peres-led Labor Party to side with American Jewry, located on the liberal side of the map, was probably not conducive to embracing Falwell, as the Likud, led by Menachem Begin, did, as part of a conservative alliance spanning both sides of the ocean. Whether Falwell's commitment and passion for working on behalf of Israel would be identical under the Peres-led Labor Party, had it won in 1977, will remain open for conjecture.

Chapter 6

ESTABLISHING THE MORAL MAJORITY AND BREAKING AWAY FROM IT

Case Studies from the 1980s of the Moral Majority's Lobby Congressional Activities

About the Decision to Enter Politics

Patricia A. Pingry, author of the book about Jerry Falwell, was asked: "How can it be that one person, who holds the answer for the nation's redemption, manages to convince people to surrender to GOD?" She answers that Falwell, a man who believed in GOD when he founded a church in an old bottle factory with 35 devotees, and since then, it has grown to 17,000 followers by 1980; a man who turned a 30-minute radio program into the most-watched televangelist program in the world; and a man who turned a college with a meager student body into a large university—never doubted how it should be done. Falwell is quoted saying:

> *I have been researching in recent years on how to transform the trend in our nation. I have always known that prayer has an important place in this, lobbying has an important role in this, and building churches has an important role in this, but there was a missing link. Why, despite the immense Moral Majority, does the government continue to move away from the path of moral values? The fact is that our people are not part of the decision-making process. So since that's the question, how can we start with this? I decided to talk to good Christian politicians, from the top level of the nation, who would teach me how to do it right. I spoke with twelve politicians from the top of the government leadership, with the best lobbyists of organizations in Washington, most of whom, incidentally, thought exactly the opposite of what I think. I talked to them anyway, so I could understand for myself how things are done correctly. I learned that the answer to that is proper organization. It's just like building a church, there's no difference. We have over 1,000 teachers and staff who teach at the Thomas Road Sunday School in our church. Those thousand do all the*

work successfully, whether I'm in town or outside. I understood that the way politics is done is from the pastor upward, not from above downward.

Pingry continues to describe how Falwell founded the organization: "[he] founded an organization in which there is a board of directors. In each of the 50 states, the local leader of the organization is appointed, with an emphasis on the respected and well-known spiritual figure in each state. The role of the chairman was to be the spokesperson for the state and its leader. The role was a voluntary one that did not interfere with the pastor's mission in the community. Those managers at the national level became important as a channel of information on political issues of interest."[1] The "Moral Majority" organization is intended to serve as a home for all those who believe in the basic values of the Ten Commandments. The organization appeals to Christians and non-believers, Republicans or Democrats, rich or poor. The basis for the establishment of the organization was the belief of its founder, Jerry Falwell, that a "liberal, radical, and noisy minority" had influenced the government through a false presentation of how other countries view us. The goal of the organization is to gather people from all walks of life who are for life, for family values, for morals, and for America, in order to create an atmosphere that will help politicians make the right decisions. Falwell believes in the power of mass media to create the atmosphere and uses communication tools at the local church level to influence the audience and public opinion. The Moral Majority was registered in 1979 as a nonprofit. The reason for its establishment as a nonprofit was to fight against the American income tax.[2]

Establishment of the Moral Majority Movement in Response to Supreme Court Rulings

The introductory chapter that discusses the 1960s presents Falwell's positions regarding his interpretation of Jesus's relationship to politics. Indeed, at the beginning of his public career, Falwell distanced himself from politics. In 1964, he wrote: "Believing the Bible as I do, I would find it impossible to stop preaching the pure saving gospel of Jesus Christ, and begin doing anything else—including fighting Communism, or participating in civil-rights reforms."[3]

---

1 Ibid., *Jerry Falwell: Man of Vision*.
2 Ibid.
3 James Price and William Goodman, "Jerry Falwell, An Unauthorized Profile," cited in Grace Halsell, *Prophecy and Politics, Militant Evangelists on the Road to Nuclear War* (Westport, CT: Lawrence Hill, 1986), 72–73.

But in the early 1970s, after two significant Supreme Court rulings, Falwell decided that it was time to establish a political force that could influence American politics.

The Supreme Court ruling in Coit v. Green

In 1969, a group of African American parents in Holmes County, Mississippi, successfully sued the U.S. Treasury Department when three tax-exempt religious schools refused to admit non-white students. The Supreme Court, in the *Coit v. Green* ruling, upheld the decision of the lower court and ruled in favor of the parents. The ruling stated that such private schools, recognized as tax-deductible donations under U.S. income tax laws, "could not prove that they did not discriminate on the basis of race in admissions, employment, scholarships, loan programs, athletics, and extracurricular programs."[4] The Supreme Court decision prompted the Internal Revenue Service to conduct detailed investigations of private schools in general and Christian schools in particular. In 1974, the IRS decided to revoke the tax-exempt status of Bob Jones University. Falwell stated that "In some states it's easier to open a massage parlor than to open a Christian school."[5] Amanda Hollis-Brusky and Joshua Wilson argue that the Supreme Court's rulings served as a catalyst for the formation of the political movement, stating that "the decision in 1974 to revoke the tax-exempt status of Bob Jones University played a decisive role in the emergence of the 'Moral Majority' movement, as it was perceived as an attack on the autonomy of Christian institutions in general, and Christian higher education institutions in particular."[6]

The Supreme Court ruling in Roe v. Wade

The *Roe v. Wade* ruling allowed for abortion under certain conditions,[7] thus outraging conservative forces in America. Falwell, who was interviewed for the "Lynchburg News" on January 23, 1973 was quoted: "I sat there staring

---

4 Coit v. Green, "330 F. Supp. 1150 (D.D.C. 1971)," available at: https://law.justia.com/cases/federal/district-courts/FSupp/330/1150/2126265/, accessed May 9, 2021.

5 J. Brooks Flippen, *Jimmy Carter, The Politics of Family, and the Rise of the Religious Right* (Athens, GA: University of Georgia Press, 2011), 200.

6 Amanda Hollis-Brusky and Joshua C. Wilson, *Separate but Faithful: The Christian Right's Radical Struggle to Transform Law and Legal Culture* (New York: Oxford University Press, 2020), 64.

7 In June 2022, the Supreme Court overturned the decision and ruled that authority over the issue of abortion will be returned to the states to decide.

at the Roe v. Wade story … growing more and more fearful of the consequences of the Supreme Court's act and wondering why so few voices were raised against it."[8]

These rulings triggered the understanding that there needs to be political awareness for Christian believers in America. In her book, Sara Diamond attributes to Falwell the creation of the Moral Majority, among other things, to help advance the legislative process of the Dornan and Ashbrook amendments, which aimed to strip the abilities of the American IRS to conduct investigations. "The legislation weakened the power of the American IRS to investigate, harass or otherwise intervene with private schools. It was a provision that held for 12 months, which means that the battle over Christian schools was not yet won, but the Moral Majority managed to generate the effect on lawmakers."[9]

For many years, the idea of religious figures' involvement in "secular" politics seemed incompatible with Christian ideas. Ten different studies conducted between 1950 and 1974 found that Evangelicals and church members negatively perceived Christians and churches that leaned toward political activity. It was also reflected in the active involvement of Evangelicals in voting in the United States where, according to data collected before the 1980 elections, only 55 percent of Evangelicals registered to vote, compared to 72 percent among non-Evangelicals.[10]

One of the closest people to Jerry Falwell was Duke Westover, who worked for him in the early days as responsible for building religious institutions and the buildings of Liberty College (now University), and from the mid-1980s, according to Falwell's order, as an organizer of tourist trips to Israel, which included tens of thousands of tourists over the years. Westover describes in his autobiography the circumstances as he saw them and talked to Falwell about the decision to get actively involved in American politics:

When Congress enacted and the Supreme Court upheld the prohibition of prayer in schools and the legality of abortion, Christians felt that the government was trying to crush biblical values. Jerry Falwell, Tim LaHaye, James Kennedy, and Charles Stanley began to meet with people with similar views who could support them toward

---

8 Randall Balmer, "The Real Origins of the Religious Right," *poltico.com*, May 27, 2014, available at: https://www.politico.com/magazine/story/2014/05/religious-right-real-origins-107133/, accessed May 9, 2021.

9 Sara Diamond, *Not by Politics Alone: The Enduring Influence of the Christian Right* (New York: Guilford Press, 2000), 66.

10 David G. Bromley and Anson D. Shupe, *New Christian Politics* (Macon, GA: Mercer University Press, 1988), 274.

the 1980 elections. After meeting with Ronald Reagan for several hours, they felt he was their candidate. Reagan and Falwell became close friends. Reagan visited Liberty University during the campaign in 1980 to gain support for his campaign appearances. [His son also crowned President Trump in 2016 and spoke about it, Ed.] Jerry was invited to the White House to sign bills and participate in events throughout Reagan's eight years in office.[11]

The 1980 presidential campaign was the first election cycle where the "born-again" phenomenon among Evangelicals and their involvement in American politics was evident. According to a survey by the American Gallup Institute in 1976, the year Carter was elected, there were about 50 million Evangelicals in the United States, with about half of them considered devout.[12] In the 1980 election, approximately 72,000 churches throughout the United States with the majority religious movement were involved.[13] It is estimated that about 2 million new born-again Evangelical voters registered and joined the 1980 election system.[14]

How Was the Mailing List Created, or—a Story About Sugar and a Horse on a Farm

As described earlier in the chapter on the founding of Liberty University, the media and all its channels were very close to Falwell's heart. He understood the importance of mass communication for conveying messages, motivating action, and raising donations. Falwell appointed Dr. Elmer Towns as the editor of Batton, which dealt with politically relevant issues circulated among pastors and conservatives in America. In his book, Towns described how Falwell's mailing list expanded thanks to a farm visit and feeding a horse sugar cubes and Milky Way bars: "As chief editor of Falwell's publications, I wrote several political stories in the early days when the Moral Majority was formed. I displayed my press credentials at the Capitol building and thus gained access to the Senate library. That is how I used to write a page and send it to one of the senators who was interested in the organization's issues." Since Jerry Falwell was named the Man of the Year by *Good Housekeeping* magazine

---

11 Duke Westover, *Wow! What a Ride: My Life and Journey with Jerry Falwell* (Alpharetta, GA: Carpenter's Press & Media, Inc., 2012), Chapter 26.
12 John Heidenry, *What Wild Ecstasy* (New York: Simon and Schuster, 1997), 224.
13 Sarah Weddington, *A Question of Choice* (Oakland, CA: The Feminist Press at CUNY, 1993), 197.
14 Laura Kalman, *Right Star Rising: A New Politics, 1974–1980* (New York: W. W. Norton & Company, 2010), 274.

in 1979, senators wanted to be positively identified with him. I started by establishing a magazine called *The Journal Champion* for Jerry Falwell, and since his mailing list grew consistently, the biweekly newspaper was distributed to over a million households. About 400,000 copies were sent to pastors. The power of the magazine provided tremendous political leverage. One of the first things I did as an editor was to expand the mailing list to pastors. Everyone knew that John R. Rice, the editor of *Sword of the Lord* magazine, held a massive mailing list of pastors in America, especially independent and fundamentalist pastors [...] I was asked by Jerry to try and obtain this mailing list and was invited to visit Dr. Rice at his farm in Murfreesboro, Tennessee. As soon as we arrived, Dr. Rice took us to the barn to feed the horses. That is how we met a horse named MacArthur, after General Douglas MacArthur. Rice warned us that he was a 'conceited horse who did not tolerate strangers' [...] I had sugar cubes and Milky Way bars in my pockets that I gave to the horse. The horse loved the sugar and loved me [...] Toward the end of that day, when we returned to Lynchburg, it was evident MacArthur liked me [...] A little later, Jerry and I lugged heavy suitcases with 400,000 data tapes about pastor lists, from a bank's vault in town, which we loaded onto a plane bound for Lynchburg. Those 400,000 pastors were the driving force behind the creation of the Moral Majority, and Jerry relied on them to rally support for Ronald Reagan in his presidential campaign against Jimmy Carter. Isn't it strange to think that GOD used sugar to help put Ronald Reagan in the White House? Of course, there were many other factors that led to Reagan's election, and I was just one of millions who supported him.[15]

The Rise to Power of Jerry Falwell and His Role in the Struggle Against President Carter

Historian Paul Matzko describes how the awakening movement started in 1975–1976: "Alarmed at the secular drift of American society, Falwell launched an Evangelistic campaign with a political edge during the bicentennial in 1975–1976. Falwell called them 'I Love America' rallies and the grand production, featuring patriotic music by a large choir from Falwell's new Liberty Baptist College (now Liberty University), toured a succession of state capitals. Falwell's campaigns and books promised to return America to the right, God-fearing track, while also attracting the attention of conservative political organizers like Paul Weyrich and Ed McAteer. Weyrich, who had founded The Heritage Foundation in 1973 with money from the

---

15 Ibid., *Walking with Giants*, 202–204.

Coors family, believed that Evangelical Christians were an untapped source of conservative voters. Ed McAteer, a sales executive for Colgate-Palmolive, introduced Weyrich to Falwell at a Dallas rally in February 1979. The rally was held in response to a local television station that had banned the popular televangelist James Robison after he had accused homosexuals of being child molesters. More than 10,000 people attended the protest rally, at which Robison introduced Weyrich as "a brother Cath-o-lic" and challenged any who had a problem with that to leave the stadium. Afterward, McAteer assembled a collection of preachers, including Falwell and local Southern Baptist preacher W. A. Criswell, to talk with Weyrich about forming a new Christian advocacy group. In response to concerns about church involvement in liberal politics, especially left-leaning judges, Weyrich commissioned a poll of Evangelical churchgoers that reported an overwhelming majority in favor of conservative activism."[16]

In his book *The Fall of the House of Bush*, Unger describes the events that led to the establishment of the movement and even the choice of its name: "In 1978, Jerry Falwell gave his first sermon on 'unborn babies, who, by the hundreds of thousands, are being murdered.' When Francis Schaeffer's film[17] 'Whatever Happened to the Human Race? Was distributed to thousands of church groups the response was extraordinary. By this time, a Gallup poll showed that one out of three Americans said they'd had a 'born-again' experience. Half the country believed in biblical inerrancy. Eighty percent saw Jesus as divine. And there were thirteen hundred Evangelical radio and TV stations with a total audience of 130 million." Unger further quotes Falwell: "Jimmy Carter was making everyone mad; he had gotten the Evangelical support two to one in 1976. This guy betrayed everything we stood for." Unger describes the popularity Falwell gained during this period: "By this time, Falwell's television ministry was booming. He had nearly eight million people on his mailing lists. But at that time, only 55 percent of Evangelicals in America were registered voters. Worse, as Falwell saw it, most of them voted the wrong way. I asked, 'How can I, without violating my ministry, without breaking the law, put this group together?' [and answered himself]: 'They will listen to me if I have the facts.'"[18] This move triggered the gathering of Evangelical colleges

---

16 Paul Matzko, *Jerry Falwell Helps Found the Moral Majority* (The Association of Religion Data Archives (ARDA), available at: https://www.thearda.com/timeline/events/event_46.asp, accessed March 9, 2021.
17 Francis Schaeffer was a Christian theologian whose film *What Happened to the Human Race* circulated among thousands of churches and sparked a wave of reactions on the subject.
18 Ibid., *The Fall of the House of Bush*, 72–73.

from around the world with influence in Washington to initiate a meeting to promote political involvement. Falwell expressed interest and scheduled a meeting in May of the same year in Lynchburg, Virginia. Among the guests were significant figures in right-wing Christian fundamentalism, like Dr. Tim LaHaye, a substantial figure in founding religious conservatism as a political force in the United States through creating organizations like "The Moral Majority" in the early 1980s. LaHaye was a prolific author who wrote dozens of books with a total volume of around 80 million copies and was the founder of The Institute for Creation Research, as well as several schools. However, he was most closely associated with the successful Left Behind series, which imagines Jesus's return to Earth in the modern era as a vision described in previous chapters, which he conceived with novelist Jerry B. Jenkins.[19] Paul Weyrich also attended the meeting. He founded The Heritage Foundation, where he served as its first president, as well as the Free Congress Foundation. During the 1970s and 1980s, he operated a private cable television channel and was an architect of the connection between Christianity and political conservatism.[20] The third partner in the meeting was Robert Billings, who founded hundreds of Christian schools and served in the Reagan administration's Department of Education. He was one of the architects of the political alliance between the conservative right and the fundamentalist Christians.[21]

Unger describes the dramatic meeting that led to the formation of the lobby, quoting Tim LaHaye: "We all made a commitment to GOD that day that for the first time in our lives we were going to get involved in the political process. So, I prayed to GOD, 'Dear GOD, we have got to get this man out of the White House and get someone in here who will be aggressive about bringing back traditional moral values.'" After the meeting had been under way for some time, Paul Weyrich spoke up. "Dr. Falwell," he said, "I believe there is a moral majority out there ready to be organized so that they see what they are battling." Weyrich continued, but Falwell interrupted. "Go back to what you said earlier," he said. He was trying to recapture a "Eureka" moment. Weyrich didn't understand what he was getting at, however, so Falwell patiently backtracked. "You started saying that out there was

---

19 Jerry Jenkins, "Died: Tim LaHaye, Author Who 'Left Behind' a Long Legacy," *christianitytoday.com*, July 25, 2016, https://www.christianitytoday.com/news/2016/july/tim-lahaye-dies-left-behind-coauthor-stroke.html, accessed March 9, 2023.

20 Announcing the Death of Paul M. Weyrich, December 18, 2008, https://policymed.typepad.com/files/weyrich-obituary.pdf, accessed March 9, 2023.

21 Robert Billings, "Moral Majority Founder," *chicagotribune.com*, June 4, 1995, https://www.chicagotribune.com/news/ct-xpm-1995-06-04-9506040245-story.html, accessed March 9, 2023.

[...] What did you say?" "I had to think," said Weyrich, recalling the historic incident. He racked his brain for a moment, and finally, he spoke. "I said, 'out there, there is a moral majority [...]'" "That's it!" said Falwell. "That's what I'm going to call the organization: The Moral Majority." Falwell viewed the expression "Moral Majority" as the name of their new organization, which sought to bridge the moral gap between Evangelical Protestants, conservative Catholics, and neo-conservative Jews. The Moral Majority founders aimed to do just that with three Catholics (Paul Weyrich, Richard Viguerie, and Terry Dolan), one Jew (Howard Phillips), and two fundamentalist Baptists (Jerry Falwell and Robert Billings). Falwell hosted the Moral Majority headquarters in Lynchburg and used his popular radio and television program, The Old Time Gospel Hour, which aired on 350 stations, to popularize the movement's idea among his wide national audience. The Moral Majority Report, sent out monthly to over 600,000 people, helped to maintain and shape American conservatism and the need for social and spiritual revival.[22]

According to Duke Westover, who was part of Falwell's inner circle, the Moral Majority setting-up meeting took place in April 1979:

> *The first meeting of the Moral Majority took place in April 1979 at the Baptist church in Indianapolis. About 2,000 pastors, priests, bishops, and rabbis attended the founding event. Falwell's first words were: 'In normal times, I probably wouldn't be caught dead on the same platform with many of you, and truth be known, many of you feel the same way about me. But we haven't come here to argue theology; we have a nation to save. After that, we can go back to fighting each other'. After laughter and applause from the audience subsided, Westover describes that the difficult situation of the Republic under Carter's presidency with an inflation rate of 16%, interest rates of 22%, 10% unemployment rates, and 70% tax rates could be understood. That same day, the religious right was born.[23]*

The Principles of the Moral Majority and Its Activity in Support of Israel

The organization was established as the Moral Majority Inc. in 1979 by Falwell and other pastors, along with politicians from the new Right. It was defined as a political framework and not as a religious one, manifested by the various streams in Christianity (Catholics, Protestants), Jewish rabbis who shared its values and people who sought to promote them politically.

---

22 Ibid., 72–73.
23 Ibid., *Wow! What a Ride: My Life and Journey with Jerry Falwell*, Chapter 16.

According to Ray Oliver Vernon, these are the credal statements of the organization and its admirers

1. believe in the separation of Church and state;
2. are pro-life (anti-abortion);
3. are pro-traditional family (anti-homosexual);
4. are opposed to illegal anti-drug trafficking and usage;
5. are opposed to pornography;
6. are pro-Israel and Jewish people worldwide;
7. believe in a strong national defense (as a deterrent to war);
8. support equal rights for women; and
9. are anti-Equal Rights Amendment (ERA) [aiming to ensure equality of rights for all citizens regardless of gender; the amendment seeks to end the legal distinctions between men and women in areas such as divorce, property, employment, and other areas].[24]

According to Falwell, as expressed in the Mission Statement on the founding day, "Moral Majority [...] is attempting to bring America to its original moral, ethical, and religious moorings, by: (a) mobilizing the grassroots or moral America in one clear and effective voice; (b) informing the moral majority what is going on behind their backs in Washington and in state legislatures across the country; (c) lobbying intensively in Congress to defeat leftwing, social-welfare bills that will further erode our precious freedom; (d) pushing for positive legislation such as that to establish the Family Protection Agency, which will ensure a strong, enduring America; and (e) helping the moral majority in local communities to fight pornography, homosexuality, the advocacy of immorality in 44 school textbooks, and other issues facing each and every one of us.[25]

Already at The Moral Majority's inception and before the 1980 elections, Falwell, on behalf of the movement's political arm, voiced its commitment to the State of Israel. The Moral Majority, which won a significant amount

---

24 Vernon Oliver Ray, "A Rhetorical Analysis of the Political Preaching of the Reverend Jerry Falwell: The Moral Majority Sermons" (Electric Church, Demagogue, 1979) (PhD diss., Louisiana State University, 1985), 86–89, available at: https://digitalcommons.lsu.edu/cgi/viewcontent.cgi?article=5071&context=gradschool_disstheses, accessed November 9, 2020.
25 Jared A. Farley, *The Politicization of the American Evangelical Press, 1960–1981: A Test of the Ideological Theory of Social Movement Mobilization* (Order No. 10817948, Miami University, 2006), 43, https://www.proquest.com/dissertations-theses/politicalization-american-evangelical-press-1960/docview/2028075851/se-2, accessed November 9, 2020.

of political competition in the 1980 presidential elections, plans to establish its own political action committee for candidates: "Our emphasis will be on supporting candidates who are in the majority, who support the State of Israel and the traditional values we cherish," Falwell said to United Press International.[26]

In the Republican primaries leading up to the 1980 U.S. presidential election, candidate John Connally seemed to be a promising candidate for the Republican nomination. According to Melani McAlister, a statement by Connally against Israel angered Falwell and caused him to revoke his support of Connally's candidacy. His comments on the State of Israel did not stem from a religious perspective: "The biblical realization of the State of Israel is not at all an issue in our relationship with it." Connally's ties with the oil industry were detrimental to his relationship with the Evangelical community. Rubinstein explains the aversion among the Evangelical movement to Connally: "the support of fundamentalist Christianity for Reagan was due to Connally and George Schultz's support of oil relations with the Arab world." Finally, although Connally raised more money for his campaign compared to the amounts raised by other candidates, he was unable to defeat the front-runner, popular conservative Ronald Reagan.

In his book, writer David Brog extensively argues for supporting Israel: "Support for Israel and the Jewish people was a central organizing principle of the Moral Majority movement." He continues: "In 1980, shortly after becoming a household name, Falwell published a political manifesto titled 'Listen, America!' Here Falwell discusses his views on all his trademark social issues: abortion, pornography, and homosexuality." And in this little book is a chapter titled: "That Miracle Called Israel" where Falwell sets forth his rationale for supporting the Jewish State. Falwell writes that Israel is a bastion of democracy in a region of despots and an ally of the United States during the Cold War, who vanquished Soviet surrogates. He details how Israel's existence is the fulfillment of a series of biblical prophecies about the triumphant return of the Jews to their land. Finally, Falwell invokes Genesis 12:3 to remind his readers that those nations that bless Israel will be blessed, while those nations that curse Israel will be cursed. In Falwell's words: "I firmly believe that GOD has blessed America because America has blessed the Jews. If this nation wants her fields to remain white with grain, her scientific

---

26 "Key West Citizen Newspaper Archives," February 18, 1983, 11, available at: https://newspaperarchive.com/key-west-citizen-feb-18-1983-p-11/ accessed November 9, 2020.

achievements to remain notable, and her freedom to continue, America must continue to stand with Israel."[27]

On March 24, 1981, the Moral Majority movement placed an advertisement in the *New York Times* which outlined the principles of the movement on a range of issues. In the context of Israel, it stated: "We support the State of Israel and Jewish people everywhere. It is impossible to separate the State of Israel from the Jewish family internationally. Many Moral Majority Inc. members, because of their theological convictions, are committed to the Jewish people. Others stand upon the human and civil rights of all persons as a premise for support of the state of Israel. Others support Israel because of historical and legal arguments."[28] Hence, Falwell operated within the framework of the Moral Majority's lobby to establish the importance of Israel as a political force at the core of the movement's activities and in a way that could deepen its political leverage to promote the U.S.-Israel relationship.

About Falwell's Political Power Before the 1980 Election

Close to the August 1980 election, in a *New York Times* profile titled "Pastor Falwell Inspires Evangelical Vote," writer Dudley Clendinen attempts to explain how Falwell tries to mobilize the Christian voice through a speech to 10,000 pastors in Dallas. According to the article, based on Moral Majority sources, around 3 million Evangelical voters across the United States have registered. Furthermore, the article claims there are around 17,000 followers in the church in Lynchburg, Virginia, and that religious prayer broadcasts are aired on 304 television stations across the United States and 100 more worldwide, with a half-hour radio broadcast airing on about 300 radio stations across the country. All that yielded a total of $56 million in donations in 1979. The audience, so claims the article, stands at around 15 million viewers across the United States. The Moral Majority Inc. raised $1.5 million in its first year, and the Political Action Committee (PAC) raised around $200,000, with separate fundraising of around $100,000 in districts interested in the Moral Majority's cause to support candidates. On Sunday and Wednesday evenings, Falwell toured the country and traveled over 5,000 miles each week on a private plane to attend hundreds of political rallies.

---

27 Ibid., *Standing with Israel: Why Christians Support the Jewish State.*
28 "Moral Majority Affirms Support for Israel, Civil Rights of Jews," JTA, March 24, 1981, available at: https://www.jta.org/1981/03/24/archive/moral-majority-affirms-support-for-israel-civil-rights-of-jews, accessed November 9, 2020.

The phenomenon of harnessing voters, which began to emerge several years before the 1980 election, was described by political researcher Albert Menendez in his book *Religion and Surveys* as "the sleeping giant of American politics."[29] Clendinen also touched on the issue of Evangelical support for President Carter, a born-again Christian, quoting Falwell as saying, "President Carter, who defines himself as a born-again Christian, won 46% of the Protestant vote, more than any other Democrat in the last 25 years except for Lyndon Johnson." He adds his assessment toward the election: "I am afraid that Mr. Carter will disappoint the Evangelicals who put him in office."[30]

The Moral Majority Blitz in the 1980 Elections

In his book, author Matthew Moen notes that liberals in America were surprised by the 1980 election campaign and were unprepared for the Evangelical Christians' blitz in the new political organization of the conservative right in America. What is unique in this context is the ability of new voters to leave behind their prior engagement and political behavior. In this context, the attitude of religious individuals toward the issue was that politics was considered a dirty business and, as such, was unsuitable for the lives of devout Christians. In 1965, Falwell himself summarized this in a sermon called "Ministers and Marches": "I believe that if we spend enough effort trying to clean up our churches, rather than trying to clean up state and national government, we would do well." That statement actually marks a long history where the church tried to stay out of the political game, and therefore the way popular recruitment of voters was done toward the 1980 elections was a complete surprise to the active liberal forces in the United States.[31]

Toward the 1980 election, an article by *The Christian Science Monitor* attempted to assess Falwell's recruitment of new voters. It charted and named the most high-profile areas for the Moral Majority: Texas, Illinois, Ohio, Florida, Indiana, Alabama, and Iowa. The article advised that efforts focused on registering new voters from the peripheral areas of those states, estimating around 30,000 to 50,000 new voters who registered in Florida and another 75,000 in Texas. Leaders of the *Christian Voice* and The Moral Majority Inc.,

---

29 Albert J. Menendez, *Religion at the Polls* (Philadelphia, PA: Westminster Press, 1977), 104.
30 Dudley Clendinen, "Rev. Falwell Inspires Evangelical Vote," *New York Times*, August 20, 1980, B22.
31 Matthew C. Moen, *The Christian Right and Congress* (Tuscaloosa, AL: University of Alabama Press, 1989).

emphasized in an interview that their main goal was to educate their public on political awareness, not to endorse candidates, but to clarify their position on moral issues so that voters could decide. However, these coalitions emphasized values that matched many positions within the Republican mainstream. Additionally, the coalitions were also tied to informing Evangelical voters about the positions of candidates for the Senate, especially when it came to well-known liberal senators running for re-election against opponents whose views aligned more closely with the moral positions of Evangelicals.[32]

Mordechai Barkai describes in the Israeli newspaper *Davar* the impact Jerry Falwell had over the 1980 elections: "In the spring of 1979, a year and a half before the elections, Falwell founded the Moral Majority movement, through which he marshaled millions of voters to pressure their candidates to embrace family values and defeat candidates who do not identify with them. On the eve of the elections, pollster Louis Harris found that Reagan had a 5-point advantage over Carter. However, without the support of the Moral Majority, Carter would have had a 1-point advantage over his rival. Falwell, although focused on his religious-political message, did not hesitate. His photograph adorned articles and magazine covers, and a week after the elections, on November 10th, he held a victory rally—not in his Southern home, but in the liberal east, on the steps of the Capitol building in Trenton New Jersey. It was a superbly organized religious-patriotic show with choirs, flags, orchestras, and television cameras. "The Moral Majority Lobby brought 4 million voters who had never voted before to the polls, and 10 million voters who would have boycotted the elections due to frustration," Falwell said, and continued, "The Christian right worked in 40 out of 50 states in the United States. Its candidates competed for 55 seats in Congress, winning 34 of those, and 12 seats in the Senate, winning 9 of those." Finally, he declared, "We will be active all over the United States, through independent branches."[33]

In his article about the political intentions behind the establishment of the Moral Majority, Brenton Cross says:

> *Falwell's Moral Majority Inc. was intended to give impetus to the approach of the 'Religious Roundtable' that was founded to empower pastors and provide them with*

---

32 Richard M. Harley, "Evangelicals May not Fall into Ranks behind 'New Right'," in *Christian Science Monitor*, October 29, 1980, available at: https://www.csmonitor.com/1980/1029/102943.html, accessed May 9, 2021.

33 Mordechai Barkai, "Right Evangelical," "Davar," December 19, 1980, page 16. The article is available at: https://www.nli.org.il/he/newspapers/dav/1980/12/19/01/article/142/?srpos=6&e=——-he-20-1-img-txIN%7ctxTI-%d7%a4%d7%90%d7%9c%d7%95%d7%95%d7%9c————-1\, accessed February 22, 2022.

a platform to inspire their community to vote for candidates who foster traditional family and moral values. Moreover, in preparation for the 1980 elections, they funded the registration of voters through phone calls that rated each of the candidates and their positions on issues relevant to the Moral Majority, and provided transportation services to polling stations for those in need. Through the establishment of the Moral Majority, Falwell tried to influence the Reagan administration to restore prayer [in schools], oppose abortions, and appoint conservative judges to the Supreme Court.[34]

To understand the impact of the "Reagan Revolution" established before the 1980 elections, various parameters of the voting ratio for the presidency in 1976 compared to 1980 are examined here. A CBS exit poll demonstrated that 17 percent of all voters defined themselves as "born-again Christians," and the distribution between them gave 61 percent to Reagan, versus 34 percent for Carter.[35] Only by comprehending the differences between the 1976 election and that of 1980 campaign, can one grasp the significance of the shift in votes from the Democratic to the Republican side. In the 1976 election campaign, Carter won 58 of the "Bible Belt" districts out of 100 districts in 12 states, but four years later, Carter managed to win only 16 of those same districts. In the 1976 election campaign, Carter managed to gather 32 districts that were outside the Bible Belt, in Illinois, Indiana, Ohio, Iowa, and Missouri. In 1980, he only managed to restore victory in five of those districts.[36]

Dividing the Spoils Following Reagan's Election in 1980

On the weekend following President Reagan's inauguration, the strategic assembly of Evangelical leaders convened to formulate a strategy and policy for the new government that was carried on the wings of believers to the White House. Journalist Marjorie Hyer reports: "Meeting in the wake of the inauguration of the president, whose election they characterized as 'a victory for GOD,' about 2,500 Evangelical Christian leaders gathered here this week to praise GOD and develop future strategy for turning the nation back to GOD. The five-day gathering at the Sheraton Washington Hotel brought together the National Association of Evangelicals and the National Religious Broadcasters, two groups of the most influential leaders of the religious movement, which includes 40 million to 50 million born-again Americans.

---

34 Brenton Cross, *Southern Baptist and Expository Preaching: Biblical Interpretation, Values, and Politics in Twentieth-Century America* (Eugene, OR: Wipf and Stock Publishers, 2021).
35 Ibid. Evangelicals May not Fall into Ranks behind 'New Right', 44.
36 Ibid.

Speaker after speaker portrayed the '80s as "the decade of the Evangelicals," a boom time for conservatives generally and particularly for those concerned with a return to traditional morality. "The sleeping giant that has lain prostrate across America is beginning to wake itself," said Reverend D. James Kennedy of Coral Ridge, Fla. "Believers in a living GOD are beginning to assert their spiritual rights," said Kennedy, whose church was the favorite of former president Richard Nixon when he visited his Florida White House. "The '80s is the decade in which this country is going to have a moral rebirth," said Rev. Jerry Falwell, founder of Moral Majority and pastor of the 18,000-member Liberty Baptist Church in Lynchburg, Virginia. Evangelist Billy Graham, whom the religious broadcasters honored by inducting into their Hall of Fame, was optimistic, too, but struck a note of caution. Noting the "high expectations in the country" that a new administration will turn the country around, Graham said, "only GOD can do that." The involvement of Evangelicals—or as Falwell prefers to call them, Christian fundamentalists—in politics was one of the themes at the hundreds of speeches, workshops and discussions. Religious Roundtable, one of a number of groups of the so-called New Christian Right, conducted a five-hour marathon on Tuesday to evaluate their role both in the past and the future. Dr. Mildred Jefferson, an antiabortion crusader, proclaimed to sustained applause that the November election was "a victory for belief, a victory for GOD." One of the high points of the meeting related to Israel was the invitation of Orthodox Rabbi Abraham Hecht, wearing a black yarmulka, who told the group in ringing tones that secularism in this country was the dangerous equivalent for the "organized religion" of communism in the Soviet Union and China and fascism in some parts of Latin America. Rabbi Hecht said, "We represent the majority of the American people who are God-fearing, tax-paying citizens of the greatest country on earth." In the wake of controversy stirred up ... when an Evangelical leader said that GOD does not hear the prayers of Jews, Evangelicals here seemed to be going out of their way to mend relations with the Jewish community. "I am a fundamentalist [Christian]," said Falwell, "but I believe in a pluralistic America. This country belongs to the Hebrew Americans, the Mormon Americans, black Americans, white Americans." Earlier at a press conference Falwell denounced antisemitism and said, "every religious leader has an obligation from GOD to preach and pray and work to the end that we put an end to hate groups like the Nazis and the Ku Klux Klan." Falwell added, "Most fundamentalist 'Bible-believing Christians are very pro-Israel and pro-Jews because we believe in the Bible'." He said that fundamentalists are "the best friend the Jews has. [...] There is not one living anti-Semite in the Bible-believing church in America." Falwell said that antisemitism is increasing in the United States and added that some of it "is a backlash at us [evangelical/fundamentalist Christians]. They see Reagan and they see us. They see that and they think that America is going to become unswervingly pro-Israel."[37]

Reagan's victory in the 1980 elections was the opening shot for the integration of "our people" on behalf of the Moral Majority in senior positions in all matters related to the management of the government's diplomatic and military system. For example, the "Moral Majority Report," the official publication of The Moral Majority Inc., published many articles emphasizing the deep connection between American Evangelicals and the State of Israel. These articles coincided with significant moments in U.S.-Israel relations during the 1980s. For example, an article dated March 1981 celebrated the integration of pro-Israeli friends in Reagan's government, including National Security Advisor Richard Allen and Alexander Haig. "With appointments like those of President Reagan," wrote Deputy Editor Daryl Edwards, "the views of the overwhelming majority of American Evangelicals can be preserved through a friendly government."[38]

One may deduce the importance the White House under Reagan's leadership attributed to the political power of Evangelicals in the context of Israel from events and seminars held on Israel-U.S. relations. A special gala held by the Reagan administration on March 19, 1984 for the Lobby in support of relations with Israel, demonstrates the importance given to the rising Evangelical power. Invitees included key activists in the Lobby and Evangelical activists. According to estimates, 150-200 key Evangelical activists participated in the conference and it is essential to discuss their importance for the administration on the one hand, and to the relationship with Israel, alongside Falwell, on the other hand. Among the guests it is worth mentioning, for example, Pat Robertson, a presidential candidate in 1988, founder of the CBN religious channels with the popular program "Club 700" and the Regent Christian University. A strong supporter of the State of Israel and of political significance in the connection between the conservative right and televangelism.[39] Jimmy Swaggart, a televangelist, who at the peak of his television career in

---

37 Marjorie Hyer, *Evangelical Christians Meet to Develop Strategy for 1980s* (January 30, 1981), available at: https://www.washingtonpost.com/archive/local/1981/01/30/evangelical-christians-meet-to-develop-strategy-for-1980s/3ee92602-35a7-413a-ae2a-bb786fb3b396, accessed May 9, 2021.
38 Deryl Edwards, "Key Posts Please Conservatives," in Moral Majority Report (MMR), Vol. 2, No. 3 (March 16, 1981), 7. (Spencer Research Library, University of Kansas, Lawrence, KA).
39 Official biography. http://www.patrobertson.com/Biography/index.asp, retrieved March 31, 2023.

the 1980s (before his involvement in a sex scandal), was broadcasted on 104 stations worldwide to millions of fans on the Christian channel he founded "The Jimmy Swaggart Telecast."[40] The couple, Jim and Tammy Bakker, who hosted a missionary television program for an Evangelical Christian organization called PTL. At its peak, their Evangelical empire generated proceeds of $130 million collected from its believers, but financial difficulties led to the collapse of the church, despite Falwell's attempt to take over the station and Jim's imprisonment.[41] The Christian right played a significant role in the Reagan administration, as demonstrated by several prominent figures: Ed McAteer, strategist and founder of the "Religious Round Table" Forum and "The Moral Majority" (both instrumental in Reagan's 1980 presidential victory), and an avid supporter of Israel, pursued a Tennessee Senate seat in 1988 and was even considered for the U.S. ambassador position during George Bush Jr.'s term; writers like Tim and Beverly LaHaye; author Hal Lindsey; lecture presiders such as National Security Advisor Robert "Bud" McFarlane and Reagan's advisor William Middendorf (Head of the Organization of American States), to name a few.

On the extent to which Jerry Falwell's role was significant in the Reagan administration, one can infer from the letter sent by Congressman Stanford (Stan) Parris to National Security Council (NSC) Director Christopher Lehman on July 7, 1983: "Attached herewith is correspondence from my advisor Donald T. Francis regarding the briefing on national security that was given to Jerry Falwell [...] I would appreciate your response to this troubling matter that justifies your attention."[42] In a response letter from Paul Thompson's office to a congressional inquiry, it was stated that "Falwell did not have security clearance or classified reports from the NSC organization, but he did receive informational briefings from Faith Whittlesey on defense and weapons proliferation last spring by Dick Boverie and Sven Kraemer."[43] These letters, found in Reagan's archives, testify to Falwell's intimacy and ability to receive information on national security matters pertaining to United States' foreign policy.

---

40 A Brief Biography of Jimmy Swaggart, jsm.org, https://www.jsm.org/jimmy-swaggart, retrieved March 31, 2023.
41 Ofra Yeshua-Lyth, the millionaire strip club owner who was accused of raping a church secretary, *Ma'ariv*, April 29, 1987. Page 5.
42 Ronald Reagan Presidential Library & Museum, MC003, Briefings-Conference (172800-173799), 173168.
43 Ronald Reagan Presidential Library & Museum, MC003, Briefings-Conference, 4850 (172800-173799).

Jerry Falwell's Political Ascent

In the 1980s, Falwell succeeded in generating political interest and an important American jargon in the political world called "Name Recognition." For example, *Good Housekeeping* magazine conducted a reader poll every year during that period. The magazine's annual poll was designed to determine the readers' "most admired person." The 1983 poll generated some surprising results: As expected, President Reagan, came in first place, just as he did in the 1982 poll. The runner-up was Rev. Jerry Falwell, who only made it to the tenth place the year before.[44]

In his book, Allen Hertzke describes the methods of the influential Evangelical lobby in Washington: "The Christian organizations operated using well advanced technological methods. They were the first to implement cutting-edge broadcasting methods to convey messages through television. The 'Moral Majority' organization, which held an extensive mailing list, was at the vanguard of these lobbying efforts. They used segmentation methods to target their audience through computer-generated call centers, and made cold calls to voters based on a focused segmentation of the various districts."[45] However, the most amazing part pertaining to such ultramodern tools brought into the political arena was already expressed in the early 1980s, in what Hertzke describes as "150,000 religious people who spoke with President Ronald Reagan before the 1984 elections, in a conference call from a headquarters established in Lynchburg, Virginia," and adds on the technological capabilities: "The organization could make up to 100,000 phone calls a week, with recorded messages tailored to the subject matter or religious inclination of the member. These recordings, 'Call your Senator now,' are even customized based on the persuasion of the listener: some of them are recordings associated with Falwell's supporters, some of them are recordings of Swaggart, and some of them are recordings of Robertson's believers." This system was set up to improve efficiency and reduce costs by creating a database of names and addresses of millions of devotees, classified by Congress districts, topics of interest, and religious background. It allowed the organization to target its mailings and reduce costs. Tracking these lists also allowed leaders to identify "hot" topics for fundraising purposes. Another important aspect described by the author in his book, was the ability to recruit supporters through the

---

44 "Odds & Ends," in *The Cincinnati Enquirer*, January 4, 1983, A6, available at: https://www.proquest.com/historical-newspapers/january-4-1983-page-6-36/docview/1894715821/se-2?accountid=12084, accessed May 9, 2021.

45 Allen D. Hertzke, *Representing God in Washington: The Role of Religious Lobbies in the American Polity* (Knoxville, TN: University of Tennessee, January 1, 1988), 50–52.

communication networks operated by Evangelical groups and movements: "New Religious Right groups have access to a huge network of Christian radio and television stations. These organizations see this as an integral part of their political strategy, as religious leaders attribute their success in mobilizing voting districts to the technology that plays a central role."[46]

Inez Schippers describes the relationship that was formed between the Republican Party and Evangelical Christians in general, and the Moral Majority in particular:

> *Among the tools that the Republican Party used to reach and grow the group of Evangelical Christians were Jerry Falwell's "Moral Majority", and similar organizations. These organizations had the ability to promote a right-wing political agenda on their radio and television networks, as well as directly in their churches. They conducted an aggressive campaign for Reagan both before the 1980 elections and leading up to his reelection in 1984. Ronald Reagan was presented as a defender of traditional Jewish-Christian values and conservatism, while his Democratic opponents were presented as driving forces of secular humanism that had destroyed American society. It appeared that the Republican tactic succeeded. Since Reagan was elected president in 1980, the party has won five out of seven presidential elections.*[47]

According to Jeff Halper, with the results of the 1980 elections, "Not only did the Zionist lobby have an open door to the White House, but also the Christian Zionists, including General Counsel Ed Meese, Defense Secretary Caspar Weinberger, Interior Secretary James Watt, and indeed Reagan himself, the Christian Zionists achieved political power for the first time." He adds that "the leading figures of the Christian Zionist movement, Lindsay, Robertson, and Falwell, gained official access to political leaders and policy-makers when they were invited by President Reagan in 1982 to provide guidance to the National Security Council," which reflects the political connection.[48]

There are also documented instances in the Israeli press that point to Falwell's growing political power as a derivative of the media coverage he received. For example, the *Haaretz* newspaper refers to an extremist leader who raises concern in American politics in general and the Jewish community in particular. For instance, in a background article titled "Falwell - A

---

46 Ibid.
47 Inez Schippers, *Politics in the Name of God—Christian Zionism, American Foreign Policy, and Israel* (Master Thesis in American Studies—Utrecht University, July 23, 2007), 40.
48 Jeff Halper, Israel as an Extension of American Empire, September 15, 2007, available at: http://www.counterpunch.org/halper11072005.html, accessed November 9, 2020.

Conservative Extremist Who Influenced Reagan," Zvi Bar'el describes Jerry Falwell as "zealous abortion opponent, and supporter of appointing Right-Wing Extremist judges for the courts." As to Falwell's influence on Ronald Reagan, Bar'el writes: "His primary importance lies in the influence he has on President Reagan. He and his community supported the latter in the elections. Now, Falwell is trying to call the debt' through Right-Wing legislation that the president must prompt or the appointment of judges and officials whose approach is consistent with Right-Wing conservatism."[49]

In principle, during Falwell's political ascent and connection to Israel, the media coverage he received was relatively limited and formulated to make readers uncomfortable. For example, Gad Becker titles his article about Jerry Falwell in "Yedioth Ahronoth," before the 1984 elections, "Look at the Red Light and Write a Big Check," and continues with a subtitle describing the contempt American Jewry feels toward him. He brings a quote attributed to Falwell: "I believe that GOD does not listen to the prayers of Jews." Becker writes in the article that "it seems that American Jewry's attitude to Falwell is closer to abhorrence and concern, rather than partnership."[50]

Toward the 1984 Elections

The Moral Majority movement led by Jerry Falwell reached the 1984 presidential campaign bearing a stance of recognition and an open door to Reagan's administration. Prior to the elections, Falwell was asked if he saw a trend of support for Israel in the Evangelical community. He replied:

> *In the past 20 years, Fundamentalists and Evangelicals, at a very rapid pace, have been 'converting' to support for Israel. This has not been a traditional position. It is a position taken today by the majority of Evangelicals and Fundamentalists in this country. Leading pastors and preachers across the nation have begun taking a very courageous stand on what they have always believed theologically but have never been willing to take a stand on practically. With every passing day, the number of supporters of Israel is outdistancing those that oppose Israel in the Evangelical-Christian community. It is my feeling is that the best friends Israel has in the world today are among Evangelical and Fundamentalist Christians. I think five years from now that consensus will be virtually unanimous.*[51]

---

49 Israel State Archives, ISA-MFA-Religion-R0003e6i, 175.
50 Israel State Archives, ISA-MFA-Religion-R0003e6i, 228.
51 "On God's Chosen People," in *The Fundamentalist Journal* 3, no. 3 (1984): 11, available at: https://digitalcommons.liberty.edu/cgi/viewcontent.cgi?article=1010&context=fun_84, accessed November 9, 2020.

According to Unger, "Still in its infancy as a political movement, the Moral Majority had registered 8.5 million voters in five years. They were powerful enough to swing presidential and senatorial elections. President Reagan appeared on the *Old Time Gospel Hour* with Falwell, who gave the benediction at the 1984 Republican National Convention. The CNP (Council for National Policy) had access to the highest powers in the land."[52]

Toward the 1984 elections, which were the first elections after the Moral Majority movement's massive success, a plan was formulated to expand Evangelical influence further. In his article, Richard Pierard quotes from "a confidential memorandum [...]." According to which, ACTV (American Traditional Values Coalition, KB), led by Louis Sheldon, Falwell's friend who operated from California to promote a conservative agenda, "intended to continue its work after the election and take advantage of the 'four more years of freedom' which GOD would give to turn America back to its traditional moral values." Pierard further elaborates about the plan, "to move the headquarters to Washington," in order to "offset the influence of the left they get through government," and to "recruit and train 'qualified Christian leaders' to run for public office at all levels [...]" The Reagan administration was influenced by Christian Right, and thus Senator Paul Laxalt, the Republican senator from Nevada and the head of the Republican Party, sent a letter on July 9 to "45,000 carefully selected ministers in sixteen states which addressed them as: 'Dear Christian Leader' and asked the recipients to 'play a significant role in what may very well be the most pivotal election of this century [...]. As leaders under GOD's authority, we cannot afford to resign ourselves to idle neutrality.' The letter further spoke about the aforementioned recipients' interaction with the community: 'help assure that those in your ministry will have a voice in the upcoming elections [...] a voice that surely will help assure the re-election of President Reagan and Vice President Bush.'"[53]

In February 1983, in anticipation of the 1984 election cycle, Falwell announced the creation of the PAC to support candidates favored by the pro-life movement who supported Israel and traditional values. In an interview with United Press International, Falwell stated that "our emphasis will be along the lines of supporting candidates who are strongly pro-life, supportive of the state of Israel and the many traditional values we espouse." Falwell further noted, "We have two years to raise it and I expect it to be in the millions." Regarding the establishment of the PAC itself, he remarked, "This will be a third entity for us for the purpose of raising funds from our constituency

---

52 Ibid., *The Fall of the House of Bush*, 75.
53 Richard V. Pierard, "Religion and the 1984 Election Campaign," *Review of Religious Research* 27, no. 2 (1985): 103.

for candidates who support pro-life and pro-family issues." When asked to refer to the timing, of establishing the PAC, Falwell responded, "We have spent the first three years registering five million voters and educating them on the issues. Now we want to get them involved in the process."⁵⁴

Clyde Wilcox conducted a study tracking the growth of political action committees (PACs) established by conservative Christian organizations between the 1980 and 1984 election campaigns. His findings demonstrate that between 1977 and 1984, there were three active PACs, two of which were associated with the Moral Majority. One was called "I Love America Pac" and the other "Moral Majority Pac," while the third was identified with the Christian Voice Moral Government Fund. The overall collection of money for the PACs was impressive, with donations increasing from just over half a million dollars in 1980 to over 1.5 million dollars. The amount of money transferred to candidates also grew, with an increase of over 400 percent between 1980 and 1984.⁵⁵

In the file prepared for the meeting between Falwell and Reagan on March 14, 1983, President Reagan's advisor, Faith Whittlesey, briefed Reagan on Falwell's significance for the administration:

Dr. Falwell, an Independent Baptist, is head of four major organizations headquartered in Lynchburg, Virginia:

- *Thomas Road Baptist Church, congregation of 19,000.*
- *Old Time Gospel Hour broadcasts, including Sunday programs on more than 400 TV stations and daily programs on more than 500 radio stations. Adding 50,000 supporters monthly.*
- *Liberty Baptist schools, with. more than 5,000 students through the college levels.*
- *The Moral Majority, a national conservative lobby with a $60 million per year budget, adding 11,000 members monthly, and a monthly newsletter that is mailed to 560,000 homes.*⁵⁶

---

54 David E. Anderson, *The Moral Majority, Which has been credited with Exercising [...]*, upi.com.
   February 4, 1983, available at: https://www.upi.com/Archives/1983/02/04/The-Moral-Majority-which-has-been-credited-with-exercising/2555413182800/, accessed November 9, 2020.
55 Clyde Wilcox, "Political Action Committees of the New Christian Right: A Longitudinal Analysis," *Journal for the Scientific Study of Religion* 27, no. 1 (March 1988): 63.
56 Ronald Reagan Presidential Library & Museum, 03/15/1983 (Case file 127515), Box 27, President Briefing Pages.

Unlike some other national conservative organization leaders, Dr. Falwell has never criticized you or the Reagan administration's policy. He has been strongly supportive on economic and social issues.

Without a doubt, the event that boosted the Moral Majority's rise to power toward the 1984 elections, as described in Westover's book, was a three-day conference held in April 1984 at the Washington Convention Center.

> *We decided that the speakers at the three-day conference would be pastors, religious leaders, congress members and senators. I hired a team of twenty people to design an event that would capture national media's attention. Three weeks before the event, Jerry called me at two in the morning and told me he wanted me to bring 3,000 students from Liberty University to Washington. The next morning, I rented 85 buses and arranged thousands of rooms in 23 hotels, with 29,000 meals for 3,000 students and faculty members. The result exceeded our expectations, as on the last day, Senator Jesse Helms arrived at the morning session, Vice President Bush spoke in the afternoon, and President Ronald Reagan was the guest of honor in the evening. The atmosphere was electrifying. Jerry ran the entire evening, and the media had to acknowledge the man sitting next to the president. It was the first time ever that the president and vice president appeared at the same event, on the same day. The next day, the "Washington Post" published a great article about the event, reporting that 26,000 people filled the hall.*[57]

The Decision to Retire from Political Life and Dissolve the Moral Majority

On January 4, 1986, Falwell announced that the "Moral Majority" would merge into a new political group called the "Liberty Federation." In a press conference, Falwell explained that "we are not disbanding or retreating, but expanding our action goals to include support for the strategic initiative of the Contras government in Nicaragua and the governments of South Africa and the Philippines."[58] A month later, on February 24, 1987, it was Falwell who gathered over 60,000 letters that he sent to the White House to support the president who was under public attack over the Iran-Contras affair. In a letter Falwell sent to Carl Anderson, the liaison to the public for the White House, he wrote: "I am sending you thousands of cards to encourage President Reagan. These cards are from many people nationwide who are

---

57 Ibid., *Wow! What a Ride: My Life and Journey with Jerry Falwell*, Chapter 24.
58 Ronald Reagan Presidential Library & Museum, Falwell Jerry, OA 18826, De Mose, Charlotte: Files.

very angry about the wave of attacks against the president in recent months." In response to his letter, Anderson noted, "I have just received a delivery of encouragement cards for the president. In our estimates, we have received about 60,000 to 70,000 cards! Thank you very much for forwarding these letters to me. It is a tremendous encouragement for us that so many Americans continue to support the president and his policy despite the difficulties. We continue to appreciate your leadership in these contexts."[59]

There are different conjectures as to the circumstances that led Falwell to give up his political activity within the framework of the Moral Majority. According to Clyde Wilcox, the main reason for Falwell's departure was a long line of scandals involving televangelists in the mid-1980s, which diminished public trust to the point where they stopped donating money:

> *Scandals involving televangelists in the latter half of the 1980s made many people skeptical about donations. Although those pastors were not necessarily politically involved, the issues raised affected fundraising efforts made by the moral majority and the efforts of Pastor Pat Robertson's campaign. One of the pastors, Jim Bakker, was charged with criminal acts in the realm of finance and sex and was even incarcerated for fraud. The criminal investigation into Bakker's financial activities revealed that he and his wife provided their dog with a heated doghouse and gold-plated faucets. Such behavior made it highly challenging for the Moral Majority to continue raising funds via direct mail, and in 1988, the money stream dried out.*[60]

It is important to emphasize that during the Moral Majority's heyday, it possessed a mailing list of 6 million addresses and approximately 500 activists in the organization.[61] Richard Leeman and Bernard Duffy also interpreted the transfer of Bakker's church to Falwell's management as a catalyst for his departure from politics but claim that some fierce power struggles were at play and propelled Falwell's departure: "Finally, Bakker was charged with

---

59 Ibid.
60 Clyde Wilcox, *Onward Christian Soldiers?: The Religious Right in American Politics* (New York: Routledge, 2018), available at: https://books.google.co.il/books?id=GxdWDwAAQBAJ&pg=PT39&dq=Falwell+Quits+as+Moral+Majority&hl=iw&sa=X&ved=2ahUKEwjLu7bTwvX3AhUhx4UKHScvBlkQ6AF6BAgHEAI#v=onepage&q=Falwell%20Quits%20as%20Moral%20Majority&f=false, accessed November 9, 2021.
61 Gene Camerik, *The Second Coming* (Bloomington, IN: IUniverse, 2007), available at: https://books.google.co.il/books?id=Yfhu4lmsKuoC&pg=PT110&dq=Falwell+Quits+as+Moral+Majority&hl=iw&sa=X&ved=2ahUKEwiOtZ_L9Pn3AhWVolwKHbl0BCI4HhDoAXoECAIQAg#v=onepage&q=Falwell%20Quits%20as%20Moral%20Majority&f=false, accessed November 9, 2021.

tax offenses and incarcerated, and his devotees perceived Falwell as responsible for the failed management of PTL-Praise the Lord church. The allegations of Falwell's failed crisis management as head of PTL became a 'holy war' between Falwell's and Bakker's followers, and from there to the remainder of the Christian Right's base. Years later, Falwell's own organizations, the 'I Love America' PAC and the 'Old Time Gospel Hour,' were fined $6,000 each for selling Bibles at an exorbitant price. Finally, in October 1987, Falwell resigned from PTL church management and later resigned from the Moral Majority."[62] According to Laura Olson and Paul Djupe, a lack of unity among believers regarding excessive involvement in politics was a major factor that led to Falwell's departure. They emphasize that "in addition, the increasingly political nature of Falwell's activities alienated some followers who did not support his evident repudiation of traditional evangelical political disengagement."[63]

On November 4, 1987, Falwell held a press conference where he announced his retirement from politics and his return to work at Liberty University, stating, "My first love is back to the pulpit, back to preaching, back to winning souls, back to meeting spiritual needs." He added, "I will never work for a candidate again [...] I will not be lobbying for legislation personally." Regarding his reasons for entering politics, Falwell said, "There was a need for breaking down the psychological barrier that religion and politics don't mix, and convincing Evangelical and fundamentalist Christians that 'it's not a sin to vote'."[64]

To what extent was Falwell significant to President Reagan? We can learn from a personal letter the latter sent to Falwell: "With deep sadness, I learned of your intention to give up the position of president of the Moral Majority and return to your Thomas Road Baptist Church in Virginia. As you know, the Founding Fathers understood the desire to create frameworks for human sexuality. These visionary men saw the country as a moral order in which religion is a central foundation. During your years as the leader of the moral majority, you provided exceptional morality and leadership as you advanced the freedom of religion and traditional Judeo-Christian values. "I want to take this opportunity to thank you from the bottom of my heart for your support and prayers for me and for my administration. Thanks to you, you

---

[62] Richard W. Leeman and Bernard K. Duffy, *American Voices: An Encyclopedia of Contemporary Orators* (Westport, CT: Greenwood Publishing Group, 2005), 151.

[63] Laura R. Olson and Paul A. Djupe, *Encyclopedia of American Religion and Politics* (New York: InfoBase Publishing, 2014), 162.

[64] "Falwell Quits as Moral Majority Head," *The New York Times*, November 4, 1987, Section A, Page 14.

helped me greatly on the road to making America a better place. Nancy and I wish you the best from the bottom of our hearts and our prayers for your continued success and happiness. May GOD bless you."⁶⁵ In 1989, the Moral Majority ceased to exist as an actual organization.⁶⁶

Falwell's Retirement to Liberty University and Adapting It to the Twenty-First Century

As mentioned, in 1987, Falwell retired from his political activities and tended to his work as president of Liberty University. That same year, he managed to secure a tax-exempt status, which he described in his autobiography as a necessity for survival: "If a tax exemption could not be granted us," he wrote, "it would have been impossible to carry out the dream of 50,000-student Christian university in Lynchburg."⁶⁷

Just as he developed modern methods for disseminating knowledge, communication, and messages through the radio and television era, it was important for Falwell to continue and remain at the forefront of technological developments. For example, Falwell was among the first to see the importance of developing a distance learning system using VHS tapes in an era when video equipment was entering almost every household in America. In so doing, he developed a methodology for disseminating knowledge for those who could not physically attend classes on campus and earn academic credit for it. Lamport and Kurian describe the system: "In 1985, Liberty University began a process that placed it at the forefront of distance learning in America, allowing students to study outside the traditional campus system and providing a solution for those who could not copy their studies to earn academic credit. The program began under the auspices of the School of Lifelong Learning under the supervision of Dr. Ron Godwin and has since become the largest distance learning program in the country among Christian universities, offering study programs to students from all 50 states and the world."⁶⁸ The *New York Times* also discussed the innovation in distance learning that he

---

65 Ronald Reagan Presidential Library & Museum, ME001, 529332, FJK.871207.1.
66 Joseph B. Tamney, *The Resilience of Christianity in the Modern World* (New York: SUNY Press, 1992), 124.
67 Alec MacGillis, "How Liberty University Built a Billion-Dollar Empire Online," *The New York Times,* April 17, 2018, available at: https://www.nytimes.com/2018/04/17/magazine/how-liberty-university-built-a-billion-dollar-empire-online.html, accessed November 9, 2021.
68 Mark A. Lamport and George T. Kurian, *Encyclopedia of Christian Education Vol. 3* (Lanham, MD: Rowman & Littlefield, 2015), 739.

developed at the university: "One educational innovation that Falwell worked on, starting in the mid-70s, was an early form of distance learning. Liberty would mail lecture videotapes and course packets to paying customers around the country—at first initially just certificate courses in Bible studies, and by the mid-80s, accredited courses in other subjects as well."[69]

The technological leap of the 2000s and the internet were the final levers that Falwell Sr. managed to promote within the university's ongoing revolution, and his heir, Falwell Jr., developed, established, and deepened the institution's commitment to adapt to the times and technological innovations. "At the beginning of the 2000s, for-profit colleges flourished: Access to the internet spread, and the Bush administration made particularly light use of regulatory oversight, even when programs routinely stripped a large share of the federal aid intended for students. Among the efforts of the Sperling model[70] was Falwell, who in 2004 began expanding the family's early learning programs on videotapes in what became known as Liberty University Online, offered to users over the internet."[71]

An article published in Politico, describes how the 2004 transition to online platforms and why the early preparations prior to the arrival of high-speed internet turned the university into an economic powerhouse: "In 2004, Liberty University entered the nascent online learning market. A close advisor of Rev. Falwell named Dr. Ron Godwin had, two decades earlier, spearheaded a remote educational program, first using VHS tapes sent through via mail and later dial-up internet. These early efforts put Liberty ahead of its competitors when high-speed internet came online. Remote learning proved to be a financial boon. The university pitched its same message of 'Christian excellence' to online students, promising a high-quality, affordable education—and today [i.e., by 2020. KB] enrolls 94,000 students online, according to Liberty figures."[72]

---

69 Ibid., *How Liberty University Built a Billion-Dollar Empire Online*.
70 The Sperling model is a model developed by John Sperling that created a degree model in correspondence as early as 1976 at the private University of Arizona. It is named after him and is called the distance or correspondence degree methodology.
71 Ibid., *How Liberty University Built a Billion-Dollar Empire Online*.
72 Maggie Severns, Brandon Ambrosino, and Michael Stratford, "'They All Got Careless': How Falwell Kept His Grip on Liberty Amid Sexual 'Games' Self-Dealing," politico.com, November 1, 2020, available at: https://www.politico.com/news/magazine/2020/11/01/jerry-falwell-liberty-university-becki-self-dealing-sex-430207, accessed November 9, 2021.

Falwell's Relationship with the Likud Prime Ministers After His Retirement from Politics

In the context of his connection to Israel, Falwell continued to keep the door open to Israeli prime ministers, especially from the political Right; for example, Prime Minister Shamir, who viewed the connection with Evangelicals in general and Falwell in particular as a passing of the baton from Menachem Begin. His advisor, Ariel Horowitz, commented on the matter, saying that "Israeli right-wing conservatives welcome the support of Evangelical Christians, especially Pastor Falwell."[73] Falwell's connection with Shamir stemmed from the former's desire to assist the latter to withstand Bush's pressure with regard to the Madrid Conference. Falwell maintained his relationship with Israeli leaders after Begin. He attempted to help Yitzhak Shamir when George Bush Sr. pushed Shamir to freeze settlement activity in the West Bank and Gaza.[74] He also developed close ties with Benjamin Netanyahu, and in April 1997, Netanyahu spoke at a conference organized by United Israel Appeal, led by Jerry Falwell and Pat Robertson.[75] Alan Dershowitz described in his book how, "When Bibi made his first official visit to the United Stated during the Clinton presidency, he made the mistake of meeting with the Reverend Jerry Falwell, the founder of the Moral Majority and a virulent critic of President and Mrs. Clinton." The Clintons were furious at Netanyahu for beginning his "visit at a Falwell event."[76] Beyond the personal anger of the Clintons, there was also a political aspect to the visit, Stephen Sizer describes how, In January 1998, when Netanyahu, the prime minister of Israel, visited Washington, his first meeting was at a conference with the Coalition for Israel's National Unity … "The crowd hailed Netanyahu 'the Ronald Reagan of Israel.' This time Falwell promised to contact 200,000 pastors and churches leaders who receive the 'National Liberty Journal' and

---

73 Zoa Lauds, *Falwell, Jewish Advocate* (June 21, 1984): 5.
74 Ibid., *Evangelicals and Israel: The Story of American Christian Zionism*, 148.
75 Ofira Seliktar, *Divided We Stand: American Jews, Israel, and the Peace Process* (Westport, CT: Greenwood Publishing Group, 2002), 160.
76 Alan M. Dershowitz, *Defending Israel: The Story of My Relationship with My Most Challenging Client* (New York: St. Martin's Publishing Group, 2019), available at: https://books.google.co.il/books?id=5V6HDwAAQBAJ&pg=PT76&dq=Falwell+Quits+as+Moral+Majority&hl=iw&sa=X&ved=2ahUKEwiOtZ_L9Pn3AhWVolwKHbl0BCI4HhDoAXoECAUQAg#v=onepage&q=Falwell%20Quits%20as%20Moral%20Majority&f=false.

ask them to 'tell President Clinton to refrain from putting pressure on Israel to comply with the Oslo Accords.'"[77]

Falwell continued to promote religious and political support for Israel during Ariel Sharon's tenure as prime minister of Israel. For example, a few days after Sharon's election in February 2001, Falwell delivered a speech called "Israel, Ariel Sharon, and the Return of Jesus," where he extolled Sharon's military capabilities as fitting the Ezekiel's Vision of the Valley of Dry Bones prophecy, which would result in a mighty army of Jews reclaiming their land.[78] Falwell rallied for Sharon in 2001, when the Bush administration requested the withdrawal of Israeli tanks from Palestinian areas, as described by Stephen Rock: "Falwell's influence was demonstrated in 2001 when President George Bush, whose government was generally supportive of Israel, called on Sharon's government to withdraw Israeli tanks from Palestinian cities in the West Bank. Falwell sent a letter of protest to the White House. Over 100,000 emails from conservative Christians were sent as a result […] Falwell said in this context: 'There are 70 million of us. And if there's one thing that can bring us all together quickly, it's when our government turns against Israel'."[79] In an interview with CBS's "60 Minutes" in 2002, Falwell said: "It is my belief that the Bible Belt in America is Israel's only safety belt right now." In the same interview, he called the Prophet Muhammad a "terrorist," which he later apologized for.[80] Falwell did not hesitate to exert pressure on the Bush administration, as Jennifer Schwirzer describes: "The latter was interviewed on 60 Minutes in October 2003, several months after the Israeli attack of the West Bank city of Jenin. Bush appealed to Sharon to withdraw from Jenin, but the pro-Israel lobby and the Christian right saw things differently. They immediately mobilized their masses to barrage the White House with more than 100,000 email messages, calls, and visits urging the president to allow Israel to defend itself. Bush grew suddenly silent toward Israel, and the activists considered it a sign of victory." Referring to this incident, Jerry Falwell

---

77 Stephen R. Sizer, *Christian Zionism: Road-map to Armageddon?* (Eugene, OR: Wipf and Stock Publishers, 2021), 91.
78 Ibid., *Allies for Armageddon: The Rise of Christian Zionism*, 178.
79 Stephen R. Rock, *Faith and Foreign Policy: The Views and Influence of U.S. Christians and Christian Organizations* (Bloomsbury, NJ: Bloomsbury Publishing USA, 2011), available at: https://books.google.co.il/books?id=q5zF8pudsAUC&pg=PT141&dq=Ariel+sharon+falwell&hl=iw&sa=X&ved=2ahUKEwjHl-fpsPz3AhVHeMAKHZYHB2MQ6AF6BAgLEAI#v=onepage&q=Ariel%20sharon%20falwell&f=false, accessed November 9, 2021.
80 "Rev. Jerry Falwell," cbsnews.com, March 29, 2005, available at: https://www.cbsnews.com/pictures/rev-jerry-falwell/14/, accessed November 9, 2021.

told the nation: "I think now we can count on President Bush to do the right thing for Israel every time."[81]

As mentioned, despite Falwell's retirement from the public sphere, he continued to maintain encouragement for action of the grassroots movement he founded, in all matters related to U.S.-Israel relations, support for the State of Israel in general, and Israeli Right-Wing leaders in particular.

Falwell's Death

On May 15, 2007, Jerry Falwell, age 73, was found dead in his office at Liberty University. He was "discovered without a pulse on Tuesday in his office at Liberty University in Lynchburg. His death was pronounced at a hospital about an hour later. Dr. Carl Moore, his personal physician, said he had a history of heart problems and probably died of cardiac arrythmia."[82]

The funeral arrangements and participants are described by the religious news agency RNS: "About 10,000 mourners bid farewell to the Rev. Jerry Falwell on May 22, [2007, K.B] remembering his influence as a pastor, political activist, and Christian educator [...] Police helicopters flew overhead and people waited for hours in line to attend his wake and funeral. More than 33,000 paid their respects to Falwell [...] first at Liberty University and later at his church. The line of people wanting to attend his funeral began forming at 4 a.m." The Evangelist Franklin Graham was quoted saying: "People have asked me, 'Franklin, do you agree with Jerry Falwell?' [...] to which he replied 'Every time he opened the Bible, I agreed with Jerry Falwell. And you know what? He opened the Bible a lot.'" Tim Goeglein, a White House liaison to Evangelicals, attended the funeral and eulogized him: "A man of vision has seen a vision fulfilled, and he is dancing with GOD in the stars this very afternoon."[83]

President George Bush released a statement to the media after Jerry Falwell's death:

---

81 Jennifer J. Schwirzer, "Mutual Back-Scratching," libertymagazine.org, July/August 2005, available at: https://www.libertymagazine.org/article/mutual-back-scratching, accessed November 9, 2021.
82 "Televangelist, Christian Leader Jerry Falwell Dies," npr.com, May 15, 2007, available at: https://www.npr.org/templates/story/story.php?storyId=10188427, accessed May 9, 2022.
83 Adelle M. Banks, "Thousands Bid Farewell to Falwell," religionnews.com, May 23, 2007, available at: https://religionnews.com/2007/05/23/thousands-bid-farewell-to-falwell/, accessed May 9, 2022.

> *Laura and I are deeply saddened by the death of Jerry Falwell, a man who cherished faith, family, and freedom. As the founder of Thomas Road Baptist Church in Lynchburg, Virginia, Jerry lived a life of faith and called upon men and women of all backgrounds to believe in GOD and serve their communities. One of his lasting contributions was the establishment of Liberty University, where he taught young people to remain true to their convictions and rely upon GOD throughout each stage of their lives. Today, our thoughts and prayers are with his wife Macel and the rest of the Falwell family.*[84]

Pat Robertson, his colleague, evangelical pastor, and candidate for the Republican Party's nomination in the 1988 election, called Falwell "a beacon on many moral issues facing our nation."[85] Rudy Giuliani, the former mayor of New York City, praised him, saying, "He was a man who set direction" and noted that "he was someone who was not afraid to speak his mind. We all owe him a great deal of respect."[86] Former Massachusetts governor and 2012 Republican presidential nominee Mitt Romney said of Falwell, "He was an American who built and led a movement based on strong principles and strong faith [...] the important legacy of his work will continue through the many organizations he built to put his faith into action."[87] The Israeli ambassador at the time, Sallai Meridor, conveyed his condolences to Falwell's family: "It was with both shock and sorrow that I learned of the tragic and sudden passing of Rev. Dr. Jerry Falwell, whose support for Israel spanned many decades."[88]

The death of Falwell also provoked criticism from his opponents. For example, journalist and publicist Christopher Hitchens expressed himself after Falwell's death in an interview with CNN: "No, and I think it's a shame

---

84 "George W. Bush Whitehouse Archive," May 15, 2007, available at: https://georgew-bush-whitehouse.archives.gov/news/releases/2007/05/20070515-8.html, accessed November 9, 2021.
85 "Moral Majority's Falwell Dies," *The Denver Post*, May 15, 2007, available at: https://www.denverpost.com/2007/05/15/moral-majoritys-falwell-dies/, https://www.thenation.com/article/archive/agent-intolerance.
86 Max Blumenthal, "Agent of Intolerance," thenation.com, May 16, 2007, available at: https://www.thenation.com/article/archive/agent-intolerance/, accessed November 9, 2021.
87 *Trump, Gop, Rightwing Media and the Southern* Strategy, the Responsible consumer, available at: https://theresponsibleconsumer.wordpress.com/gop-racism-beyond-trump/, accessed November 9, 2021.
88 Ron Kampeas, "Falwell Left Jews with Mixed Feelings," JTA.com, May 15, 2007, available at: https://www.jta.org/2007/05/15/united-states/falwell-left-jews-with-mixed-feelings, accessed November 9, 2021.

there's no hell for him to go to [...] The anti-life of Jerry Falwell proves only one thing: that you *can get away with the most extraordinary offenses to morality and truth in this country if you'll just get yourself called Reverend.*"[89] People like that "should be out in the street, shouting and hollering with a cardboard sign and selling pencils from a cup."[90] Criticism of his style also sounded in the Jewish world. For example, Reform Rabbi David Saperstein expressed concern about Falwell's attitude toward Judaism: "Many Jews were deeply concerned by the divisive rhetoric that he used, the politicization of faith, and efforts to Christianize America."[91]

Beyond Jewish and secular criticism, a noteworthy voice of dissent emerged from within the Evangelical world itself, offering a theologically grounded alternative vision of faith and politics.

Among the most prominent theological critics of Falwell from within the Evangelical world was Jim Wallis, founder of the progressive Christian organization *Sojourners*. In his book *God's Politics*, Wallis argued forcefully against the dominance of the religious Right in American faith discourse: "It is true that some of the religious Right's leaders are indeed theocrats—those who would impose their versions of morality on the nation if they ever had the chance."[92] Wallis sought to offer an alternative Christian voice—one focused on social justice, peace, and economic fairness—challenging the notion that religious belief should naturally align with conservative politics. His theological critique developed into active political engagement. In the fall of 2004, Wallis launched a national campaign directly aimed at undermining the monopoly of figures like Falwell, Pat Robertson, and James Dobson over Christian political identity. Under the slogan "God is Not a Republican. Or

---

89 Two days after the terrorist attack on America, Falwell was quoted saying, "What we saw on Tuesday, as terrible as it is, could be minuscule if, in fact, God continues to lift the curtain and allow the enemies of America to give us probably what we deserve." He then blamed liberal bodies, saying, "I really believe that the pagans, and the abortionists, and the feminists, and the gays and the lesbians who are actively trying to make that an alternative lifestyle, the ACLU, People for the American Way, all of them who have tried to secularize America, I point the finger in their face and say, 'You helped this happen.'" He later apologized for the interpretation given to this statement.
90 "Christopher Hitchens on Rev. Jerry Falwell's Death," *CNN*, May 15, 2007, available at: https://www.youtube.com/watch?v=52yTqMcwuQE, accessed May 9, 2022.
91 Ibid., *Falwell Left Jews with Mixed Feelings*.
92 Jim Wallis, *God's Politics: Why the Right Gets It Wrong and the Left Doesn't Get It* (San Francisco: HarperOne, 2006), 37.

a Democrat," he raised $400,000 in two months and ran full-page ads in the *New York Times* and in the hometown newspapers of Falwell and his allies.[93]

Political scientists and historians who have commented on Falwell's role in shaping American politics and society have highlighted his role in building the conservative movement in American politics. For example, upon his death, Matthew Wilson, a political scientist at Southern Methodist University in Dallas, commented: "Jerry Falwell, more than anyone else, was responsible for recruiting and mobilizing the most important mass political movement of the past 30 years. His Moral Majority truly propelled the Republican Party to power."[94] William Martin, a political scientist from Rice University, says that with the establishment of the Moral Majority, Falwell became one of the first Evangelicals to use their religious influence for political purposes. "He legitimized voting and participation in the political arena, something that was not common and often considered a bad thing, especially for the most conservative Evangelicals and Fundamentalists," Martin said in an interview. "Although it was not a true populist organization, the Moral Majority played a significant role in reaching millions of people who previously did not register to vote. Therefore, he played a significant role in bringing in the conservative Protestants into the political arena." Martin said Falwell also illustrated "the importance of regular communication with people through mass media and the role of mega-churches in such a movement. He was an energetic, wise religious leader capable of leading processes. And for me, one of the most amazing things about his life was how he built this church from scratch and turned it into a true powerhouse."[95] Mark Rozell from the Public Policy Department at George Mason University discussed Falwell's influence during the Republican primaries leading up to the 2008 election: "If you want to see his legacy, look at that recent Republican debate where almost every candidate shifted right with regard to social issues."[96] Historian Douglas Brinkley

---

93 Amy Sullivan, "The Good Fight," *Washington Monthly*, March 2005, available at: https://washingtonmonthly.com/2005/03/01/the-good-fight-2/, accessed June 10, 2025.

94 Lisa Anderson and Margaret Ramirez, "Evangelist Falwell Dies at 73," deseret.com, May 16, 2007, available at: https://www.deseret.com/2007/5/16/20018917/evangelist-falwell-dies-at-73, accessed May 19, 2022.

95 Ibid.

96 Ed Stoddard, "Falwell Legacy to Live on in U.S. Politics," reuters.com, May 16, 2007, available at: https://www.reuters.com/article/us-usa-falwell-legacy-idUSN15 42938020070515, accessed May 19, 2022.

from Rice University in Texas said about Falwell, "He set the tone, direction, and momentum of the 1980s."[97]

His partner and collaborator, Duke Westover, summed up in his book the life's work he had built: "On July 2, 2006, Thomas Road Baptist Church celebrated its 50th anniversary and the first service in the new building with over ten thousand attendees. In addition, since it was the 203rd anniversary of the United States, there was a giant fireworks display above the Liberty University football stadium. We tried to count the number of people who came, and it was much more than 30,000. Jerry Falwell was a giant visionary, larger than life. Unlike most visionaries, he had the privilege of seeing his vision and dreams come true [...] In 50 years, under the leadership of Jerry Falwell, the church managed to raise and spend about five billion dollars for the following purposes:

- Elim Home for Combating Drugs and Alcohol Abuse.
- The "Old Time Gospel Hour" television program, which was the longest-running religious program on television worldwide.
- Liberty Christian Academy enrolls around 2,000 students.
- Liberty House, which serves as a home for unmarried mothers.
- Liberty University, the world's largest Evangelical Christian university, has a total enrollment of 50,000 students.
- Thousands of churches have been planted worldwide.
- More than three million people have declared that they have found religion through the outreach efforts of Jerry Falwell and his emissaries."[98]

In life and in death, both those who revered and those who abhorred Falwell could not ignore the immense and lasting impact he left on American society, politics in general, and conservatism in particular. His ability to build a populist movement that influenced both local politics and U.S. relations with Israel was undeniable.

---

97 David Walsh, "Jerry Falwell, Founder of the Right-Wing Moral Majority, Dead at 73," wsws.org, May 17, 2007, available at: https://www.wsws.org/en/articles/2007/05/falw-m17.html, accessed May 13, 2022.
98 Ibid., *Wow! What a Ride: My Life and Journey with Jerry Falwell*, Chapter 40.

Chapter 7

A FOLLOW-UP STUDY ON LIBERTY UNIVERSITY GRADUATES WHO HAVE PLANTED CHURCHES

Methodology and Approach

As previously stated, and according to the LCN network website, around 2,000 churches were established by Liberty University graduates throughout the United States and approximately 4,800 churches. Falwell's vision/estimate was planting 5,000 new churches. This original qualitative study is a mere example or model that does not presume to indicate the full extent of the phenomenon but shines a spotlight to illustrate Falwell's strategic action and offers a case study to understand better the ripple effect and influence caused by the conservative political force in particular and the American political system in general. The study only examined churches established by Liberty graduates throughout the United States. In cases where an alum planted more than one church, the sampled church was the first one he planted during his studies or postgraduation.

Liberty University alumni were tracked via two primary sources: The first was student newspapers, alum publications, and official university publications found in the Falwell archive at Liberty University. These covered mainly graduates who completed their studies in the 1970s and 1980s. The second was a LinkedIn search, which is not limited by time, hence including even recent graduates. After identifying the graduate's name and the church they planted, additional background information was reviewed, like the exact church's address, city and state, year of establishment, the number of worshippers in the first prayer service, and as many historical details as exist on the pastor who founded the church. The benchmark set to indicate the size of the community was the number of followers the church had on Facebook. The idea stemmed from the understanding that most church followers do so because they belong to that church and that given the spread of COVID-19 pandemic, many prayers were conducted in the virtual space. Approximately 200 graduates were sampled. The data collected was input into the ArcGIS

Pro system to extract insights on trends in the expansion of university graduates and into the Gephi system to generate insights on various correlations that would be available for future reading and research in the United States-Israel blog, and is also attached as hard-copy appendix to this work.[1] Eli Yitzhak describes social media research as a "Spatial Revolution" or spatial modeling, noting, "Through advanced technologies, the basic human need for a presence in space has become real and accessible to the public more than any previous era."[2]

The second part of the study focuses on qualitative research of responses to questionnaires sent to dozens of pastors who agreed to answer questions and be interviewed, along with historical materials found about pastors in church sites, archives, and throughout the web. The pastors' responses helped to understand how such seminarians, or as Falwell called them, "young timothies," implemented what they absorbed from Falwell and Towns as students on their way to becoming leaders of a local church and their involvement in motivating their communities to support and identify with the State of Israel.

The Graduates' Expansion Trend

As can be seen from the map below, Falwell's layout of expansion, starting in Jerusalem, moving to Judea, then Samaria, and finally to the edge of the earth, appears in the form of connections pertaining to graduates who have become church planters, in proximity to the "mother base" in Lynchburg, Virginia. Out of approximately 200 graduates sampled, 27 chose to plant churches in the state of Virginia, thus essentially becoming the central hub adjacent to that of Liberty University, from which graduates emerge after their studies. Neighboring states include North Carolina with 14 churches, Pennsylvania with 17, and Maryland with 8, as shown in Figure 7.1.

One can also learn how the church planting movement has spread from the heat map in Figure 7.2, showcasing the geographic area of the southeastern United States. The highlighted areas on the map represent the geographic region starting at the Lynchburg area and extends slightly southward and northeastward. The combination of these maps and the fact that most graduates chose to cluster in this area indicates their preference to serve in relatively close geographic proximity and in a system of building influence circles. Other centers beyond these regions are Florida, with 12 churches;

---

1 Kobby Barda, "Data of Liberty U," us-israel.org.il, available at: https://us-israel.org.il/2022/03/02/data-of-liberty-u/, accessed March 1, 2022.
2 Eli Yitzhak, "The Digital Revolution in the Geotechnology and Geoinformatics Space: Background Article." Horizons in Geography, 2018, 173. Hebrew Text.

Figure 7.1 Map showing the number of churches per state.

Figure 7.2 Heat map of the spread of Liberty graduates.

Tennessee, with 9; Texas, with 8; and Ohio with 8. Interestingly, even when centers are established in these states, they are usually established relatively close to each other in urban proximity and appear on the map as red hotspots, as shown around Dallas, Texas.

Another way to witness the spread and relative proximity of radius around the orb's core (representing the size and center of gravity in relation to the country) is Figure 7.3, which shows small spheres and satellites representing the names of the churches and their distance from the center point. For example, in the blue sphere, which represents the state of Virginia, one can see the proximity of the churches, some of which are very close to the hub, that is Liberty University. A similar distribution can be seen in the green sphere, which represents Pennsylvania; the purple sphere, which represents North Carolina; and the red sphere, which represents Texas. The light purple spheres of Tennessee represent an anomaly in the context of church distribution. These churches are scattered relatively far from the center, forming a network of several medium-sized hubs.

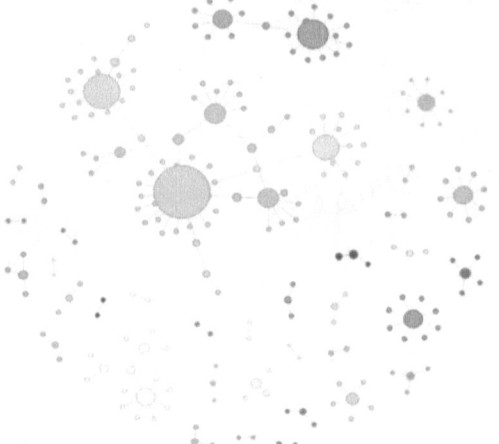

Figure 7.3 Church proximity by state size.

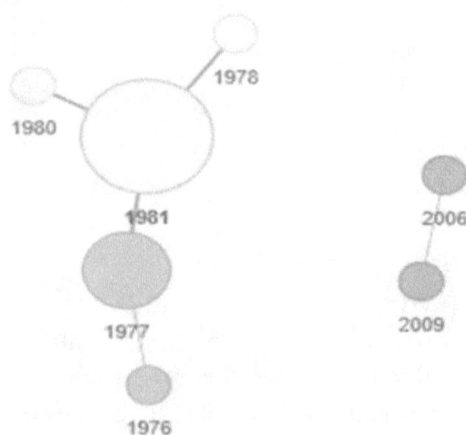

Figure 7.4 The number of graduates who planted churches as a function of the year the church was established.

Figure 7.4 shows the most productive years of the church planting process, and one can see that at least in the context of the 200-sample group of graduates, the launch to plant churches was at its peak was in the late 1970s and 1980s. At that time, Falwell was intensely involved in promoting and advancing his church planting vision.

There are clear connections and an evident pattern according to which the graduates acted. I will examine why and how these connections were formed by tracking the action patterns of those graduates and answering how they connected to Falwell's vision.

Liberty University Graduates and Church Planting

In his book that guides pastors on church planting, Elmer Towns explains what he believes is the ideal model for church planting:

> It should be noted that many who want to start church planting do so without an understanding of the philosophy of the church [...] I was asked by a Liberty graduate how to solve a certain problem. I smiled and answered, 'WWJD.' He thought I meant the acronym for What Would Jesus Do, but I answered in the negative. The words WWJD stand for What would Jerry do, and then I explained: "Jerry Falwell is not GOD, nor is he the perfect model for starting a church, but he did manage to build one of the top 10 most successful churches in America. Use Jerry as your model—not because he is perfect, but because he overcame difficulties and built a church. Let Jerry be your model."[3]

Indeed, the stories told by the pastors in the questionnaires and the background materials written about them or their church planting process showed an unmistakable pattern of repetition of the same characteristics, narratives, philosophy, and history of Jerry Falwell, which helped establish a network of churches according to his image and vision. The first part will focus on planting the churches themselves, as it is based on testimonies written by pastors about the process they went through in planting churches or, alternatively, written about them as part of the description of the relevant church's history. The second part, deriving from questionnaires sent to pastors by email, will focus on the context of the pastor's personal experiences with Israel, how he was educated at Liberty University, and the mediation of the topic to the community established around the church he planted. These means provide a better understanding of the church planting process, its spread in the United States on the one hand, and how Israel was incorporated into the overall narrative that passed to the local population that uses the religious services of the church founded by Liberty University graduates on the other hand. This helps to explain the institutional uniformity seen among Liberty-trained pastors, many of whom modeled their ministries on a singular archetype rooted in Falwell's example. As historian Mark Noll has observed, "These institutions were created for specifically religious purposes; many are successful, some remarkably so, in promoting those goals. Virtually without exception,

---

3 L. Elmer, *Towns, Planting Reproducing Churches* (Shippensburg, PA: Destiny Image, 2018), 221.

however, they were not designed to promote thorough Christian reflection on the nature of the world, society, and the arts."[4]

Closeness Forms a Family That Leads to a Mission

Examining Falwell's biography reveals how the university president educates his graduates. The idea of community life still thrives on campus, creating the initial connection between people with similar backgrounds. A few examples demonstrate the merging of the preaching to family life, on the one hand, and the ability to promote the planting of churches to help spread the message Falwell sought to encourage, on the other hand. In an interview with Johnnie Moore, Falwell's assistant from the late 90s until his death, Liberty graduate who served as the university's Senior Vice President, he talked about the overall atmosphere on campus that fostered familiarity for the purpose of marriage. According to Moore, it was "Got to get the ring by the spring" atmosphere, encouraging the creation of a family unit.[5]

That is how, for example, Don Meckley from Altoona, Pennsylvania, and his wife Lisa Mendendelk from Maryland met on the Liberty University campus. After graduation, the couple planted a church called Ministries of Emmanuel Community Church in Bayville, New Jersey, which now has about 750 followers on Facebook. Their daughter Ashley also studied at Liberty, where she met her husband Hunter, who works at Liberty University, and she works at the Heritage Baptist Church in Lynchburg.[6] Another story of a couple whose relationship was woven on campus and turned into a mission of community planting is that of Stacy Bearden and his wife, Janine. Stacy grew up in East Tennessee and married his wife Janine while still studying at Liberty. He graduated from Liberty with a degree in Business Management and a master's degree in Arts and Christian Leadership from Liberty Theological Seminary. In 2000, Stacy went on a church planting mission and has since served in four different churches. He has also been involved in planting three new churches in Tennessee, North Carolina, and

---

4 Mark A. Noll, *The Scandal of the Evangelical Mind* (Grand Rapids, MI: Eerdmans, 1994), 16.
5 Kobby Barda, "Interview with Johnny Moore," us-israel.org.il, available at: https://us-israel.org.il/2022/02/21/%d7%a8%d7%90%d7%99%d7%95%d7%9f-%d7%a9%d7%a0%d7%a2%d7%a9%d7%94-%d7%a2%d7%9d-%d7%92%d7%99%d7%9e%d7%99-%d7%9e%d7%95%d7%a8, accessed March 1, 2022.
6 "Pastor Don Meckley," available at: https://www.eccbayville.org/pastor-don-meckley , accessed March 1, 2022.

South Florida. He is currently the pastor of Providence Church in Knoxville, Tennessee, with a community of about 1,300 followers on Facebook.[7]

Another couple who met on campus, married and embarked on a church planting journey, is the Garman family. The couple met on Liberty University and have been married since 2001. Colby Garman graduated with a BA in Biblical Studies. Annie, his wife, writes a blog for North American pastor's wives. Together with another Liberty alumnus, Clint Clifton, also involved in church planting, they founded Pillar Church of Dumfries in Virginia in 2010, which serves a community of 939 followers on Facebook.[8] Colby and Clint also host a "Church Planting Podcast" broadcasted on various platforms and advises on how to plant communities.

Liberty University community does not only foster men's and women's acquaintance on campus but also families who decide to study together the subject of planting communities. Gabe and Kari Turner, a married couple, agreed in the summer of 2007 to move to Lynchburg, Virginia, where both enrolled as full-time students in a seminar at Liberty. They completed the seminar in the spring of 2009, and on June 15, 2009, moved to Charlottesville, VA, to lead a church planting team in establishing The Point Church. Graduates and students from Liberty University, as well as residents of Charlottesville and the surrounding counties, joined them in founding the church, which helped expand the community to another church in the city of Louisa as part of a local church expansion, which now has 6,265 followers on Facebook.[9]

All Beginnings Are Difficult

As we remember, Jerry Falwell completed his studies in 1956 and turned to establishing a church. He tried to convey to his students how he was forced to "pioneer" the establishment of the church, through hardships and obstacles, he tried to convey to the students. This is how he addressed the difficulties he faced at the beginning of his journey as a church planter in his book:

> In the 1950s, there was a building of the Donald Duck Bottling Plant that was empty. We entered the building, opened the door, and a wave of dust swept us outside.

---

[7] "Meet the Elders," available at: https://providencechurch.com/elders, accessed March 1, 2022.
[8] "Missional Leadership Team," available at: https://pillardumfries.com/leadership/, accessed March 1, 2022.
[9] Available at: https://www.thepointva.com/pastorgabe, accessed March 1, 2022, "Pastor Gabe."

> *The building was empty except for broken shelves, rusty pipes, and boxes in the corner of the room, in a deserted environment, but we did not pay attention to that [...] 'We don't have the money to purchase the property,' I explained, 'but we want to execute a leasing deal starting today with a purchase option.' The deal was signed and, for a week, the community rallied to help us renovate the place [...] On Wednesday, June 27, 1956, our community gathered and held an inaugural meeting for our church. We adopted bylaws, elected the three treasurers, and chose the name of the church: Thomas Road Baptist Church. We believed that GOD was with us from the beginning and asked for His guidance in every step we took.[10]*

Falwell's story is replicated in hundreds of cases, as an inspiration for young graduates who go out into the field to plant churches.

The motivational theme of humble beginnings is a common thread in the stories of churches established/planted by Liberty graduates. The importance of starting, no matter the format, place or atmosphere, is the primary storyline for dozens of such tales, like the Victory Baptist Church in Winthrop, Maine, founded by Pastor Jeff Clark, for example. According to the church's website, Clark began attending Liberty College in Lynchburg, Virginia. He would occasionally return home on weekends and preach to those who gathered at the Chick residence. Upon completing his studies at the college, he became the first pastor of Victory Baptist Church. The church by this time had already bought some property with a barn on it. The barn was remodeled and became the church building. The first official prayer meeting was held on Father's Day 1976. Pastor Clark grew the church, and the desire for a Christian school was awakened. The church purchased a property in Winthrop that was an old bar. Once again, the church members worked on remodeling. This time, they turned an old bar into a school. In just a short time, the church decided to sell the barn and move to the school until they could build a new auditorium.

The theme of community involvement in the purchase and renovation of a building as part of the church planting vision also appears in the story of Dr. Freddie Young of Grand Strand Baptist Church in Myrtle Beach, South Carolina. The church's website states, "Our church first met on Wednesday, April 2, 1975, in a rented warehouse in the Myrtle Beach Industrial Park. Ninety-five people were present. Our church had 172 Charter Members (those joining within 90 days). Our present location, on Hospitality Lane, is on five acres of land that was donated by Nick & Lena Mae Lucas (charter members) back in 1976. Pastor Young was our founding pastor, but GOD

---

10 Ibid., *An Autobiography*, 195–6.

called him to Hendersonville, NC, in early 1979, but the Lord returned him back to us in June 1986. He has enjoyed fruitful ministry here, once again, since that time. To GOD be all the glory!"[11]

Similar to Falwell's story of purchasing the building by leasing, funding the purchase of the church is described in the case of Ocean County Baptist Church, founded by Pastor Rick Dinoff. The community's involvement in resource mobilization is described on the church's website:

> *In the summer of 1980, Pastor Rick Dinoff and his family moved to Toms River, NJ, for the purpose of starting an independent Baptist church. They spent several months visiting and sharing the gospel with families in Toms River. On November 30, 1980, the Ocean County Baptist Church held its first service as a church in the East Dover Elementary School. The church had its signing service in 1981 with sixteen families signing as Charter Members. Under the leadership of Pastor Dinoff, the church continued to grow. In 1982, they purchased the property on which the church is presently located for fifty-nine thousand dollars. The ground breaking ceremony for the first building, 8,352 square feet, was held on June 20, 1982. The congregation of our church would meet there and pray over the land for GOD's blessings. The construction was financed through a bond program.*[12]

An element that repeats itself in some of the stories emphasizes the contribution of the land or building by people in the community for the development of the church, as part of the community's development, involvement, and growth. That is also evident in the story of Epping Bible Church, planted by Pastor Ron Townsend: "In 1981, Ron Townsend was approached by a family from Epping who shared the need for a Bible preaching church in their town. After praying and seeking counsel, Ron decided to accept the call and start a church in a town that needed to hear the Gospel! They began with just a few families meeting in a church building in Camp Hedding, and a little later, they were able to start using a vacant church building on Bedee Road in Epping. It was a small church, with only an outhouse as a restroom! After meeting there for several years, they were told that the church building would need to be taken down as the town was planning to put a highway in. The Sanville family of Epping was one of the families impacted by the start up church. They decided to donate two acres of land to Epping Bible to be

---

11 "Our Story," available at: https://www.grandstrandbaptist.com/about-us, accessed March 1, 2022.
12 "Church History," available at: https://ocbcministries.org/church-history/, accessed March 1, 2022.

able to put a trailer for the Townsend's to live in as well as eventually build a church."[13]

The story of Central Baptist Church in Victoria, VA, and Pastor Pat Fortner, also demonstrates land donation, as part of the community's involvement in the renovation and construction of the building, generating ripples of influence that Falwell mentioned in his vision for church planters: "November 7, 1979, Pat Fortner received approval from the Victoria High School to use Room #104 for the purpose for religious use. Central Baptist Church officially began January 27, 1980! C.O. Dunnavant on September 19, 1980, drew up a 'deed of Gift' for 2.23 acres to Central Baptist Church. Mr. Dunnavant constructed the foundation and main structure. Mr. Earl Pinchback completed the interior and finished work to the building. October 7, 1985, C.O. Dunnavant deeded 3 more acres to Central Baptist Church. Many local people in Lunenburg County have been assets to the growing of our church."[14]

On the Importance of Marketing in the Life of a Pastor

On the one hand, Falwell saw great importance in the ability to convey the message through direct marketing to help draw the community. On the other hand, he greatly valued the global external circle facilitated by mass media tools, which brought about the realization of his vision, as stated in his speech at the church in Antioch. The idea of footwork to engage the local community appears in many testimonials, some of which were previously mentioned. However, in this context, it is important to mention field work testimonials, including knocking on doors and creating ripples of influence.

For example, the story of the establishment of Harvest Baptist Temple by the Gass brothers from the town of Danville, as reported:

> *In May of 1977, two men were finalizing their plans to start a church in the Rogue Valley. Pastor Bob and Pastor Mike had just graduated from seminary in Lynchburg, Virginia and were led of GOD to start an independent Baptist church in Medford, Oregon. After some deliberation and much prayer, Pastor Bob and Pastor Mike named the new church Harvest Baptist Temple. This name would convey their mission of starting a soul-winning church! The first service took place on June 19, 1977 at the Holiday Inn Convention Center. Sunday school started at 9:45 a.m. and worship at 11:00 a.m. God blessed with 35 people in attendance. Each week,*

---

13 "How It Started," available at: https://www.eppingbiblechurch.org/copy-of-what-we-believe, accessed March 1, 2022.
14 "Church History," available at: http://www.centralvictoriava.com/91412.html, accessed March 1, 2022.

Pastor Bob and Pastor Mike knocked on thousand doors of homes in the Rogue Valley, inviting folks to church! As a result of their efforts, the church grew and it soon became evident that a new location would be needed to accommodate the growing congregation. About a month later, Harvest Baptist Church moved from the Holiday Inn to the Girl Scout Center across from the newly constructed North Medford High School. This building held about 75 people plus room for a nursery. GOD blessed mightily as the pastors continued to knock on doors during the daylight hours, and visit people in the evenings. The church was officially organized on August 14, 1977, with 100 people in attendance and seventy signing the newly drafted constitution. Harvest Baptist Temple was officially born.[15]

Another case of aggressive recruitment of neighborhood residents, which later translated into fundraising through the sale of securities, is demonstrated in the story of New Life Church, planted by Pastor Ronald Riggins:

In the fall of 1975, Ronald Gene Riggins, a native of Atlanta, Georgia, who had just completed his training at Lynchburg Baptist College (now known as Liberty University), was seeking the Lord's direction for a place of service. After an extensive period of prayer and exploration, an invitation was received from a gentleman to come to New Cumberland, Pennsylvania and start a church [...] By knocking on doors and other forms of advertisements, the first service was announced. Would anyone come? Yes, 21 people came for Sunday School, 42 to the Morning Worship Service, and 25 came back for the Evening Service. Thus, was born an infant church [...] From the very beginning the Lord provided both people and finances. Within a month the church was able to support its Pastor. On February 8, 1976 the church was officially organized with Dr. Jerry Falwell as its guest speaker. At that time, 51 people became charter members. For four months the church met in the old Fairview Township building until it went up for sale [...] On April 3, 1977 the church purchased its [...] present property of over 11 acres. After completion of a successful bond program, construction of a new building was begun.[16]

Falwell understood the importance of using mass media to reach people's hearts and was even quoted as saying, "A pastor has to be media-savvy if he's going to reach everybody. I don't mean to be ugly and harsh, but to be forthright and candid. And the result is that people that don't like you start listening."[17] As someone who led the importance of adapting the church to

---

15 HOW IT ALL STARTED..., hbtmedford.org, available at: https://hbtmedford.org/our-story, accessed March 1, 2022.
16 "History," available at: nlcfamily.org/about-us/history/, accessed March 1, 2022.
17 Andrew L. Johns, *A Companion to Ronald Reagan* (Hoboken, NJ: John Wiley & Sons, 2015), 211.

mass media, we find the various interpretations given by pastors to social media tools in the digital age. For example, Pastor Ryan Johnson and his wife Megan planted New City Church in Lawrenceville, Georgia, from scratch in 2015. The New City Church website includes an audio library of the Covenant called "Genesis," featuring dozens of chapters in which Johnson speaks to more than 10,000 followers on Facebook.[18] Pastors' ability to communicate with their congregations in the modern era has become an integral part of their daily work. For example, the richness of operation of 10 social media platforms, targeting different age groups, such as TikTok and Instagram for the younger audience, and more traditional tools like Facebook, Twitter, and YouTube, with significant and engaged followings, is the twenty-first-century equivalent of the color TV studio revolution that Paul Crouch established in the early 1970s at Liberty University. In total, Dr. Gabriel Powell holds tens of thousands of followers who follow his church and his personal platforms.[19] The creativity of modern church planters establishes direct connections with the audience of devotees with a particular emphasis on visibility, such as North Star Church in Kennesaw, Georgia, which has an App that broadcasts live video content to mobile devices. Mike Linch, who planted the church in 1997, has developed an impressive ability to transmit content and live broadcasts from a studio.[20] Mike testifies about the path he took on his special website, where he records guests in programs broadcasted to thousands of his followers on social media: "I have the most amazing family and work in the world [...] I am married to my best friend Ann, whom I met in 1991 at Liberty University."[21] In an interview with him titled "How to Connect with the Community," it was written that "Mike shares how his church became a center of activity in the community. By building a bridge from the church to the community, his team works hard to bring information to people. He explains how church leaders can be active in the community and teach others how they can also be influential leaders."[22]

---

18 "Messages," available at: Messages – New City Church (newcitychurchatl.org), accessed March 1, 2022.
19 Encounter Atlanta, available at: https://solo.to/encounteratlanta?fbclid =IwAR03FY6AB_m9ig0u7FIut2U8PHdlVrBUZSgCWqYjnxy5JV1n5Em4I 2HMK9o, accessed March 1, 2022.
20 App – Northstar Church – GA (subsplash.com).
21 "About," available at: About – NorthStar Church | Kennesaw, GA, accessed March 1, 2022.
22 "Episode 11: Connecting the Church to the Community," available at: Church Outreach & Connecting to Your Community | The Ship Podcast (injoystewardship .com), accessed March 1, 2022.

Falwell's famous paraphrase used to describe the circles of influence of a pastor, when he establishes a local community, from which he can later spread to other churches in the immediate, medium, and distant vicinities, brought theoretical thinking into action. For example, in the case of Rooted Church, founded by Pastor Rodney Rambo:

> *At late summer 2014 a small group of families began gathering together to pray and dream of planting a church in Northwest Arkansas. After a year of praying, planning, and meeting together, that small group of families began gathering weekly for worship. In late 2015, Rooted Church started gathering informally on Sunday evenings in the Johnson Baptist Fellowship building. After a season of sharing a space, Johnson Fellowship decided to join with Rooted Church and in turn, graciously gave their building to this new gospel work. On January 3rd, 2016 Rooted Church was officially founded. A short time later, on August 13th, 2017, we commissioned and sent one of our Missional Communities out to plant Rooted Church (SWMO) in Joplin, Mo. Since those early days, our story continues to unfold as we seek to reach NWA, Joplin, and see more churches planted across our region and the world.*[23]

Notable emphasis was placed by Falwell on promoting integration within disadvantaged neighborhoods, particularly the African American community, as a focus of the university named "Liberty." *The Fundamentalist* newspaper presented in the first issue of 1987 the first conference held at Liberty University regarding the urban spread of churches among young leadership. The main presenter at the conference was African American, Pastor John Perkins, founder of the Voice of Calvary Ministries organization, who specialized in evangelizing the black community since 1962. According to the organization's website, since its establishment in 1975, it has recruited over 30,000 volunteers from diverse cultural, ethnic, and racial backgrounds to live among West Jackson, Mississippi residents. Young leaders from all races attended the conference with the goal of increasing faith-based activity in African American community centers. Perkins highlighted the importance of the three Rs at the conference. The first R stands for *Relocation*, which is essentially the decision to establish a community where there is a need for spiritual leadership among Black communities. These can be areas or urban neighborhoods where there is an African American population in need of spiritual guidance, as well as in remote countries or districts where there is a lack of trained ministers to spread the gospel. The second R is *Reconciliation*, which occurs between individuals and between the leader and followers. The

---

23 "The Story of Rooted Church," available at: https://www.rootedchurch.com/our-story1.html, accessed March 1, 2022.

third R is the need for *Redistribution* of knowledge, resources, time, talent, and wealth where they are needed. His deputy, Lem Tucker, added that "the goal of the conference is actually connection. People come here from both sides of the racial and cultural divide. Usually, people gather according to these characteristics, but this conference allows us to meet and talk." According to the article, the conference brought together more than 6,000 students and staff who participated in thinking and exploring new options. The way in which these students are allowed to participate is through a connection during the summer break by working in churches in such areas. This program was created to plant churches, and generate conferences and introductions. Students studying for a degree in urban religious development receive academic accreditation for their practical experience in churches during the summer.[24]

A great current example can be found in the case of African American Pastor Ken (Kenneth) Richardson, a Liberty graduate. In March 2014, Ken and his wife, Victoria, packed up their home in North Carolina and moved to a missionary house in the suburbs of Philadelphia, Pennsylvania. In August 2015, "GOD called" Ken and Victoria to plant a church and provide holistic services in South Philadelphia's Wilson Park community. Wilson Park is a public housing neighborhood in South Philadelphia designed for families and seniors, with development properties consisting of high-rise and low-rise buildings, with a total of 727 units ranging in size from one to four bedrooms. After the couple received the call to plant a church in South Philadelphia, they were told that it would be very difficult to gain the community's trust, let alone access their facilities. On Tuesday, August 11, 2015, the couple knocked on the door of the housing manager and were immediately answered. In that autumn, the couple began to pray and serve in the community. It quickly became clear that the couple was in the right place, but there was a need for a place to gather for worship and fellowship. In June 2016, a lease contract was signed for a building, and renovations began. On July 10, 2016, the first prayer meeting was held, during which two women received Jesus. "The following week, another decision was made for Jesus, and the three of them were baptized in our third church service […] GOD continues to expand the borders of the Neighborhood Church with many church ministries in Kenya, Africa. We are now one church in six locations: Neighborhood Church—Philadelphia, Pennsylvania (USA), Neighborhood Church—Igar Town (Kenya, Africa), Neighborhood Church—Sangera (Kenya, Africa),

---

24 Angela Elwell Hunt, "First Urban Summit Held at LU," *The Fundamentalist Journal* 6, no. 1 (1987): 61, available at: https://digitalcommons.liberty.edu/cgi/viewcontent.cgi?article=1003&context=fun_87, accessed November 29, 2020.

Neighborhood Church—Mgena (Kenya, Africa), Neighborhood Church—Kiagware (Kenya, Africa), and Neighborhood Church—Riteke (Kenya, Africa). In addition, GOD provided an opportunity to offer training to pastors and leaders in Kenya, Africa, and India."[25]

The Importance of Israel in the Daily Lives of Liberty University Graduates Who Lead Churches

As described and outlined in the methodology section, an email was sent to those pastors whose email addresses could be located, requesting their participation in an online survey that included several short questions about their and their communities' perceptions toward Israel. Their answers offered a glimpse into the daily operations of those sent by Liberty University and how Israel is prioritized among the communities they serve. The questions were identical for everyone, and the answers were condensed to understand the pastors' approach to their community in the context of Israel. This section is the qualitative questionnaire in which the different responses were interwoven to understand the central importance of Israel in the agenda of the Liberty University pastors and how it is communicated to their congregations.

Question: Did Israel serve as a significant topic discussed during your studies at Liberty University?

Jeff Swart, an expert Liberty University church planter, said: "As a student at Liberty, I was very aware of Dr. Jerry Falwell, Dr. Elmer Towns, Dr. Harold Wilmington, and the University's pro-Israel stance. I was aware of their pro-Israel viewpoint through hearing them speak on the issue, their libraries, and their statements to the media."[26] Pastor Edward Cantu adds, "I definitely remember leaders like Dr. Falwell and Pastor John Hagee discussing the need for America's support of Israel. I'm sure it had some influence on me and my

---

25 "History," available at: https://www.theneighborhoodchurch.net/history, accessed March 1, 2022.
26 Kobby Barda, "Interview with Jeff Swart, Specialist in Church Planting from Liberty University," available on us-israel.org.il at: https://us-israel.org.il/2022/02/18/%d7%a8%d7%90%d7%99%d7%95%d7%9f-%d7%a2%d7%9d-jeff-swart-%d7%9e%d7%95%d7%9e%d7%97%d7%94-%d7%9c%d7%a9%d7%aa%d7%99%d7%9c%d7%aa-%d7%9b%d7%a0%d7%a1%d7%99%d7%95%d7%aa-%d7%9e%d7%90%d7%95%d7%a0%d7%99%d7%91/, retrieved on February 22, 2022.

developing stance on our relationship."²⁷ Pastor Keith Gardner of First Free Will Baptist Church said,

> *During my studies at Liberty University, I had the opportunity to travel to and visit Israel on several occasions and received credits for international studies. The information I learned from my visits to Israel reinforced my deep appreciation for Israel's sovereignty as a nation. It was clear to me as a student that Israel was still GOD's chosen people. For Americans, especially American Christians, there was a responsibility to support Israel and stand by Israel regardless of how it was perceived by other countries. I greatly appreciate Israel's struggle for independence and GOD's providence in preserving Israel's history. I saw in the Old Testament the historical documentation of Israel.²⁸*

> *Question: After graduation, did you work to strengthen your knowledge about Israel? Do you feel it is something you did for the benefit of your community?*

Pastor Wayne Kuenzle spoke about strengthening knowledge for the community:

> *My preaching and teaching since 1979 have focused on reaching those who listen with the hope of the message of Jesus Christ. Jesus was a Jew in faith, and perfect practice of Judaism in the context of Israel and its past and present history, was critical. My message to people I knew and loved was to conveying the message of the gospel and my love for Israel. GOD has given me a full life to tell the story of the gospel, and a big part of that is the necessity to support Israel from then until now. I led two groups from my sphere of influence on trips to Israel, and they all came back with a stronger recognition of the importance of Israel and the need for support from the United States.*

He continues to describe his activities with fellow believers: "We talked with the community about Israel. We believe that we have a responsibility to pray

---

27 Kobby Barda, "Interview with REV. Edward E. Cantu from the Family Worship Centre," us-israel.org.il, available at: https://us-israel.org.il/2022/02/16/%d7%a8%d7%90%d7%99%d7%95%d7%9f-%d7%a2%d7%9d-rev-edward-e-cantu-%d7%9e%d7%9b%d7%a0%d7%a1%d7%99%d7%99%d7%aa-family-worship-center/, retrieved on February 22, 2022.

28 Kobby Barda, "Interview with Pastor Keith Gardner from the First Free Will Baptist Church," available at: https://us-israel.org.il/2022/02/15/%D7%A8%D7%90%D7%99%D7%95%D7%9F-%D7%A2%D7%9D-%D7%94%D7%A4%D7%A1%D7%98%D7%95%D7%A8-keith-gardner-%D7%9E%D7%9B%D7%A0%D7%A1%D7%99%D7%99%D7%AA-first-free-will-baptist-church-%D7%91-28-%D7%9C%D7%99%D7%95/, accessed February 22, 2022.

for the peace of Jerusalem as it is written in the book of Psalms. We encouraged and led our people on educational tours to Israel."²⁹

Pastor Swart also answered that question:

> *I feel that I have had a part in my opportunities to speak in various churches and gatherings of church organizations. I have spoken hundreds of times about the fact that Israel was, is, and will always be GOD's chosen people. I surveyed the messages that I shared around the world (in 70 countries) in the past year, and discovered that I have spoken more than 12,000 times, and 20% of these messages are significantly or minimally related to Israel. Handwritten messages of these messages have been distributed to thousands of people over the past 45 years and have often been published in church newspapers. I have led four tours in Israel, taking more than 120 people with me to introduce others to the wonders of the Jewish nation and people.*³⁰

Pastor Keith Hudson lists the religious and political reasons for his support of Israel, as he presented to his devotees: "I have consistently spoken about our commitment to stand with Israel. First, they are our strong allies in covenant, second, they exist in the commandment of GOD, and third, GOD has promised blessings to those who bless the children of Abraham."³¹

The importance and centrality of Israel, including in his role as a military chaplain, also arose in the responses given by Pastor Charles Mallory: "First, I would say that I am 'pro-Israel' and have consistently advocated for the chosen people of GOD, during my tenure as a pastor in various churches across 12 different states here in the United States, including during my time as a military chaplain [...] I would classify myself as 'pro-Israeli' and active in supporting the Jewish people and the flag with its traditions and holidays."³²

Pastor Robert (Bob) Fritch spoke of the importance of a pastor's personal connection, created as a result of visiting Israel and a sense of commitment. He is the founder of the Watchmen for Zion Ministries organization, operating

---

29 Kobby Barda, Interview with Wayne Kuenzle, available at: https://us-israel.org.il/2020/07/26/%d7%a8%d7%90%d7%99%d7%95%d7%9f-%d7%a2%d7%9d-%d7%94%d7%90%d7%91-wayne-kuenzle-%d7%9e%d7%99%d7%95%d7%9d-%d7%94-24-7-2020/, accessed February 22, 2022.
30 Ibid., interview with Swart.
31 Kobby Barda, Interview with Pastor David Keith Hudson from FBC Hayden church, available at: https://us-israel.org.il/2022/02/16/%d7%a8%d7%90%d7%99%d7%95%d7%9f-%d7%a2%d7%9d-%d7%a4%d7%a1%d7%98%d7%95%d7%a8-david-kaith-hudson-%d7%9e%d7%9b%d7%a0%d7%a1%d7%99%d7%99%d7%aa-fbc-hayden/. The article was not accessible as of February 22, 2022.
32 Kobby Barda, Interview with Charles Mallory, available at: https://us-israel.org.il/2022/02/18/%d7%a8%d7%90%d7%99%d7%95%d7%9f-%d7%a2%d7%9d-charles-mallory/, retrieved on February 22, 2022.

to make Israel's significance accessible through explaining it to Evangelical believers: "My support for Israel was more of a divine thing that happened to me after my first visit there in 1976, where I saw the land, and its people entered my heart."[33]

Finally, Pastor Dave Earley mentioned: "We talked to the community about Israel and addressed it. We believe that it is our responsibility to pray for the peace of Jerusalem as written in the book of Psalms. We encouraged our people to go on educational trips to Israel, led by myself."[34]

> *Question: With regard to political involvement, do you remember receiving candidates for various positions and encouraging your community to explain the importance of the relationship between Israel and the United States through prayer, conversations with such representatives, and hosting candidates or politicians in the church?*

Paster Gardner talked about the connection between love for Israel and political motivation: "One of the topics that I emphasize is the relationship that GOD has with the Jewish people and the covenant promises of the Bible. These covenant promises of GOD have implications in the international arena (hence the stunning victory in the Six-Day War of 1967 and the establishment of Israel as a nation in 1948)."[35]

Pastor Swart talked about political activism: "I went to the state legislature and spoke on behalf of several issues, including the sovereign right of Israel to exist. I also spoke privately with numerous national and state legislators and encouraged the pro-Israel stance." [36]

Fostering activism is also a part of Pastor Kuntzle's role, as he notes: "I encouraged our community to call or write to senators and the president to move the US embassy to Jerusalem. I don't know how many actually did, but the fact is that the embassy was eventually moved."[37]

---

33 Kobby Barda, Interview with Rev. Robert Fritch from "Watchmen for Zion Ministries," us-israel.org.il, available at: https://us-israel.org.il/2022/02/16/%d7%a8%d7%90%d7%99%d7%95%d7%9f-%d7%a2%d7%9d-rev-robert-fritch-%d7%9e-watchmen-zion-ministries/, retrieved on February 22, 2022.
34 Kobby Barda, The Story of Dave Early, available at: https://us-israel.org.il/2020/12/02/%d7%a1%d7%99%d7%a4%d7%95%d7%a8%d7%95-%d7%a9%d7%9c-%d7%94%d7%9b%d7%95%d7%9e%d7%a8-%d7%94%d7%93%d7%a8-%d7%93%d7%99%d7%99%d7%91-%d7%90%d7%a8%d7%9c%d7%99/, retrieved on February 22, 2022.
35 Ibid., Interview with Pastor Keith Gardner from the First Free Will Baptist Church.
36 Ibid., Interview with Jeff Swart, Specialist in Church Planting from Liberty University.
37 Ibid., Interview with Wayne Kuenzle.

Question: Do you remember if you or your community voiced your opinion on the recognition of Jerusalem as the Capital of Israel?

Swart talks about his commitment to recognizing Jerusalem: "Yes, I remember the topic well and spoke publicly about Jerusalem being the eternal capital of Israel. I wrote letters to my fellow congressmen and personally spoke to them about it. The issue of Israel's right to the land and its capital Jerusalem, not Tel Aviv, are issues that I am very passionate about!"[38]

Kuenzle talks about his visit to Jerusalem at a young age as a deep consciousness-raiser:

We talked a lot about moving our embassy to Jerusalem, both in my circles of influence and as part of the material taught on the vital importance of the United States' position for Israel. My opinion is that Israel's capital should always be Jerusalem. Here, King David conquered the land for the temple, and his son Solomon built the temple [...] We visited Israel for the first time, I believe, in 1983. I was then a younger pastor and returned to my church with so many wonderful stories. We went with a non-denominational group, but my wife and I extended our trip by four days to stay in Israel, revisit some of the places we visited on the tour, and try to explore new places. It made such a big change in my life and ministry. The tour to Israel opened up a new perspective on the meaning of Israel for Americans and the world. Since then, I have taught and preached about GOD with a much greater understanding.[39]

---

38 Ibid., Interview with Jeff Swart, Specialist in Church Planting from Liberty University.
39 Ibid., Interview with Wayne Kuenzle.

Chapter 8

FINDINGS AND DISCUSSION

The Republican primary candidate for the 2016 elections, Donald Trump, arrived at Liberty University on January 18, 2016, one week before the first primaries in Iowa. He was introduced to the students by Jerry Falwell Jr., the university's president and son of Jerry Falwell Sr., who followed in his father's footsteps and echoed Reagan's visit to the campus in 1980.[1] During the speech, where Trump was portrayed by the popular conservative broadcaster Sean Hannity as the "defender of Christianity," the candidate pledged to defend believers in the United States and around the world.[2] In that same speech, Trump explicitly responded to the dangers of the nuclear deal with Iran and even vowed to cancel it. The support he received from Falwell Jr. on the eve of the first primaries held in Iowa on February 1, 2016, was of significant value. Falwell Jr.'s political stance and support of Trump were extensively discussed in the American media, mainly in terms of the damage such support could have on Republican Senator Ted Cruz from Texas, whose father was an Evangelical pastor and should have received this portion of the Republican Party voters in the primaries. "This support [for Trump, K.B.] is a blow to Ted Cruz, less than a week before the primaries in Iowa, in which he needed the support of conservative Christians."[3] Trump highly appreciated the support he received from Falwell Jr., and on January 30, 2016, at a rally before the first primaries in Iowa, when Falwell stood beside him on stage, Trump boasted at a Sabbath rally in Davenport, where Falwell introduced him, "'Now I'm leading with the evangelicals,' and to be honest, I think

---

1 Falwell Jr. was ousted from his position as university president after a sex scandal in which he was involved with his wife and a pool boy who had worked at a hotel they owned was leaked to the media in August 2020.
2 Trump on Political Correctness and Christianity, available at: https://www.youtube.com/watch?v=gNao_WOjKb4, accessed February 22, 2022.
3 Jessica Taylor, "Trump Nabs Endorsement of a Top Evangelical Leader," *NPR*, January 26, 2016, available at https://www.npr.org/2016/01/26/464435834/trump-nabs-endorsement-of-top-evangelical-leader, accessed November 29, 2021.

that was the amazing spirit and support of Jerry."⁴ At Trump's proclamation convention before the Republican Committee, Falwell Jr. spoke about the commitments he received from candidate Trump that related to his father's legacy: "In 1984, my father, Jerry Falwell, stood at this convention before the proclamation of Ronald Reagan's candidacy and led a prayer, after which Reagan won the election by a landslide. Over 30 years later, I stand here, praying that history will repeat itself and bring Donald Trump's election [...] Since 2007, Liberty University has become the largest and most prosperous Christian university in the world [...] A vote for Trump is a vote against Iran, which threatens to reach nuclear weapons [and destroy Israel, K.B]."⁵

On June 21, 2016, candidate Trump decided to establish a body called the "Evangelical Executive Advisory Board," which served as an advisory body to the president on matters related to the core concerns of the Evangelical community in the United States, a community that was extremely important to Trump. In an interview with him, Johnnie Moore, who was the personal aide to Falwell Sr. and Deputy Vice President of Communication at Liberty University, explained what happened behind the scenes of that initiative: "When Trump asked Paula [Paula White, an evangelical TV personality] to organize the committee, Paula called Tim Clinton, who is the president of the Association of Christian Counselors, and a graduate of Liberty, and Clinton called me. It can be determined that two out of the first three organizers of the advisory body are graduates of Liberty University."⁶ Trump himself announced the establishment of that body on June 21, 2016, in a statement to the media that read: "Today, the campaign of Donald J. Trump announced the formation of a new advisory council that convened to provide advisory support to Mr. Trump on issues important to Evangelicals and other people of faith in America [...] Members of the council will meet regularly. Certain members of the advisory council will be exclusively responsible for managing Mr. Trump's private meeting with hundreds of established Christian lead-

---

4 Jay Bouchard, "Christianity on Stage in Iowa: Jerry Falwell Jr. Joins Trump for Weekend Rallies," *Medill Report*, January 31, 2016, available at: https://news.medill.northwestern.edu/chicago/christianity-on-stage-in-iowa-jerry-falwell-jr-joins-trump-for-weekend-rallies/, accessed November 29, 2021.

5 "Jerry Falwell Jr., President of Liberty University, Speaks at the Republican National Convention," available at: https://www.youtube.com/watch?v=5YcOz2J7vuE, accessed November 29, 2021.

6 Kobby Barda, "Interview with Johny Moore," https://us-israel.org.il/, available at: https://us-israel.org.il/2022/02/21/%d7%a8%d7%90%d7%99%d7%95%d7%9f-%d7%a9%d7%a0%d7%a2%d7%a9%d7%94-%d7%a2%d7%9d-%d7%92%d7%99%d7%9e%d7%99-%d7%9e%d7%95%d7%a8/, accessed February 22, 2022.

ers that were announced today in New York." In the statement, Trump was quoted as saying: "I have such tremendous respect and admiration for this group, and I look forward to continuing to talk about the issues important to Evangelicals and all Americans, and the common-sense solutions I will implement when I am President."[7] It is no coincidence that so many Liberty University alumni appeared on Trump's advisory list. On September 5, 2017, after Trump entered office, the *National Catholic Reporter* ran an article titled "Key players in Trump's evangelical advisory panel" and analyzed the list of 17 members on the panel. Four members from that influential list are Liberty University alumni, including the son of Jerry Falwell Sr., who then served as the president of Liberty University, Jerry Falwell Jr., the pastor and personal aide to Falwell Sr., Johnnie Moore, the president of the Council for National Policy Tony Perkins, and the president of the National Hispanic Christian Leadership Conference, Tim Clinton.[8] The significant number of approximately 23.5 percent of Liberty University graduates, from a list of advisors to the president, constitutes the "whisperers in his ear" on issues that have become the agenda of President Trump's presidency, particularly with regards to the "evangelical base." When asked about the importance of Jerusalem to President Trump, as a result of the advisory council's agenda, born out of Falwell's vision to influence American politics through the grassroots movement, Moore explained that

> *Zionist Christianity existed before Falwell, but the intersection of Zionist Christianity and local American politics, which makes all the difference, did not exist before Falwell. He created the infrastructure, and we are all his 'Timothys', continuing his legacy. The spirit of Falwell Sr. has loomed over all of us [...] He has two great legacies, one of which is the establishment of Liberty University, and the other, which is his greatest legacy, is the issue of Zionist Christian politics, and the system that he created that was deep and stable between Israeli heads of state and Jerry Falwell Sr [...] Immediately after the inauguration, we were in a meeting at the White House, Vice President Pence came in and invited us to the President. The Vice President*

---

7 "Press Release – Trump Campaign Announces Evangelical Executive Advisory Board," www.presidency.ucsb.edu, available at: https://www.presidency.ucsb.edu/documents/press-release-trump-campaign-announces-evangelical-executive-advisory-board, accessed November 29, 2021.

8 Adelle M. Banks, "The Key Evangelical Players on Trump's Advisory Board," ncronline.org, available at: https://www.ncronline.org/news/key-evangelical-players-trumps-advisory-board, accessed November 29, 2021.

took us to the Roosevelt Room, and in our first conversation, what came up? The issue of Jerusalem and its importance.[9]

On August 17, 2020, the American president spoke at a rally held in Oshkosh, Wisconsin, and told his supporters, "We moved the United States Embassy to the capital of Israel, Jerusalem," and added, "It is for the Evangelicals. You know, the Evangelicals love it more than the Jews do. It's incredible. It's true. But we did it. We did it. And the Golan Heights, don't forget the Golan Heights."[10]

This statement by President Trump is the connecting thread between Falwell's 1971 vision of building an academic institution that would spread Christianity and its values throughout the United States and moving the U.S. embassy to Jerusalem by creating an effective and significant political force. The ability to connect the dots over time, with the starting point in the summer of 1971 with 141 students traveling to Israel so they could "get a feel" for the importance of the land of the Bible in daily life, through the vision of planting 5,000 new churches in the United States by those emissaries ("the Timothies") nurtured by Falwell, so they could influence local American politics. The tools used were legislation, speeches, and decisions on conservative issues in general, and the issue of Israel in particular, that could grow, through planting churches and communities, to millions of politically engaged people at all levels of American politics. This ability to establish a university, has grown to its current size, with millions of graduates and hundreds of thousands of enrolled students, alongside the integration of graduates into the political mainstream, media, religion, social and business spheres. The push for moving the embassy to Jerusalem began in the 1980s, through legislation in 1995, and culminated in two recent key points: First, in January 2016, when Jerry Falwell Jr., the crown prince of Trump's Republican Party candidacy for the presidency, touted and promoted the move in congressional hearings, following in his father's footsteps, who had done so throughout the 1980s; Second, in Trump's decision to move the embassy from Tel Aviv to Jerusalem, pleasing the Evangelical base that Falwell helped galvanize. Connecting these dots revealed the intersection between vision on the one hand, and ability, on the other hand—leading a significant change in the foreign relations map of the United States.

---

9 Ibid., Interview with Johnnie Moore.
10 Tovah Lazaroff, "Trump: We Moved the Capital of Israel to Jerusalem for the Evangelicals," jpost.com, August 18, 2020, available at: https://www.jpost.com/american-politics/trump-we-moved-the-capital-of-israel-to-jerusalem-for-the-evangelicals-639034, accessed November 29, 2021.

Summary and Recommendations for Future Research

This study aimed to examine the real-time influence of Falwell on American politics in the 1980s, but with even greater intensity, more than 50 years after the cornerstone was laid for Liberty University, to examine the future design capabilities of conservative politics in the United States. The ability to explore the infrastructure that was laid as part of its vision to create political power through pastoral education for the planting of communities and the construction of circles of influence in the community in general and the support for Israel, in particular was demonstrated through the information about over 200 pastors and their organization, collected through intensive data-mining, which illustrates its methodology over the years in practice. On the other hand, by presenting the qualitative research data that dealt with Israel's centrality in the eyes of pastors, it was possible to get a glimpse into the daily lives of the communities established by those pastors who left the university to develop circles of influence.

In this context, regarding the church planting functions and congregations, the most remarkable and essential components should be emphasized: the media and the shaping of consciousness developed by Falwell, starting with the radio, then establishing a TV studio, and finally, distance studying via videotapes and the Internet. This process and Falwell's ability to harness communication to spread the grassroots movement could explain many processes nowadays in diverse domains. The centrality of such strategies as "church planting" or "community planting" substantially changed American political marketing strategy. It insists on utilizing the means of communication and shaping consciousness to impact not only political bureaucracy but mainly identity and social perception. In this case, it is not only about competition between political actors for support of their agendas but a fundamental change in the system of American political marketing that focuses on a fundamental shift in American social order and design. In this realm, much of the focus concentrated on changes in social identity and the functioning of Political candidates who can potentially change the current social order.

It is impossible to ignore the ongoing influence of the Evangelical movement on a wide range of issues, even 15 years after Falwell's death. Donald Trump's rise to power as the Evangelical movement's candidate, at the expense of Senator Cruz, a pastor's son, and Trump's choice of Mike Pence as his VP running mate and Mike Pompeo as Secretary of State—both of whom come from the same Evangelical community, demonstrate the power and importance of that political group, which embarked on its political quest during the 1970s. This grassroots movement, which raised several banners including the fight against abortions and the appointment of conservative judges, brought concern about Israel to the forefront of the political agenda based on the beliefs of those voters. A struggle that began in the 1980s in newspaper editorials, speeches before Congress, hearings, and finally legislation in 1995 to move the embassy to Jerusalem, was successful in completing the move of the embassy to Jerusalem on May 14, 2018.

It is no coincidence that all presidents until Trump, including Trump himself (in June 2017), signed the postponement of the embassy move from Tel Aviv to Jerusalem every six months. Donald Trump, who rode the wave of the Evangelical movement all the way to the White House, actually fulfilled the commitment that every presidential candidate until then was forced to violate. Donald Trump was aware that failure to move the embassy to Jerusalem would position that strong and influential political movement against him. Eventually, President Trump moved the embassy to Jerusalem and, as he himself testified, it was only for that community' sake.

A future study of Falwell's grassroots movement, founded through Liberty University, should address its impact on American politics, a subject not discussed in this work, especially on the issue of abortions. Analysis of the movement's levers of pressure implemented to overturn the *Roe v. Wade* decision, reversed by the current composition of the Supreme Court, will provide a better understanding on how the conservative movement acted to fulfill this core value in the activity of the Evangelical conservative movement.

Another topic that would be relevant for future study is a comparative examination of whether the activation method demonstrated through the data collected and the research methodology appeared among other pastors responsible for the establishment of academic institutions, such as Pat Robertson, who founded Regent University in Virginia, or Oral Roberts, who founded Oral Roberts University in Tulsa, Oklahoma. Was it unique to Falwell, or part of a broader trend of constructing grassroots movements through the training of pastors and their return to the community with a missionary and political vocation? In the context of Evangelical support for the State of Israel—a later movement, such as CUFI founded by John Hagee in 2004, is still considered relatively young from a historical perspective, but undoubtedly took part in President Trump's decision to move the embassy to Jerusalem and as such, it is worthy of future study in the appropriate historical time frame.

Finally, in recent years, there has been an apparent phenomenon of crowd contraction among Evangelicals and, simultaneously, a loosening of their connection to the State of Israel (especially Gen Z). A survey conducted in early 2023 by the Washington Research Institute PRRI, which examined religious beliefs in the United States, indicated a dramatic decline, nearly 40 percent, in the number of people identifying themselves as Evangelicals in less than two decades from ~23 percent of the total American population in 2006 to 13.6 percent in 2022. Ron Dermer, former Israeli ambassador to Washington, was quoted in May 2021, saying: "Israel should invest more in Evangelical Christians than it should in U.S. Jews. 25% of Americans are Evangelicals. U.S. Jews are more critical of Israel than the evangelicals." However, the idea that Israel can and should rely on the Evangelical community, even at the expense of American Jewry support, does not correspond with the significant changes this religious persuasion has undergone in the past two decades. Dermer's first argument that around one-quarter of Americans are Evangelicals (~80 million people) was valid in 2006. Since then, their numbers have shrunk to around 30 million, mainly living in distinct Republican (Red") states with less electoral influence. The second argument that Evangelicals are less critical of Israel compared to American Jewry is also far from accurate. A study conducted recently by Dr. Mordechai Inbari of UNCP University, who follows the Evangelical Gen Z, demonstrates that the support rate for Israel has dropped among young people aged 19–29 from 75 percent to 33 percent within two years. Thus, the trend among young Evangelicals "convenes" into the general one of American Gen Z's: Increased criticism of Israel and a significant increase in support for the Palestinian narrative. The automatic support given to Israel by the "divine promise," which was so crucial in the past, is much less significant in the eyes of the new generation of Evangelicals. Now, a new generation emerges who does not feel the same religious commitment of their parents to uncompromising support in Israel.

Thus, future research would have to examine the grassroots movement's resilience, whereby Israel has been considered the cornerstone of Evangelical community life, and the possibility of such support in the future, as part of the relationship between Israel and the United States, through a Zionist Christian movement.

BIBLIOGRAPHY

Primary Sources
Archives

Falwell Family Papers, The Jerry Falwell Library, Liberty University Archives.
LCN for church planting and pastoral care.
Archives Library Information Center (ALIC).
Pat Robertson Biographical, Political Resources & Ministry Activity at the Special Collections & Archives of Regent University.
The Congressional Record Index, Library of Congress.
The Jacob Rader Marcus center of the American Jewish Archives, MS-603: Rabbi Marc H. Tenenbaum Collection, 1945–1992. Series A: Writings and Addresses. 1947–1991.
Jimmy Carter Presidential Library & Museum.
Ronald Reagan Presidential Library & Museum.
George H. Bush Presidential Library & Museum.
George W. Bush Presidential Library & Museum.
Spencer Research Library, University of Kansas, Lawrence, KA.

Hebrew/Israeli Archive

Menachem Begin Archive
Israel State Archives
Ministry of Foreign Affairs
Office of the Prime Minister
Ministry of Tourism Library
The Knesset Archive
Central Bureau of Statistics Autobiographies

Autobiographies

Falwell, Jerry. *Building Dynamic Faith* (Nashville, TN: World Publishing Inc., 2005).
Falwell, Jerry. *Listen America!* (New York: Bantam Books, 1981).
Falwell, Jerry. *Strength for the Journey: An Autobiography* (New York: Simon & Schuster, 1987).

Literature:

Amstutz, Mark. *Evangelicals and American Foreign Policy* (New York: Oxford University Press, 2014).

Anderson, Irvine H. *Biblical Interpretation and Middle East Policy: The Promised Land, America, and Israel, 1917–2002* (Gainesville, FL: University Press of Florida, 2005).

Ariel, Yaakov. *Evangelizing the Chosen People: Missions to the Jews in America, 1880–2000* (Chapel Hill: University of North Carolina Press, 2000).

Beattie, Kirk J. *Congress and the Shaping of the Middle East* (New York: Seven Stories Press, 2015).

Blackstone, William E. *Jesus Is Coming* (Chicago: F.H. Revell, 1878).

Bowers, Morris Glen. *Israel: The 51st State: The Unspoken Foreign Policy of the United States of America* (Bloomington, IN: IUniverse, 2005).

Brenner, Michael. *In Search of Israel: The History of an Idea* (Princeton, NJ: Princeton University Press, 2018).

Brog, David. *Standing with Israel Why Christians Support the Jewish State* (Lake Mary, FL: Front Line, 2006).

Bromley, David G., and Anson D. Shupe. *New Christian Politics* (Macon, GA: Mercer University Press, 1988).

Browne, Blaine T. *Modern American Lives: Individuals and Issues in American History since 1945* (Armonk, NY: M.E. Sharpe, 2008).

Camerik, Gene. *The Second Coming* (Bloomington, IN: IUniverse, 2007).

Carenen, Caitlin. *The Fervent Embrace: Liberal Protestants, Evangelicals, and Israel* (New York: NYU Press, 2012).

Carlisle, Jamin Christopher. *A Dangerous Friendship: Jewish Fundamentalists and Christian Zionists in the Battle for Israel* (Master's Thesis, University of Tennessee, 2007).

Carpenter, Joel A. *Revive Us Again: The Reawakening of American Fundamentalism* (New York: Oxford University Press, 1997).

Curtiss, Richard H. *Stealth Pac's: How Israel's American Lobby Seeks to Control U.S. Middle East Policy* (Washington, DC: American Educational Trust, 1990).

Clark, Victoria. *Allies for Armageddon: The Rise of Christian Zionism* (New Haven, CT: Yale University Press, 2007).

Cohn-Sherbok, Dan. *The Politics of Apocalypse: The History and Influence of Christian Zionism* (Oxford: One World, 2006).

Crouse, Eric. *American Christian Support for Israel: Standing with the Chosen People, 1948–1975* (Minneapolis, MN: Lexington Books, 2014).

Cross, Brenton. *Southern Baptist and Expository Preaching: Biblical Interpretation, Values, and Politics in Twentieth-Century America* (Eugene, OR: Wipf and Stock Publishers, 2021).

Diamond, Sara. *Not by Politics Alone: The Enduring Influence of the Christian Right* (New York: Guilford Press, 2000).

Dochuk, Darren. *From Bible Belt to Sunbelt: Plain-Folk Religion, Grassroots Politics, and the Rise of Evangelical Conservatism* (New York: W. W. Norton, 2011).

Dowland, Seth. *Family Values and the Rise of the Christian Right* (Philadelphia: University of Pennsylvania Press, 2015).

D'Souza, Dinesh. *Falwell, Before the Millennium: A Critical Biography* (Washington, DC: Regnery Gateway, 1984).

Du Mez, Kristin Kobes. *Jesus and John Wayne: How White Evangelicals Corrupted a Faith and Fractured a Nation* (New York: Liveright Publishing, 2020).

Durbin, Sean. *Righteous Gentiles: Religion, Identity, and Myth in John Hagee's Christians United for Israel* (Boston, MA: Brill, 2018).

Durham, Martin. "The American Right and Israel." *The Political Quarterly* 82, no. 4 (2011): 609–617.

Evans, Mike. *The History of Christian Zionism: 2 Volumes* (Phoenix, AZ: Time Worthy Books, 2014).

Falwell, Macel. *Jerry Falwell: His Life and Legacy* (New York: Howard Books, 2008).

Farley, Jared A. *The Politicization of the American Evangelical Press, 1960–1981: A Test of the Ideological Theory of Social Movement Mobilization* (PhD diss., Miami University, 2006).

Findley, Paul. *They Dare to Speak Out: People and Institutions Confront Israel's Lobby* (Toronto: Lawrence Hill Books, 1985).

Fisher, Netanel. "The Fundamentalist Dilemma: Lessons from the Israeli Haredi Case." *International Journal of Middle East Studies* 48, no. 3 (2016): 531–49.

Flint, Betty Gail. *Thomas Road Baptist Church: A Study of the New Fundamentalism* (Dissertations, Theses, and Masters Projects, College of William & Mary – Arts & Sciences, 1978).

Flippen, J. Brooks. *Jimmy Carter, the Politics of Family, and the Rise of the Religious Right* (Athens, GA: The University of Georgia Press, 2011).

Fox, Richard W. *Reinhold Niebuhr: A Biography* (New York: Pantheon Books, 1985).

Garrison, David V. *Church Planting Movements: How GOD is Redeeming a Lost World* (Midlothian, VA: WIGTake Resources, 2004).

Ginsberg, Benjamin. *The Fatal Embrace: Jews and the State* (Chicago, IL: University of Chicago Press, 1993).

Goldman, Samuel. "GOD's Country: Christian Zionism in America." *Haney Foundation Series* (Philadelphia, PA: University of Pennsylvania Press, 2018).

Goldman, Samuel. *Zeal for Zion: Christians, Jews, & the Idea of the Promised Land* (Chapel Hill, NC: UNC Press Books, 2009).

Grzegorzewski, Mark G. *The Christian Zionist Lobby and U.S.-Israel Policy* (Graduate Theses and Dissertations. University of South Florida, 2010). https://scholarcommons.usf.edu/etd/3671/.

Hagee, John. *The Battle for Jerusalem* (San Antonio, TX: Thomas Nelson Inc., 2001).

Halsell, Grace. "Onward Christian Zionists." *Journal of Palestine Studies* 21, no. 3 (1992): 110–111.

Halsell, Grace, H. Halsell, and Allen Kathleen Hamilton. *In Their Shoes* (Fort Worth, TX: TCU Press, 1996).

Harding, Susan Friend. *The Book of Jerry Falwell: Fundamentalist Language and Politics* (Princeton, NJ: Princeton University Press, 2000).

Hasten, Hart N. *Shall Not Die! A Personal Memoir* (Jerusalem: Geffen Books, 2003).

Haynes, Jeffrey. *Handbook on Religion and International Relations* (Northampton, MA: Edward Elgar Publishing Inc., 2021).

Haynes, Stephen R. *Reluctant Witnesses: Jews and the Christian Imagination* (Louisville: Presbyterian Publishing Corporation, 1995).

Heidenry, John. *What Wild Ecstasy* (NY: Simon and Schuster, 1997).

Hertzke, Allen D. *Representing GOD in Washington: The Role of Religious Lobbies in the American Polity* (Knoxville, TN: University of Tennessee Press, 1988).

Hollis-Brusky, Amanda and Joshua C. Wilson. *Separate but Faithful, The Christian Right's Radical Struggle to Transform Law and Legal Culture* (New York: Oxford University Press, 2020).

Hummel, Daniel G. *Covenant Brothers: Evangelicals, Jews, and U.S.-Israeli Relations* (Philadelphia, PA: University of Pennsylvania Press, 2019).

Ice, Thomas. *The Case for Zionism: Why Christians Should Support Israel* (Green Forest, AR: New Leaf Publishing Group, 2017).

Isaac, Eli. "The Digital Revolution in the Geo-Technology and Geo-Geography Space: Background Article." *Horizons in Geography* (2018–2019): 172–189.

Kaell, Hillary. *Walking Where Jesus Walked, American Christians and Holy Land Pilgrimage* (New York: NYU Press, 2014).

Kalman, Laura. *Right Star Rising: A New Politics, 1974–1980* (New York: W. W. Norton & Company, 2010).

Kyle, Richard G. *Apocalyptic Fever: End-Time Prophecies in Modern America* (Eugene, OR: Wipf and Stock Publishers, 2012).

Lamport, Mark A. and George T. Kurian. *Encyclopedia of Christian Education-Vol.3* (Lanham, MD: Rowman & Littlefield, 2015).

Leeman, Richard W. and Bernard K. Duffy. *American Voices: An Encyclopedia of Contemporary Orators* (Westport, CT: Greenwood Publishing Group, 2005).

Link, William A. *Righteous Warrior: Jesse Helms and the Rise of Modern Conservatism* (New York: St. Martin's Press, 2008).

Lowe, George E. *Stalking the Antichrists (1965–2012) Volume 2* (Bloomington, IN: Xlibris Corporation, 2013).

Marsden, George M. *Fundamentalism and American Culture* (Oxford: Oxford University Press, 2006).

Marsden, George M. *Understanding Fundamentalism and Evangelicalism* (Grand Rapids, MI: William B. Eerdmans, 1991).

Marty, Martin E. and Frederick E. Greenspahn. *Pushing the Faith: Proselytism and Civility in a Pluralistic World* (Chestnut Ridge, NY: Crossroad, 1988).

Massing, Michael. *The Storm over the Israel Lobby* (New York Review of Books 53.10, 2006): 64.

McAlister, Melanie. *Epic Encounters: Culture, Media, and U.S. Interests in the Middle East since 1945* (Berkeley: University of California Press, 2001).

McDermott, Gerald R. *The New Christian Zionism: Fresh Perspectives on Israel and the Land* (Downers Grove, IL: IVP Academic, 2016).

McDonald, Becky Ann. *Falwell and Fantasy: The Rhetoric of a Religious and Political Movement* (PhD thesis, The Ohio State University, 1987).

Mearsheimer, John J. and Walt Stephen M. *The Israel Lobby and U.S Foreign Policy* (New York: Farrar, Straus, and Giroux, 2007).

Menendez, Albert J. *Religion at the Polls* (Philadelphia: Westminster Press, 1977).

Merkley, Paul C. *Christian Attitudes towards the State of Israel* (Montreal and Kingston: McGill-Queen's University Press, 2001).

Merkley, Paul Charles. *Christian Attitudes towards the State of Israel* (Montreal: McGill-Queens University Press, 2007).

Moen, Matthew C. *The Christian Right and Congress* (Tuscaloosa, AL: University Alabama Press, 1989).

Nederveen-Pieterse, Jan. "The History of a Metaphor: Christian Zionism and the Politics of Apocalypse / L'Histoire d'une métaphore: le sionisme chrétien ET la politique de l'apocalypse." *Archives Des Sciences Socials des Religions* 75 (1991): 75–103.

Neuhaus, Richard John. *The Naked Public Square: Religion and Democracy in America* (Grand Rapids, MI: William B. Eerdmans Publishing Company, 1984).

New, David S. *Holy War: The Rise of Militant Christian, Jewish and Islamic Fundamentalism* (Jefferson, NC: McFarland, 2002).
Olson, Laura R. and Paul A. Djupe. *Encyclopedia of American Religion and Politics* (New York: InfoBase Publishing, 2014).
Parr, Steve R. *Sunday School that Really Excels* (Grand Rapids, MI: Kergel Publications, 2013).
Ray, Vernon Oliver. *A Rhetorical Analysis of the Political Preaching of the Reverend Jerry Falwell: The Moral Majority Sermons, 1979 (Electric Church, Demagogue)* (PhD diss., Louisiana State University, 1985).
Rock, Stephen R. *Faith and Foreign Policy: The Views and Influence of U.S. Christians and Christian Organizations* (New York: Bloomsbury Publishing USA, 2011).
Roussos, Sotiris. *Religion and International Relations in the Middle East* (Basel: MDPI, 2020).
Ryan, Michael A. and Karolyn Kinane. *End of Days: Essays on the Apocalypse from Antiquity to Modernity* (Jefferson, NC: McFarland & Co., 2009).
Rubinstein, W.D. *The Left, the Right and the Jews* (New York: Routledge, 2016).
Schippers, Inez. *Politics in the Name of GOD – Christian Zionism, American Foreign Policy, and Israel* (Thesis Master American Studies – Utrecht University, 23 July 2007).
Schoenbaum, David. *The United States and the State of Israel* (New York: Oxford University Press, 1997).
Seliktar, Ofira. *Divided We Stand: American Jews, Israel, and the Peace Process* (Westport, CT: Greenwood Publishing Group, 2002).
Shapira, Anita. *Israel: A History* (Waltham, MA: Brandeis University Press, 2012).
Shilon, Avi. *Menachem Begin: A Life* (New Haven: Yale University Press, 2012).
Simon, Merrill. *Jerry Falwell and the Jews* (New York: Jonathan David Publishers, 1984).
Sizer, Stephen R. *Christian Zionism, Road Map to Armageddon* (Leicester: Inter-Varsity Press, 2006).
Sizer, Stephen R. *Christian Zionism: Road-map to Armageddon?* (Eugene, OR: Wipf and Stock Publishers, 2021).
Sizer, Stephen R. *The Promised Land: A Critical Investigation of Evangelical Christian Zionism in Britain and the United States of America since 1800* (Middlesex University PhD thesis, 2002).
Smillie, Dirk. *Falwell Inc.: Inside a Religious, Political, Educational, and Business Empire* (New York: St. Martin's Press, 2008).
Smith, Robert O. *More Desired than Our Own Salvation, The Roots of Christian Zionism* (New York: Oxford University Press, 2013).
Snider, William D. *Helms and Hunt. The North Carolina Senate Race* (Chapel Hill, NC: UNC Press, 1984).
Snowball, David. *Continuity and Change in the Rhetoric of the Moral Majority* (Santa-Barbara, CA: ABC-CLIO, 1991).
Spector, Stephen. *Evangelicals, and Israel: The Story of American Christian Zionism* (New York: Oxford University Press, 2009).
Steinberg, Alan J. *American Jewry and Conservative Politics: A New Direction* (Ann Arbor, MI: The University of Michigan Press, 1988).
Stewart, Caitlin. "Patriotism, National Identity, and Foreign Policy." *United States Foreign Policy and National Identity in the 21st Century* (Oxford Shire: Taylor & Francis, 2009).
Strober, Deborah H. "Israel at Sixty: An Oral History of a Nation Reborn." *Independence* (Kentucky: John Wiley & Sons, 2008).

Tadayeski, John Charles. *Evangelicals and the Republican Party: A Reinforcing Relationship for Israel* (Louisiana State University Master's Theses, 2005).

Tamney, Joseph B. *The Resilience of Christianity in the Modern World* (Albany, NY: SUNY Press, 1992).

Thomas, Michael. *American Policy toward Israel: The Power and Limits of Beliefs (LSE International Studies Series)* (London: Routledge, 2007).

Thomas, V. C. *The GOD Dilemma: To Believe or not to Believe* (Bloomington, IN: Xlibris Publishing, 2009).

Towns, Elmer. *Planting Reproducing Churches* (Shippensburg, PA: Destiny Image Publishers, 2018).

Towns, Elmer. *What's Right with the Church: A Manifesto of Hope Destiny Image Publishers* (Shippensburg, PA: Destiny Image, 2009).

Unger, Craig. *The Fall of the House of Bush: The Untold Story of How a Band of True Believers Seized the Executive Branch, Started the Iraq War, and Still Imperils America's Future* (New York: Scribner, 2007).

Wald, Kenneth D., and A. Calhoun-Brown. *Religion and Politics in the United States* (Lanham, MD: Rowman & Littlefield, 2014).

Weber, Timothy P. *On the Road to Armageddon: How Evangelicals Became Israel's Best Friend* (Grand Rapids, MI: Baker Academic, 2004).

Weddington, Sarah. *A Question of Choice* (Oakland, CA: The Feminist Press at CUNY, 1993).

Westover, Duke. *Wow! What a Ride: My Life and Journey with Jerry Falwell* (Alpharetta, GA: Carpenter's Press & Media, Inc, 2012).

Williams, Daniel K. *GOD's Own Party: The Making of the Christian Right* (New York: Oxford University Press, 2010).

Wilcox, Clyde. *Onward Christian Soldiers? The Religious Right in American Politics* (New York: Routledge, 2018).

Windt, Theodore Otto, Jr. "*A New Foreign Policy*": *President Jimmy Carter's Speech at Notre Dame, May 22, 1977.* A Paper Presented in Honor of Everett Lee Hunt, eric.ed.gov, 20 November 1989. Available at: https://files.eric.ed.gov/fulltext/ED314767.pdf accessed at June, 9, 2021.

Young, Neil J. *We Gather Together: The Religious Right and the Problem of Interfaith Politics* (New York: Oxford University Press, 2016).

Articles

Drozdíková, J. "History of the Future." In *Asian and African Studies* 16, no. 1 (2007): 81–101.

Finney, M.T. "Christian Zionism, the US and the Middle East: A Sketch and Brief Analysis." In Sandford, M., (ed.). *The Bible, Zionism and Palestine: The Bible's Role in Conflict and Liberation in Israel-Palestine.* Bible in Effect, 1 (Dunedin, New Zealand: Relegere Academic Press, 2016): 20–31.

Goldman, Shalom. "Christians and Zionism: A Review Essay." *American Jewish History* 93, no. 2 (2007): 245–260.

Hyser, Raymond M., and J. Chris Arndt. "The Christian Right's Call to Action." In *Voices of the American Past: Documents in U.S. History.* 5th ed. Vol. 2 (Boston, MA: Wadsworth Cengage Learning, 2011).

Kellstedt, Lyman. "The Falwell Issue Agenda: Sources of Support among White Protestant Evangelicals." *Research in the Social Scientific Study of Religion* 1 (1988): 68–92.

Miller, Paul D. "Evangelicals, Israel and US Foreign Policy." *Survival* 56, no. 1 (2014): 7–26.

Mouly, Ruth W. "Israel: Darling of the Religious Right." *Humanist* 42, no. 3 (1982): 5.

Price, James, and William Goodman. "Jerry Falwell, An Unauthorized Profile," cited in Grace Halsell, *Prophecy and Politics, Militant Evangelists on the Road to Nuclear War* (Westport, CT: Lawrence Hill, 1986).

Rynhold, Jonathan. "Evangelicals and Christian Zionism: Standing with Israel." Chapter In *The Arab-Israeli Conflict in American Political Culture* (Cambridge: Cambridge University Press, 2015): 95–115.

Shindler, Colin. "Likud and the Christian Dispensationalists: A Symbiotic Relationship." *Israel Studies* 5, no. 1 (2000): 153–182.

Varisco, Daniel Martin. "Evangelicals and Israel: The Story of American Christian Zionism." *The Middle East Journal* 63, no. 2 (2009): 330–331.

Wagner, Donald E. *Evangelicals and Israel: Theological Roots of a Political Alliance* (The Christian Century 115.30. 1998): 120–123.

Wagner, Donald E. "Evangelicals and Israel: Theological Roots of a Political Alliance." *The Christian Century* (November 4, 1998): 1020–1026.

Wagner, Donald E. "For Zion's Sake." *Middle East Report* 223 (2002): 52–57.

Wagner, Donald E. "The Alliance between Fundamentalist Christians and the Pro-Israel Lobby: Christian Zionism in US Middle East Policy." *Holy Land Studies* 2, no. 2 (2004): 163–187.

Wallis, Jim. *The Soul of Politics: A Practical and Prophetic Vision for Change* (San Fransico: HarperSan Francisco, 2006).

Wigoder, Geoffrey. "The Churches and the State of Israel." *The Month* 32, no. 1 (1999): 3.

APPENDICES

Appendix A—Data of Liberty Graduates Who Planted Churches

*Excel spreadsheet data can be accessed on the blog.[1]

#	Name of Grad	source	Name of church	address	City	Stat	Year establish	facebo	Attend	Current Attendence
2	Jeff Clark	Church planting Mag. 1981	Victory Baptist Church	1170 US Route 202	Winthrop	ME	Nov. 17, 1976	5334	57	130
3	Billy Price	Church planting Mag. 1981	Faith Baptist Church	311 Jackson Drive	Covington	VA	August 3, 1975	1915	28	
4	Don Reynolds	Church planting Mag. 1981	Calvary Baptist Church	1120 Market Street	Denton	MD	1974	364	8	
5	David M. Rhodenhizer	Church planting Mag. 1981	Calvary Road Baptist Church	6811 Beulah St.	Alexandria	VA	1979	1173		
6	Daren Ritchey	Church planting Mag. 1981	Cornerstone Baptist Church	930 FREDERICK STREET	CUMBERLAND	MD		1047		
7	Ronland Sanding	Church planting Mag. 1981	Highland Baptist Church	27476 HAYWARD BLVD.	HAYWARD	CA		151		
8	James Shriver	Church planting Mag. 1981	Calvary Baptist Church	308 McClellandtown Rd.	Uniontown	PA	1979	966		
9	Jhon Wesley Price	Church planting Mag. 1981	Temple Baptist Church	15157 Inspiration Dr.	Abingdon	VA	1975	15		
10	Leslie Smith	Church planting Mag. 1981	Victory Baptist Church	4125 Indian River Rd	Virginia Beach	VA		201		
11	Kurt Strong	Church planting Mag. 1981	Freeseport Baptist Church	2810 W Pearl City Rd	Freeport	IL	1978	297	1	150
12	George Sweet	Church planting Mag. 1981	Atlantic Shores Baptist Church	1861 Kempsville Rd	Virginia Beach	VA	1981	2819		
13	David Tels	Church planting Mag. 1981	Liberty badpist church	6501 W Lake Mead Blvd	Las-Vegas	NV	Sep. 11, 1977	3667	88	
14	William R. Trotter	Church planting Mag. 1981	Open Door Baptist Church	3576 Luce Road	Cassadaga	NY	1981	235		
15	Marvin Wood	Church planting Mag. 1981	HARVEST BAPTIST CHURCH	951 Woodland Way	Hagerstown	MD	July 18.1981	32		
16	Frank D. Papandrea	Church planting Mag. 1981	Union County Baptist Church	4 Valley Road	Clark	NJ	1976	298		
17	T.D Worthington	Church planting Mag. 1981	Freedom Baptist Church	300 Country Day Rd	Goldsboro	NC	1979	636		200
18	Steve Ray	Church planting Mag. 1981	Holy Mountain Baptist Church	3121 Ashley Street	Kingsport	TN	1976	156		
19	Bobby R. Andrews	Church planting Mag. 1981	Lighthouse Baptist Church	55 Jason St	Rocky Mount	VA		174		
20	Russ Merrin	Church planting Mag. 1981	Heritage Baptist Church	5th Ave, Bay Shore	Long Island	NY	Aug 9, 1981	240	55	
21	Tim Setliff	Church planting Mag. 1981	THREE RIVERS BAPTIST CHURCH	449 S Atlantic Ave.	Pittsburgh	PA	April 10, 1981	392		
22	DAVID ANDERSON	Church planting Mag. 1981	Victory Church	North Platte	Sarasota	FL	1981	279	15	
23	Al Henson	Church planting Mag. 1981	Lighthouse Baptist Church	210 Battle Rd.	Nashville	TN	1978	983		
24	Clayton Jones	Church planting Mag. 1981	LIGHTHOUSE BAPTIST CHURCH	State Route 108.	Viola	TN	Aug 27, 1982	42		
25	James Hartman	Church planting Mag. 1981	Lee's Summit Baptist Temple	2614 NW Chipman Rd.	Lee's Summit	MO	1981	452		
26	Ronnie Riggins	Church planting Mag. 1981	New Life Church	530 Big Spring Rd.	New Cumberland	PA	1977	488		
27	Danny Chamberland	Church planting Mag. 1981	Topsham Baptist Church	52 Roman Rd.	Topsham	ME	Nov. 1st., 1978	1055		
28	Tom Hauser	Church planting Mag. 1981	Open Door Baptist Church	350 Chili-Scottsville Road	Churchville	NY	1977	1422	36	
29	Otis Hill	Church planting Mag. 1981	OPEN DOOR Family Church	1761 Mcfarland Blvd N	Tuscaloosa	AL		622		
30	John Houghton	Church planting Mag. 1981	Clay First Baptist Church	1676 Triplett Ridge Road	Clay	WV	1982	429		
31	Sam Huntley	Church planting Mag. 1981	Bedford Baptist Church	1518 Oakwood Street	Bedford	VA		233		
32	Jerry Jhonston	Church planting Mag. 1981	Albemarle Baptist Church	1685 Roslyn Ridge Rd.	Charlottesville	VA		556		
33	Dean Lamphers	Church planting Mag. 1981	Open Bible Baptist Church of Chatham	20669 US Highway 29	Chatham	VA		499		
34	Mike Grooms	Church planting Mag. 1981	Shenandoah Valley Baptist Church	4699 Valley Pike	Stephens City	VA		176		
35	Keith Mariett	Church planting Mag. 1981	Susquehanna Valley Baptist	1796 48	Oneonta	NY	1979	104		
36	Daren Ritchey	Church planting Mag. 1981	Grace Bible Church of Altoona	164 Laurel Ln.	Altoona	PA		332		
37	Tom Miller	Church planting Mag. 1981	Faith Baptist Church of Mission Texas	1302 Doherty Ave	Mission	TX	1978	508		
38	Carl Godwin	Church planting Mag. 1981	Calvary Community Church	4400 N. 1st Street	Lincoln	NE	June 10, 1973	1626	5	
39	Davy Mayo	Church planting Mag. 1981	Lycoming Valley Baptist Church	location Location	Montoursville	PA		411		
40	Larry Lusk	Church planting Mag. 1981	Hendrix Road Baptist Church	825 Co Rd 457	Florence	AL		505		
41	Raymond Barber	Church planting Mag. 1983	Worth Baptist Church	4699 Valley Pike	Fort Worth	TX		2248		
42	Denise Allison	Church planting mag. 1983	Centre Church	848 Science Park Rd.	State College	PA		972		
43	Larry Benette	Church planting mag. 1983	Calvary Baptist Tabernacle	Stokes Ferry Rd.	Salisbury	NC		210		
44	James Boling	Church planting mag. 1983	Greenwood Baptist Church	Greenwood School District	Greenwood	SC		347		
45	Harold F Crowell	Church planting mag. 1983	Plainville Baptist Church	62 South St	Plainville	MA	January 13, 19	309	42	
46	James J. Jenkins	Church planting mag. 1983	Calvary Bible Church	6968 Sweeney Road	Greig	NY	spring of 1980	278		
47	Larry Lamberth	Church planting mag. 1983	Harvest Baptist Church	3741 S. Church St.	Burlington	NC		2514		
48	Ronald W. Laughlin	Church planting mag. 1983	Harvest Baptist Church	5501 OH-45	Salem	OH		66		
49	Charls Loveday	Church planting mag. 1983	Shekinah Church	394 Glory Road	Blountville	TN		504		
50	Mark Luso	Church planting mag. 1983	Friant Foothill Bible Church	17836 North Friant Road	Friant	CA		88		

---

1 Kobby Barda, "Data of Liberty U," https://us-israel.org.il, available at: https://us-israel.org.il/2022/03/02/data-of-liberty-u/, accessed March 1, 2022.

#	Name	Source	Church	Address	City	State	Date	Count	
50	Mark Lugg	Church planting mag. 1983	Friant Foothill Bible Church	17836 North Friant Road	Friant	CA		88	
51	Beryl McKisic	Church planting mag. 1983	Calvary Baptist Church	7850 Scottsville Road	Scottsville	VA		260	
52	Robert C. Norris	Church planting mag. 1983	Bethel Baptist Church	754 E Rockhill Rd	Sellersville	PA		742	
53	David overton	Church planting mag. 1983	Mitchell Hollow Mission Church	Mill St	Windham	NY		271	
54	Richard Parker	Church planting mag. 1983	Cornerstone Baptist Church	5860 Three Notch Rd.	Mobil	AL		409	
55	Tom Sica	Church planting mag. 1983	Open Door Church	826 S Keyser Ave	Scranton	PA		197	
56	Randy Stewart	Church planting mag. 1983	Bluegrass Baptist Church	812 E Loudon Ave	Lexington	KY	1977	110	
57	Wayne Taylor	Church planting mag. 1983	Valley View Baptist Church	17471 Main Street	Buchanan	VA		304	
58	Bruce Teare	Church planting mag. 1983	Lighthouse Baptist Church	243 Kent St.	Saltville	VA		475	
59	Ron Townsend	Church planting mag. 1983	Epping Bible church.	243 Pleasant St	Epping	NH	1984	369	
60	Ronald Gene Riggins	Church planting mag. 1983	New Life Church	530 Big Spring Rd.	New Cumberland	PA	February 8, 19	478	51
61	Bob Johnson	Church planting mag. 1983	Capital Church	10233 Leesburg Pike	Vienna	VA	1984	1,446	
62	Donnie Cantwell	Church planting mag. 1983	Open Door Baptist Church	7151 Belmont Rd	Richmond	VA		413	
63	Pastor Young	Church planting mag. 1983	Grand Strand Baptist Church	350 Hospitality Lane	Myrtle Beach	VA	April 2nd, 1975	1843	95
64	Dr. David Wood	Church planting mag. 1983	Heritage Baptist Church	1570 60TH ST SE,	KENTWOOD	MI		214	
65	Johnnie Brewer	Church planting mag. May -19	New Life Baptist Church	Lloyd Ave	White Marsh	MD		850	
66	Rick Dinoff	Church planting mag. May -19	Ocean County Baptist Church	Old Freehold Rd.	Toms River	NJ	November 30,	527	16
67	Kirk D. Divietro	Church planting mag. May -19	First Baptist Church of Belvidere	155 Pequest Road	Belvidere	NJ		214	
68	Larry Ellis	Church planting mag. May -19	Fallstown Baptist Church	242 State Park Rd.	Troutman	NC		645	
69	Pat Fortner	Church planting mag. May -19	Central Baptist Church	57 Merryman Drive,	Victoria	VA	November 7, 1	1196	
70	Ronn Read	Church planting mag. May -19	Lighthouse Baptist Church	1419 Kochs Lane	Quincy	IL		120	
71	Richard VanHuss	Church planting mag. May -19	New Life Church	2159 Ironworks Rd.	Winchester	KY		654	
72	Robert Gass	Church planting mag. May -19	Harvest Baptist Temple	2001 S. Columbus	Medford	OR	June 19, 1977	553	35
73	Cliff Hartley	Church planting mag. May -19	Gateway Baptist Church	S 6th St	Ironton	OH		256	
74	Moses Yoder	Church planting mag. May -19	Carrollton Baptist Temple	1211 Lincoln Ave NW	Carrollton	OH		345	
75	Steve Malenick	Church planting mag. May -19	Manassas Baptist Church	8730 Sudley Rd.	Manassas	VA		1124	
76	Jhon Catwrite	Church planting mag. May -19	Calvary Independent Baptist Church	716 Amosland Rd.	Morton	PA		295	
77	Melvine Campbell	Church planting mag. May -19	Jordan Baptist Church	3708 PARKWOOD AVE.	LYNCHBURG	VA		309	
78	Red Brwer	Church planting mag. May -19	Fellowship Baptist Church	3661 US-60	Barboursville	WV		3201	
79	James Boling	Church planting mag. May -19	Greenwood Baptist Church of Greenwo	Deadfall Rd E,	Greenwood	SC		358	
80	Paul & Robert Gass	Liberty University 1977-78 Y	Harvest Baptist Temple	2001 S. Columbus	Medford	OR	June 19, 1977	538	35
81	Donald Jasper Ellison	Liberty University 1977-78 Y	Maynard Baptist Church	1195 Juliette Rd,	Forsyth	GA		630	
82	Pastor Galagher	Liberty University 1977-78 Y	Maranatha Baptist Church	2204 Tuggle Rd	Farmville	VA		20	
83	Pastor Elness	Liberty University 1977-78 Y	First Baptist Church	450 3rd Ave S	Windom	MN		326	
84	David B. Overton	Liberty University 1977-78 Y	Mitchell Hollow Mission Church	893 Mill St.	Windham	NY	1976	277	
85	Mike Linch	Linkdin	North star Church	3413 Blue Springs Rd.	Kennesaw	GA	Jan. 1997	6573	
86	Jim Mustain	Linkdin	Loving Community	Dublin St	Lewisville	TX	Jun. 2014	482	
87	David Cole	Linkdin	Oak Tree Church	24400 NE Colbern Road	Lee's Summit	MO		564	
88	Keith Gardner	Linkdin	First Free Will Baptist Church	2426 South Charles Blv.	Greenville	NC	May 19,2007	259	
89	Paul W Newell	Linkdin	ChurchForFamily	10478 BEAUMONT Ave.	CHERRY VALLEY	CA	2002	231	
90	Don Meckley	Linkdin	Emmanuel Community Church	331 Wheaton Ave.	Bayville	NJ		750	
91	Jason Hauffe	Linkdin	Grace Fellowship of Waxahachie	1313 West Main Street	Waxahachie	TX	Apr. 2011	91	
92	Wayne Kuenzle	Linkdin	First Baptist Cedar Hill	602 W Belt Line Rd,	Cedar Hill	TX	Aug. 1994	511	
93	Ryan Johnson	Linkdin	Perimeter Church	9500 Medlock Bridge Road	JOHNS CREEK	GA		10,000	
94	Chris Phillips	Linkdin	First Baptist Cedar Hill	8270 E Northfield Blvd, #145	Denver	CO	Nov 4, 2018,	991	
95	Steve Rowe	Linkdin	Eaglebrook Church	1025 Margaret Street	Woodruff	WI	Jan. 2008	234	
96	Dan Underhill	Linkdin	Cornerstone Church	14913 Murfin Road	Lakeway	TX		796	
97	Eugene Miller	Linkdin	Living Hope Community Church	22H West Route 313	Perkasie	PA		1,882	

APPENDICES

#	Name	Linkdin	Church	Address	City	State	Date	Number
97	Eugene Miller	Linkdin	Living Hope Community Church	22H West Route 313	Perkasie	PA		1,682
98	Russ Olmon	Linkdin	Lake point Church	3540 Emporium Circle	Mesquite	TX	2004	50,793
99	Ron Snyder	Linkdin	House Church	5624 Deer Park Road	Reisterstown	MD	Jan. 2016	83
100	Bill Kimbley	Linkdin	Life Church 2 42	16762 FM455	Forestburg	TX	Dec. 2015	327
101	Ed Stetzer	Linkdin	Milcreek Community Church	4444 Sterrettania Rd	Erie	PA	1994	1,058
102	Dayton Hartman	Linkdin	Redeemer Church	2020 Old Mill Road	Rocky Mount	NC	Sep. 2013	2,248
103	Christopher Wells	Linkdin	New City Church	2675 W. MAIN ST.	BOISE	ID	Jan. 2021	852
104	Daniel Bryan Lewis	Linkdin	RELIANCE CHURCH	1235 28th Ave N.	St. Petersburg	FL	Jul. 08, 2013	537
105	Jeff mueller	Linkdin	Restore Church	1603 Locust St	Yankton	SD	Aug. 2015	910
106	MICHAEL GUYER	Linkdin	Treasuring Christ Church	4100 Carpenter Road	Ypsilanti	MI	Mar. 2018	571
107	Dr. Tom Bartlett	Linkdin	Celebration Church	164 Celebration Way	N. Wilkesboro	NC	Jan. 2007	1,623
108	Dr. James R. Riley	Linkdin	House of Prayer Baptist Church	1640 N 48th St.	Baton Rouge	LA	Mar. 2016	1,168
109	Chuckk Gerwig	Linkdin	Crossroads Church	161 Plaza La Vista, Suite 10	Camarillo	CA	Jan. 1987	1,432
110	Andrew Green	Linkdin	Faith Baptist Church of Kokomo	600 S Dixon Rd	Kokomo	IN	Aug. 1986	460
111	Keith Cabral	Linkdin	BridgePointe Christian Church	855 Waterman Ave	East Providence	RI	Dec. 2014	2,950
112	Joe E. Alvarado	Linkdin	Eternal Rock Church	7703 Wyandot St	Denver	CO	Jan. 2005	830
113	John Chaney	Linkdin	Northwoods Community Church	10700 N Allen Rd.	Peoria	IL	Mar. 25, 1990	941
114	Gabe Dodd	Linkdin	The Branch Church Dahlonega	385 Riley Rd	Dahlonega	GA	Jan. 2014	638
115	Ken Richardson	Linkdin	The Neighborhood Church	2516 SYNDER AVENUE	Philadelphia	PA	Jul. 2016	436
116	Parker Manuel	Linkdin	Pinewood Church	1905 15th St	Boulder	CO	23 Dec. 2016	1,526
117	Raymond Hudson	Linkdin	City Center Church	3201 Shattuck Ave	Berkeley	CA	Apr 2019	918
118	Steve Davis	Linkdin	OXFORD VALLEY COMMUNITY CHURCH	1249 W Maple Ave	Langhorne	PA	Jul. 2002	962
119	Ron Davis	Linkdin	Sumter bible church	1765 CAMDEN HWY	SUMTER	SC	May 2002	392
120	Brady Arneson	Linkdin	Waikiki Beach Gathering	2735 Kalakaua Ave	Honolulu	HI	Sep. 2019	964
121	Ernest Smith	Linkdin	Front Range Christian Church	3954 Trail Boss Ln.	Castle Rock	CO	Aug. 2013	2,286
122	Larry Snyder	Linkdin	Living Legacy Church	228 McCorkle Road	Hershey	PA	Jun. 2006	292
123	Chuck Musselwhite	Linkdin	The Village Chapel	3915 Constellation Rd	Lompoc	CA	Jan. 2007	945
124	Derrick E. Young	Linkdin	Unity Baptist Church	12158 Pulaski Rd	Jacksonville	FL	Jun. 2010	573
125	Scott Mayo	Linkdin	Bridge Church	3168 Indian River Rd.	Virginia Beach	VA	Apr. 2000	5,010
126	Kevin Maloney	Linkdin	Grace Road Church	440 East Ave	Rochester	NY	Jan. 2009	3,889
127	Russ Atter	Linkdin	Cafe 420 Ministries, Inc.	420 Washington St.	Eau Claire,	WI	Aug. 2006	284
128	Nicolaas Jones	Linkdin	Grace Hill Church	901 Locust St.	Herndon	VA	Apr. 2016	622
129	Vincent Torres	Linkdin	Blaze Christian Fellowship	6 Bisbee Ct.	Santa Fe	NM	Jan. 2012	1,120
130	Dr. Joey Cook	Linkdin	City Church	766 Harkrider St	Conway	AR	Aug. 2013	2,585
131	Noah Lee	Linkdin	Redemption Church Missoula	1601 South 6th St	W Missoula	MT	Nov. 2011	390
132	Donald Morgan, Jr	Linkdin	Core Church	315 N 20th St	Guthrie	OK	Jan. 2012	615
133	Jason McKinney	Linkdin	ONE Church	3815 Woodbine Ave	Cincinnati,	OH	Apr. 2015	339
134	Gregory K Tyree	Linkdin	Gracepointe Baptist Church	568 Winesap Rd	Madison Heights	VA	Oct. 2005	261
135	Tim York	Linkdin	Grove Free Will Baptist Church	10543 Cedar Grove Rd.	Smyrna	TN	Jun. 2010	848
136	Chase Ward	Linkdin	Mountain Vista Baptist	1750 Mountain St	Carson City	NV	Sep. 2015	580
137	Dave Brunelle	Linkdin	The Rock Community Church	9403 Garfield Blvd	Garfield Heights	OH	Jul. 2002	575
138	Dr. Troy Johnson	Linkdin	R3 Church	15556 Summit Ave	Fontana	CA	Jul. 2013	454
139	Steve Hobbs	Linkdin	Redeeming Grace Baptist Church	269 Green St.	Royersford	PA	Dec. 2002	186
140	Steven Rathers	Linkdin	For All Believers Bible Church	1006 E Hoover Ave	Mesa	AZ	Sep. 2009	177
141	Chad Clement	Linkdin	RH Church Tallahassee	8116 Killearn Plaza Cir	Tallahassee	FL	Oct. 2013	995
142	Ryan Vanderford	Linkdin	HOPE CHAPEL UPC	8610 MS-178	Olive Branch	MS	Jan. 2015	1,745
143	Leroy Childress	Linkdin	GRACE CHURCH LANSING	2740 Indiana Ave	Lansing	IL	Aug. 2015	551
144	Dan Adams	Linkdin	RiverTown Church	3044 San Pablo Rd S	Jacksonville	FL	Oct. 2007	633
145	Nick Scott	Linkdin	CenterPointe Church	105 Pride Ave	Bunker Hill	WV	Aug. 2013	690
146	David Cole	Linkdin	Oak Tree Church	24400 NE Colbern Rd.	Lee's Summit	MO	Sep. 2013	563

#	Name	Source	Church	Address	City	State	Date	Amount	
145	Nick Scott	Linkdin	CenterPointe Church	105 Pride Ave	Bunker Hill	WV	Aug. 2013	690	
146	David Cole	Linkdin	Oak Tree Church	24400 NE Colbern Rd.	Lee's Summit	MO	Sep. 2013	563	
147	Joseph Wong	Linkdin	Living Stone Community Church	3100 S Goldenrod Rd.	Orlando	FL	Sep. 2008	197	
148	Donald Bryan	Linkdin	First Pentecostal Church of Slidell	388 Robert Boulevard	Slidell	LA	Nov. 1982	1,097	
149	Danny Tice	Linkdin	Bay Shore Community Church	36759 Millsboro Hwy	Millsboro	DE	Nov. 1981	2,714	
150	Brian Remsch	Linkdin	Connection Church	2 US-40 ALT	Middletown	MD	Feb. 2011	215	
151	D Patrick McCoy	Linkdin	Cornerstone Baptist Church	3683 Pious Ridge Rd	Berkeley Springs	WV	Nov. 2013	52	
152	Dwayne Hodges	Linkdin	Redeemed Voices Church	1031 W 3rd St.	Davenport	IA	Sep. 2018	708	
153	Rustin McClure	Linkdin	Faith Connection Covenant Church	1803 Wilson Dr.	Washington	KS	Jan. 2013	324	
154	Robert Martinez	Linkdin	Redemption Hill Baptist Church	8 Launfal St.	Albany	NY	Feb. 2015	840	
155	Mike DeGuzman	Linkdin	Community Bible Church Of Ocala	3200 SE 17th St	Ocala	FL	Sep. 2010	324	
156	Steve Marfia	Linkdin	Legacy 242	398-300 Summit Ave.	Westville	NJ	Jun. 2014	419	
157	Kenneth Caldwell	Linkdin	NOW FAITH FELLOWSHIP CHURCH	603 Elnor St	PLANT CITY	FL	Jan 17, 2002	135	
158	Dennis Garcia	Linkdin	The People Church	401 Irene St.	Moriarty	NM	Feb. 2012	524	
159	Jua Robinson	Linkdin	Heart Change Fellowship	455 Arborway	Jamaica Plain	MA	Jun. 2006	707	
160	Josh Knorr	Linkdin	The Point Church	155 Hansen Rd	Charlottesville	VA	Apr. 2009	6,156	
161	Michael Brinkley	Linkdin	Palmwood Church	7900 Red Bug Lake Rd	Oviedo	FL	Oct. 2014	346	
162	Ted Williams	Linkdin	New Journey Church	3123 New Hope Rd	Columbus	OH	Dec. 13, 2007	1,082	
163	Greg Fentress	Linkdin	Living Waters Church Of God	2228 Bypass Road	Pocomoke City	MD	May 5, 2016	571	
164	Tim Coleman	Linkdin	The Point Church	13801 Innerarity Point Road	Pensacola	FL	Jun. 2006	1,719	
165	Gerald Faulkner	Linkdin	Innovate Church	1508 Enochville Rd	Kannapolis	NC	Jan 2019	195	
166	Reginald Brown	Linkdin	GRACE COMMUNITY CHURCH	91 Town Square Pl	Vacaville	CA	Apr. 2007	557	
167	Dr. Gabriel Powell	Linkdin	Encounter Atlanta	4209 Northeast Expy	Doraville	GA	Aug. 2014	14,945	
168	Dayton Hartman	Linkdin	Redeemer Church NC	1431 Old Apex Rd	Cary	NC	Aug. 2013	347	
169	Clint Nolder	Linkdin	Foundation Christian Church	30-A East Washington St.	Newman	GA	Jan. 2017	2,765	
170	Cary Weaver	Linkdin	Verge Church	Grant Ave	Jonesboro	AR	Sep. 2012	1,141	
171	Barry Jude	Linkdin	New Day Church SBC	696 N Fairfield Rd	Beavercreek	OH	Jan 2009	304	27
172	Josiah Potter	Linkdin	CrossPointe Church Peachtree City	401 Dividend Dr E.	Peachtree City	GA	Jun. 2012	517	
173	Frank Brown	Linkdin	Summit Leadership	3104 Hanover Rd	Johnson City	TN	Jan. 2002	2,104	
174	Steve Smith	Linkdin	Grace Church	2320 Sleepy Hill Road	Lakeland	FL	1992	497	
175	Ernie Banks	Linkdin	Eden Village Church	312 Williamson St	Savannah	GA	Feb. 2011	572	
176	Michael D. Peoples	Linkdin	Abundant Life Church	3301 E Coliseum Blvd	Fort Wayne	IN	Mar. 2014	1,678	
177	Michael Cunningham	Linkdin	Grace Church	Juab School District	Vineyard	UT	Sep. 2019	718	
178	Dr. Michal Downing	Linkdin	Behind The Walls Ministry	1077 Eastern Blvd	Henderson	NC	Aug. 2009	142	
179	Cecil Day	Linkdin	Lighthouse - Indian Springs	7061 Sparks Ln	Hamilton	OH	May. 2001	417	
180	Craig Dyson	Linkdin	CONVO Church	919 Birchwood Cir	Sparks	NV	Jan. 2018	1,116	
181	James Santiago	Linkdin	Reading City Church	644 Penn Ave	West Reading	PA	Oct. 2009	1,302	
182	David Lewkowicz	Linkdin	Bridge Church Hendersonville	580 Upward Rd.	Flat Rock	NC	Nov. 2012	1,418	
183	Dylan Dodson	Linkdin	Lifepointe Church	9500 Durant Rd	Raleigh	NC	Sep. 2015	2,904	
184	Joel Rissinger	Linkdin	Mill Pond Church	2175 Berlin Tpke	Newington	CT	2008	419	
185	Michael Bethel	Linkdin	Haven of Hope	864 Grand Ave	New Haven	CT	Jul. 2006	1,755	
186	Keith McQueen	Linkdin	Powerhouse Church Of Indianapolis	3105 Hovey St	Indianapolis	IN	Aug. 2012	3,315	
187	Gerald Faulkner	Linkdin	Innovate Church	1508 Enochville Rd.	Kannapolis	NC	Ja. 2019	194	
188	Jake Thornhill II	Linkdin	Mosaic Community	1036 S Josephine Boyd St.	Greensboro	NC	Sep. 2018	378	
189	Rodney Rambo	Linkdin	Rooted Church	2630 N. Highview,	Joplin	MO	Aug 13, 2017	438	
190	Bliss Spillar IV	Linkdin	Redemption City Church Frederick	3301 EASTERN AVE.	BALTIMORE	MD	Nov 2014	1,601	
191	Ronnie Coleman	Linkdin	SoulQuest Church	1119 Old Humboldt Rd.	Jackson	TN	2014	7,128	
192	Rudy Rivero	Linkdin	New Dawn Church	17200 NW 87th Ave.	Miami	FL	Aug.1981	613	
193	Timothy J. Behrens	Linkdin	Colton True Life	30205 S Wall St	Colton	OR	Jan. 2014	776	

#	Name	Source	Church	Address	City	State	Date	Amount	
193	Timothy J. Behrens	Linkdin	Colton True Life	30205 S Wall St	Colton	OR	Jan. 2014	776	
194	Nathan Miller	Fundamentalist Mag.	Hot Springs Baptist Church	737 Virginia Ave	Hot Springs	VA	1986	216	
195	Allen McFarLand	The Fundamentalist Journal	Calvary Baptist Church of Portsmouth	2117 London Blvd	Portsmouth	VA	1983	280	
196	Robert Bates	Fundamentalist Journal Volu	Heritage Baptist Church	10 Chenault Ford Rd	Fayetteville	TN	1980	257	
197	Rick Flowers	Fundamentalist Journal Volu	Lighthouse Baptist Church	3145 N Thompson Ln	Murfreesboro	TN	1981	977	
198	Ricky Eason	Fundamentalist Mag.	7 Hills Community Church	3114 Memorial Ave.	Lynchburg	VA		296	
199	Carl Godwin	Sheperd's Journal	Calvary Community Church	4400 N. 1st Street	Lincoln	NE	June 10, 1973	1826	5

Appendix B—Stenogram of a Conversation Between Falwell and a Team of Pastors with Menachem Begin

```
Interview with Prime Minister Menachem Begin, conducted 11:00 A.M. on
Tuesday, April 18, 1978, in the Prime Minister's office in Jerusalem.


Please sit down, ladies and gentlemen.
I welcome you to Jerusalem and I understand you are coming from Cairo.
That is correct, yes sir.
It is a propitious time to hear what's going on in Cairo.
Yes.
We would like to introduce our group to you so you will know who we are.
First, it's nice to talk to a real _____. We are pleased to talk t
men of great truth. We admire you. We appreciate you and we are very
thankful to God for you. You are a great person. This is Dr. Jerry Falwel
from the United States and Lynchburg, Virginia -- on his telecast and
television program -- his program reaches about 15 million people a week
This is a good man. He is one of your excellent employees. This is Dr.
Toser from Covenant Presbyterian Church near Perdue University; Dr. and
Mrs. Montgomery -- Dr. Montgomery is a theologian, philosopher and
_____. This is his wife, Joyce. It is always nice having the wome
with us. Vivian Toser, who is the wife of Dr. Toser over here. Mr. Menge
who is an economist and industrialist. Roger Elwood, who is the editor an
```

publisher of Inspiration Magazine; Mr. and Mrs. Wilkerson - - Mr. Wilkers is from California. His organization is Melody Land, which is across from Disney Land, so he has an excellent time at all times. Back here is Nelson Keener who is also from Virginia and Paul Polmyrie from California - - and we are very pleased to be your guests.

I asked my friends who are on their feet to bring in a few chairs and let them sit down.

Thank you very much. In other words, I get here _____ _____ after this presentation.

Dr. Falwell has a message for you from Mr. Sadat (I read about it). We will start there.

Mr. Prime Minister, we represent a group of Americans called evangelicals We are conservative Christians in America who accept the Bible to be the inspired, infallible Word of God. We are followers of the Lord Jesus Christ, whose death, burial and resurrection we've accepted as our atonement for sin and acceptance into the family of God. There are some 46 million professing evangelicals in America who are of like mind and faith. We came at the invitation of the Egyptian and Israeli governments, sponsored by those governments, to represent these people in, first of al finding out what is happening. We have no magic solutions and we haven't come here as diplomats. We have come here as men of God to offer our prayers, our conciliatory efforts, and to communicate today to you our deep admiration and respect for you as Americans. We do believe this is God's land and we believe that you are God's people. And we are honored to be here. Our first visit was to Egypt, and the President was in Aswan. We were flown down to Aswan, where we met with President Sadat on the veranda of the rest home there. We had a very delightful time with him and I must say that we were very impressed with his warmness - - his warmth, his sincerity - - and his very expressed desire for peace, all of which you two have talked about in detail. In the course of our conversation he asked us to convey to you three basic things, and he did it very graciously and very respectfully. He asked us to reaffirm to you that he still very earnestly desires peace, and his efforts will continue in that direction. However, he, in expressing his concern over the Sinai matter, was very rigid in his statement regarding the settlements and the security. He was pleased, he said, when you expressed to him that you were willing to give back the Sinai. He was displeased when he learned that the Israelis were going to provide the security. His words were, "this is a violation of my soil and my sovereignty." He seemed to indicat that he would not negotiate that point. Secondly, he said that he felt th there could be no peace unless the Palestinian problem was resolved. However, on a positive note, he offered no prescription for the solution. He made no demands. He simply very ambiguously said, "the situation must be solved," but he made no demands or prescriptive requests of you. Finally, he advised us that he planned to build, on Mount Sinai, where Moses received the Law, three buildings: a church, a synagogue, and a mosque. And he asked us to ask your cooperation. And that is the message from President Sadat to Prime Minister Begin.

Thank you very much for this message. It is most interesting. As far as _the latest idea_ is concerned, there could be a problem I am very grateful to you for the words you uttered _in Recognition for the Book of the Books which we all Believe_. It is the source of our life, it's eternity. Some people accuse me, perhaps some of my colleagues, that we quote the Bible from time to time. What an accusation! I only can say I plead guilty, but I don't apologize. No reason to. It is really the Book which gave us our life -- not only our past, also our future. And I am very happy that we have full understa from it. _____ met many times -- people of good will -- Christians who understand our cause, support it wholeheartedly, and therefore, I want to express to you my gratitude. And now as far as the problem of peace is concerned. If you would go now to Cairo I would give you also a message to President Sadat. And I would say like this: I remember and I will not forget the wonderful days in Jerusalem and in _Ismailia_. President Sadat made in November only a short remark, almost by the word of mouth, that he will be prepared to come even to Jerusalem and speak to the _____ in order to avoid _one casualty_ amongst his sons. His sons referred to soldiers of the Egyptian _____. I read about it the following day. I took the time to read it. And every day I sent another invitation to President Sadat to come. Ultimately, through the good offices of the American ambassador, I got the question whether I can send him a formal, written invitation. Of course, I said, and I sent him such a very cordial invitation. And that is how President Sadat came here, addressed the _____, and I had with him a long talk of several hours. The atmosphere was wonderful in Jerusalem, created both by President Sadat and by our government and people. First of all, we said to each other, no more war and secondly, which is very important to stress, we have differences of opinion, but we shall negotiate. That was the summing up, actually, between President Sadat and myself of the Jerusalemite meeting.

Which was absolutely positive. As a result, the government of Israel elaborated and produced a peace plan. It was praised in the United States I brought it in December to President Carter; I showed it also to _Ranking_ Senators; went then to Britian and then I went to Ismaili and in Ismailia we had a wonderful conference and meeting - - it was even a meeting of minds. We understood each other; we consulted each other; we agreed that two committees be formed, joint Egyptian-Israeli committee a political and a military one to deal with _____ _____us how to achieve peace. So my first message would be to President Sadat _____ _would have been or would be_ that the days of Jerusalem and of Ismailia will always be with me and I will not forget th They were good days for Egypt, for Israel, for mankind, and for peace. The difficulties arose later. And as you used the two words, rigid and would not negotiate -- the three words -- excuse me for my mistake and correction - - and ambiguity, I must dwell on them, because they are collected with a very _peacemaking_ and explain then what the difficulties are now. I hope there will be other _____ but if President Sadat is rigid on the problem of the settlements, I have to explain why we asked to negotiate; why he shouldn't say non-negotiable, as we do not say non-negotiable.

If I may ask you to turn around - -- The settlements for the Israelite are in this region of the Sinai Peninsula. It is a very small area, as yo can see, in comparison with the Sinai Peninsula. For the sake of peace, we suggested to President Sadat that we, ~~offer to accept~~ *after a certain transient Per* _____ international bord which is here, and all the Sinai Peninsula will go to Egyptian rule. Now here we have settlements *and closer this problem between the Niet and between* _____. We have also a few settlements but it appeare also the main problem is to make sure of the freedom of navigation. What we suggested is - - to make things simple and to say them simple. That in these two very small areas there should be united _____ I start from the south because there was war after war as a result of the illegal, *illegitimate* closure of the Tehran Straits and in 1956 there was a war and in 1967, ten years later, there was a war only because we were denied access to our harbor through the Straits, which of course are an international waterway. Now we were more forthcoming than any othe government of my country in the past, because since 1968 decision was taken that that strip of land in the south which I showed, should be unde Israeli control and we gave it up. United _____ and also there in the northern part. This is our complete ~~repeat~~ *Proposal*. The whole Sinai

Peninsula ultimately will go to Egypt, and there will be two zones of United Nations, and actually I already explained the vital issue of the future and national security; in the south should be always free access to the international waterway. And I only add a few words about the zone in the north because we had permanent bloodshed from the Gaza Strip. For 19 years we want to stop it, we want to make peace and we want to prevent any so-called government into the Gaza Strip and it would be, no doubt, _____ were it not for that little zone which should be under the United Nations control; and then, if that shouldn't exist with our settlements there is no transgression, there is no trespassing; it is a matter of making sure that peace will be real. Everybody will understand that after all the wars we won't have real peace this is our striving, and we want it with all our hearts. When I brought this proposal to President Sadat, including demilitarization, etc., he really told me that for him to accept that proposal about the zone in the North, But he summed up, we shall discuss it, we shall negotiate Now, as you yourself said, on this he has got a rigid position and said that cannot be negotiated. I can't agree to that. It should be negotiated because the peace plan is forthcoming, everybody admitted it, and to say us, just dismantle them and go away and connection with the Gaza Strip would be a very dangerous matter to the future. There is reason to believe that peace wouldn't be assured at all. So what I would like to say here, in response to the message -- let us negotiate. _____ started negotiating -- through the military committee in Cairo; through the ~~military~~ *Political* committee in Jerusalem -- but those indecisions were suddenly interrupted by the decision of President Sadat. And the Egyptian delegation was withdrawn. I *Already*, in my second letter to President Sadat, we exchange lately letters, suggested to him to renew those two committees and the negotiati within the framework of those two committees. Let us sit down, let us reason together, let us look for a way; I think this is the reasonable way to do and to try to achieve an agreement -- all over the world this is the way in the matter to achievement an agreement. You can't say to one side, you give me certain things and no negotiations -- that is not the way to try to find out the place for an agreement. It's a completely different matter, which, of course, cannot be accepted. Here I would like to explain to you, ladies and gentlemen, is the difficulty. We want to negotiate negotiations without interruptance. And also I explained how vital this issue is to us when you point the way of our future security and keeping _____ .

Now you said that President Sadat spoke to you about what he termed the Palestinian question, and then you used the word, he was ambiguous about it, ~~and~~ that he didn't put it in concrete terms. What about ambiguity we had much, but I can only assure you that there is no ambiguity whatsoever. We cannot even afford ambiguity on this issue. And here I must again, with your permission, go to the map.

This is Samaria and Judaea - - those are two names that are very well known to you. From the Bible. As you can see, this is the mountains, this is the Valley of Jordan and this is the _____. Here the bulk of our population is. If this mountain _____ _____ by Mr. Arafat, then we face immortal danger, for obvious reasons. We had, for 19 years, permanent bloodsheds from that part of the land; the line was absolutely indefensible; there were permanent _____ and therefore, when we are asked to go back to that line behind the mountains, it would be only nine miles or ten miles from the seashore - - now you come from the United States of America -- what is nine miles in the United States of America? But here it would be our lifeline, perhaps priceless. _____

APPENDICES

11

With all the experience we have about airlifts to Angola, to _____ B

to _____, from Modessa to this part of the land, it is a matter of

two hours _____ cargo jet

plane - -supersonic jet plane -- two hours. This part of the land would

become a solid base, ~~d?~~ against us, day in and day out. The whole

civilian population of our country would be in the range - - directly

threatened with their lives. There cannot be any ambiguity about it.

We must know clearly what's our future. Therefore, we have a different

suggestion. And in Ismailia I had good words from President Sadat about

our plan. The second part of our plan is <ins>Called Autonomy, or</ins>

<ins>Self-rule</ins> for the Palestinian Arabs. So that they can

in Judaea, Samaria, also in the Gaza Strip, elect their own administrativ

council, _____ departments, dealing with all the affairs

of the daily life, we will not interfere whatsoever -- only we ~~will~~ <ins>Shall</ins> have

responsibility to secure it. So the Palestinian Arabs will have <ins>Self-Ru</ins>

<ins>or Autonomy</ins>. I will ask you later to bring these pamphlets

to distribute amongst our friends, and ~~because~~ <ins>of course</ins> the Palestinian Jews

should have their security.

That is the _____, <ins>that was the idea</ins>. And again it was praised

at the time. There cannot be any ambiguity about it. Now lately we are faced with these two demands. We should say in advance, in a declaration of principles, that we will withdraw out of those ~~alliances~~ lines of 4th of June, 1967, and there should be _____

_____ wires usually brought our self-determination, but, again, no ambiguity -- it means exactly that. Such was our peace plan. Such it is. It wasn't yet negotiated. We didn't get down to proposals. Now I can't understand when, for instance, President Sadat talked to you and made things completely simple. They will withdraw to those lines; they will gi me Sinai and we will dismantle the settlements and there will be peace. The impression is, well, this is the chance. My dear friends, please understand, it is not so in reality. In what source does our peace proposal endanger Egypt? Not atall. Not one Egyptian man is in danger. Not one Egyptian woman. Not atall. Now I can say this about all other nations -- where is the nation which ~~that~~ is endangered by our peace proposal? Not atall. But when we speak about us, our lives are in danger; the lives of our children are in danger. When President Sadat says that he will dea with our security, I can tell him, with all due respect, he couldn't guarantee the security of his own friend, _____

_____, and got killed by the very same people who want to kill our children. Again, at a glimpse of this man you will see that it is our home - - to repeat, it is our life. That is the difference. Therefore, we are not rigid; we cannot be ambiguous. We want to negotiate. My message to President Sadat, if you have an opportunity to send it back, is, let us renew the spirit of the days of Jerusalem and Ismailia when we met and shook hands and decided to call each other, "my friend" - - as he called me so. And only a few months ago in Ismailia there was a placard - - I didn't see, but I was told - - with my name and the man of peace. I didn't change. I am the same man. (I saw it. You did see it. I didn't) (And he agrees.) (Yes.) I didn't change. And it is the same peace plan. Let us review those days of understanding. Then there is a real reason to believe that there will be peace.

We believe that.

Yes. Of course it may take some time, some negotiating process; that is natural. You don't have peace with two sentences. Let me again repeat the statement by President Sadat. The ambiguous sentences. You go back to those lines preceding the six-day war and then you will have peace. We will not. In those lines and with those demands we will have the opposite of peace. There will be permanent bloodshed. We have the experience, we see it, we know the people, we can see what happened in Lebanon. We can see what happened in our country only several weeks ago on the road _____

and we can read the charter. You should know, my dear friends, there is

now one country in the world, this little country, against which there

is a written document to the effect that it must _disappear_.

We have nearly 140 members of the United Nations; I think it's a

characteristic fact to stress and there is one and one only of this

country against whom there exist a written charter -- Israel must be

wiped off the map. We must take it very seriously. We do take it seriousl

So I would like to end on a hopeful note and say again, I am very gratefu

to you for your message. I had to analyze the statement made by

President Sadat to me. I also send him greetings and it is my suggestion

that we renew first the spirit of Jerusalem and Ismailia and then the

negotiations within the framework of the two committees he and I agreed

to establish in ~~the summer~~ December, 1977, when we met at a very good conference

in Ismailia.

INDEX

Abrahamic Covenant 79
Accords, Oslo 130
Akenson, Donald 8
Allenby Bridge 69
Alroey, Gur 1
American Civil Liberties Union (ACLU) 14
American Dispensationalist Movement 25
American Jewish Committee 61
American Jewish Congress 77
American Traditional Values Coalition 122
Anderson, Carl 124
Arens, Moshe 49
Ariel, Yaakov 10
Armstrong, Herbert 71
Atherton, Alfred 70
Atlantic Shores Baptist Church 40
Avnery, Uri 78

Bakker, Jim 124
Bakker, Tammy 118
Balfour Declaration 46
Baptist Church (Thomas Road) 19–20, 22–28, 40–42, 47, 54, 116, 126, 132, 135, 144–47
Baptist College 19, 28–29, 41, 43, 106, 147
Bar'el, Zvi 120
Barkai, Mordechai 114
Barnett, Tony (Pastor) 40
Bearden, Stacy 142
Becker, Gad 121
Begin Heritage Center 64, 97
Begin, Menachem 1, 3, 5, 50, 59–99, 129
Bell, Nelson 15
Berger, Marshall 81
Bible Baptist College 18
Billings, Robert 108–9
Blackstone, William 5
Blitzer, Wolf 67

Blue Ridge Mountains 116
Bob Jones University 28, 103
Bonney, Richard 91
Born Again Christians 9, 50
Boverie, Dick 118
Bowers, Morris 55
Brenner, Michael 98
British Mandate 59
British Palestine Exploration Fund (PEF) 11
Brock, Alex 56
Brog, David 47, 63, 111
Brown, Bruce 90
Brownfeld, Allan 92
Burg, Avraham 82
Bush Administration 128, 130
Bush, George Jr 118
Bush, George Sr 129
Butler, John Washington (Christian) 12
Byrd, Harry Jr 62

Calvary Ministries 149
Camp David Accords 56, 89
Cantu, Edward (Pastor) 151
Carenen, Caitlin 75
Carey, Hugh 76
Carlson, Carol 6
Carter, Jimmy 60–61, 65, 67, 106–7
Cassell, Arthur 56
Catholic Church 54, 60
Central Baptist Church 146
Central University 19
Century America 10–11
Christian Academy 22, 47
Christian Council on Palestine 13
Christian Embassy 64, 83
Christian Lobby 6
Christian Right 50–51, 60, 77–78, 114, 116, 118, 122, 126, 130
Christian Zionism 5, 8–9, 11, 16, 26, 60

Christianity Today 15
Church Planting 1–3, 5, 26, 32, 34–37,
    41–42, 138, 141–43, 148, 161
Civil Rights Act 22
Clark, Jeff (Pastor) 144
Clendinen, Dudley 112
Clifton, Clint 143
Clinton, Tim 158
Cold War 111
Connally, John 111
Conservative Movement 86, 134, 162
Cook, Eli 1
Cross, Brenton 114
Crown Prince Hassan 69
Cruz, Ted 156

Dalton, John 62
Darby, John Nelson 8
David, King 155
Defense Committee 88
Defense Secretary Caspar Weinberger
    93, 120
Democratic Party 55, 70
Dermer, Ron 163
Dershowitz, Alan 129
Diamond, Sara 104
Dinoff, Rick (Pastor) 145
Dinsbeer, Jack (Pastor) 19
Dixon, Gene 25
Dobson, James 133
Dochuk, Darren 68
Dolan, Terry 109
Donahue, Phil 95
Donald Duck Bottling Plant 143
Donald Trump 4, 53, 156, 158, 161–62
Dream City Church 40
Drinan, Robert 96
Drozdikova, Jarmila 8
Du Mez, Kristin 15
Duffy, Bernard 125
Durbin, Dick 52
Durbin, Sean 88

Earley, Dave (Pastor) 150
East Dover Elementary School 145
Eckstein, Yechiel (Rabbi) 77
Edwards, Daryl 117
Edwards, Jonathan 32
Ehrlich, John (Pastor) 41
Eldar, Akiva 80, 81
Emmanuel Community Church 142
Epping Bible Church 145
Equal Rights Amendment (ERA) 110

Evangelical Protestants 68, 107
Evangelical Right 67, 86
Evans, Roland (Journalist) 98

Falwell, Carey 17
Falwell, Helen 17
Falwell, Jerry 2–3, 5, 17, 19–21, 25–28, 39,
    41, 48–51, 54, 56, 59–60, 62, 64–65,
    67, 71–72, 74, 76–79, 82, 88, 91, 94,
    96–97, 102, 104–7, 109, 116, 118–21,
    130–35, 141, 143, 147, 151, 156, 158–60
Falwell, Macel 49
Family Protection Agency 110
Family Values 15–16, 114
Farhi, Michael 75
Findley, Paul 52
First Baptist Church 40
First Free Will Baptist 152
First Gulf War 91
Fisher, Netanel 25
Flint, Betty Gail 28
Foreign Relations Committee 55, 57
Fortner, Pat (Pastor) 146
Free Congress Foundation 76, 108
Friedman, Murray 77, 95
Friendship Fund 77
Fundamentalist Christians 52, 77, 108,
    117, 121, 126
Fundamentalist Journal 36

Gardner, Keith (Pastor) 152
Garman, Colby 143
Garrison, David 32
General Allenby 11
George Mason University 134
Giuliani, Rudy 132
Godwin, Ron 127–28
Goeglein, Tim 131
Good Samaritan 62
Graham, Billy 1, 5, 14, 16, 116
Grand Strand Baptist Church 144
Grassroots Movement 42, 51, 80, 131,
    161–63
Gray, Bob 28
Greek Orthodox 70
Growing Church 27, 36, 39–41, 47

Hagee, John 151, 162
Haig, Alexander 117
Halim, Abdel 72
Halper, Jeff 120
Hamilton, Allen Kathleen 91
Hannity, Sean 156

INDEX

Harris, Louis 114
Harvest Baptist Church 147
Hashemite Kingdom 55
Haynes, Jeffrey 93
Haynes, Stephen 25
Hechler, Reverend William 1
Hecht, Abraham (Rabbi) 116
Helms, Jesse 55–56, 124
Heritage Baptist Church 142
Heritage Foundation 106, 108
Hertzke, Allen 119
Herzl Institute 58
Herzl, Theodor ix
Hirschson, Avraham 77
Hitchens, Christopher 132
Hollis-Brusk, Amanda y 103
Holy Land 11, 47–51, 57, 61, 66–67, 90
Holy Land Studies 66
Holy Scriptures 7, 19
Horowitz, Ariel 129
Horowitz, Mordechai 82
Horwitt, Nathan George 75
Howard Phillips 109
Hudson, Keith (Pastor) 153
Hummel, Daniel 16, 51, 60
Hunt, Jim (Governor) 56
Hurwitz, Harry 64
Hyer, Marjorie (Journalist) 115

Idaho Frank Church 76
Igar Town 150
Inbari, Mordechai 163
Independent Baptist 123, 145–46
Interior Secretary James Watt 120
International Bible Seminar 41
Israel, Agudath 88
Israel Christians 64
Israel Lobby 52, 130
Israeli Pilgrimage Committee 49

Jackson, Jesse 55–56
Jefferson, Mildred 116
Jefferson, Thomas 21
Jerusalem Embassy Act 53–54
Jesus Christ 23, 90, 102, 152
John, Richard 24
Johnson Baptist Fellowship 149
Johnson Fellowship 149
Johnson, Lyndon 113
Johnson, Ryan (Pastor) 148

Kadishai, Yehiel 64
Kansas City Baptist Temple 19

Katz, David 7
Kennedy, James 104, 116
Kinane, Caroline 15
Kincheloe, Joe 85
Knesset Member Ora Namir 88
Koch, Ed 76
Kolleck, Mayor Teddy (Jerusalem) 55
Kranz, Herzel (Rabbi) 75
Ku Klux Klan 116
Kuenzle, Wayne (Pastor) 152
Kyle, Richard 66

Labor Party 61, 83–84, 99
Landmark Church 85
Leeman, Richard 125
Leibman, Sarah Yeshayahu 14
Lewis, Samuel 89
Liberty Baptist Church 41, 116
Liberty Baptist College 28–29, 41, 106
Liberty Baptist Found 37
Liberty Christian Academy 135
Liberty Church Network 42
Liberty College 42, 54, 104, 144
Liberty Graduates 41, 137–55
Liberty Journal 35, 37, 129
Liberty Theological Seminary 142
Liberty University 1–3, 5, 21, 28–31, 34–36, 39–42, 47, 49, 51, 53, 92, 103, 105–6, 124, 126–28, 131–32, 137–51
Likud Party 60–61, 66
Linch, Mike 148
Lincoln, Abraham 91
Lindsey, Hal 6, 118
Littman, Gil (Journalist) 88
Local Super Church 34
Love America Pac 123
Lucas, Lena Mae 144
Lynch, Colonel Charles 18
Lynch, John 18
Lynchburg Baptist College 28–29, 147
Lynchburg Christian Academy 22
Lynchburg College 18
Lynchburg News 103
Lynchburg Oil Company 21

MacArthur, Douglas (General) 106
Madrid Conference 129
Mallory, Charles (Pastor) 153
Martin, William 134
Meckley, Don 142
Medal, Jabotinsky 75–77, 90
Meese, Ed (General Counsel) 120
Melodyland Christian Center 71

Mendendelk, Lisa 142
Menendez, Albert 113
Meridor, Sallai 132
Middendorf, William 118
Milky Way 105
Moen, Matthew 24, 118
Montgomery, John 71
Mooneyham, Lamar (Pastor) 92
Moore, Carl 131
Moore, Johnnie ix, 142, 158–59
Moral Majority 4–5, 42–43, 49, 52–54, 58, 74–75, 77–78, 82–83, 93–94, 96, 102–35
Mouly, Ruth 95
Mountain View 19

Netanyahu, Benjamin 129
New, David 85
New Life Church 147
Niebuhr, Reinhold 5, 13
Noll, Mark 141
Norman, Don 50
North Star Church 148
Nostra Aetate 78
Novak, Robert 93

Ocean County Baptist Church 145
Old Time Gospel Hour 20, 27, 30, 37, 42–43, 90, 109, 122–23, 135
Olson, Jason 6
Olson, Laura 126
Oral Roberts University 162

Palestinian Authority 67
Palestinian Homeland 65–67
Park Avenue Baptist Church 19
Parsons, David 64
Pate, Macel 21
Paul, Apostle 23
Paul, John (Pope) 72
Pence, Mike 161
Peres, Shimon 80–83, 99
Perkins, John (Pastor) 149
Peters, Roberta 75
Phoenix First Assembly 40
Pierard, Richard 122
Pieterse, Jan 59
Pillar Church of Dumfries 143
Pinchback, Earl 146
Poleg, Revital 82
Pompeo, Mike 161
Powell, Gabriel 148

Pratt, Frank 21
Prior, Michael 67
Professor Al Mansfeld 72
Providence Church 143

Rabin, Yitzhak 14
Radio Victory Liberty 30
Rambo, Rodney (Pastor) 149
Reagan, Ronald 4, 43, 67, 75, 78, 105–6, 111, 119–121, 124, 129, 158
Regent Christian University 117
Religious Right 16, 109, 120, 133
Republican National Convention 122
Republican Party 4–5, 15, 51–52, 60, 62, 120, 122, 132, 134, 156, 160
Richter, Ken 38
Ridge, Coral 116
Riggins, Ronald (Pastor) 147
Roberts, Oral 162
Robertson, Pat (Pastor) 117, 125, 129–30, 133, 162
Robertson, Roland 95
Robison, James 107
Rock, Stephen 128
Roman Catholic Church 54, 60
Romney, Mitt 132
Rosenne, Ambassador Meir 81
Rozell, Mark 134
Ryan, Michael 15

Sadat, Anwar 52, 68–70, 72
Samuels, Larry 63
Saunders, Harold 70
Sawyer, Cathy 82–83
Schippers, Inez 120
Schultz, George 111
Schwirzer, Jennifer 130
Scorsese, Martin 80
Shalev-Khalifa, Nirit 12
Shalheveth, Rami 12
Shamir, Yitzhak 80, 129
Sharon, Ariel 49, 91, 130
Sheldon, Louis 122
Shindler, Colin 68
Shmulevitz, Matityahu 62
Simon, Merrill 48
Sizer, Stephen 53, 129
Snowball, David 98
Southern Baptist 117
Southern Methodist University 134
Soviet Union 116
Spatial Revolution 138

Staley, George 85
Stanley, Charles 104
Stewart, Kathleen 67
Swaggart, Jimmy 117–18
Swart, Jeff 151
Sweet, George (Pastor) 40

Theological Seminary 19, 142
Thomas, Cal 54, 93
Thomas, Michael 25
Thompson, Paul 118
Timothy, Young 36, 39
Towns, Elmer 26, 34, 41, 105, 141, 151
Townsend, Ron (Pastor) 145
Tucker, Lem 150
Turner, Kari 148
Turner, Ted 42

Unger, Craig 86
United Israel Appeal 129
Untermeyer, Esther Antin (Judge) 75
Uris, Leon 75

Vernon, Ray Oliver 110
Victory Baptist Church 144
Viguerie, Richard 109
Virginia Polytechnic Institute 18

Wagner, Donald 8, 60
Wallis, Jim 133
Washington, George 91
Westover, Duke 104, 109, 135
Weyrich, Paul 106
Whittlesey, Faith 118, 123
Wiesel, Elie 75
Wilcox, Clyde 123, 125
Wilson, Joshua 108
Wilson, Matthew 134

Yitzhak, Eli 138
Young, Freddie 144
Young Pastors Movement 47

Zeltzer, Eddie 14
Zion Ministries 153

www.ingramcontent.com/pod-product-compliance
Lightning Source LLC
Chambersburg PA
CBHW021142230426
43667CB00005B/217